D1003354

Praise for
ANY NIGHT OF THE WEEK

'Toronto was always weirder than anyone thought. It's a major-label town where the thriving underground has been routinely written out of official histories – until now. Jonny Dovercourt is in a unique position to connect the T-dots through decades of freak-flag-fliers. This long-overdue document, rich with personal stories, is also just a great read. Every Canadian music fan should read it.'

– Michael Barclay, author, *The Never-Ending Present*;
co-author, *Have Not Been the Same*

'Toronto has long been one of North America's great music cities, but hasn't got the same credit as L.A., Memphis, Nashville, and others. This book will go a long way towards proving Toronto's place in the music universe.'

– Alan Cross, host, the *Ongoing History of New Music*

'The sweaty, thunderous exhilaration of being in a packed club, in collective thrall to a killer band, extends across generations, platforms, and genre preferences. With this essential book, Jonny has created something that's not just a time capsule, but a time machine – as you take in his keen insights into the (r)evolution of the city's independent music scene, you're there, on the floor, pogoing or pumping your fist or just imperceptibly swaying with folded arms, in a sea of other fans taking in the best fucking band you've ever seen on a stage.' – Sarah Liss, author of *Army of Lovers*

'A dizzyingly thorough map of scenes and spaces that collectively assembled the fabric of Toronto's musical identity. Since no one else was paying attention, we often only had our own comrades to witness our creative impulses, creating a parochial fishbowl that only recently is open to the rest of the world. This book is a mad web of cross-references, baby steps, and a real love story to a place that was forced to DIY, but chose to DIT – Do It Together – creating a community model that is still part of the local psyche.'

– Don Pyle, musician, Shadowy Men on a Shadowy Planet, and author, *Trouble in the Camera Club*

'Jonny Dovercourt, a tireless force in Toronto's music scene, offers the widest-ranging view out there on how an Anglo-Saxon backwater terrified of people going to bars on Sundays transforms itself into a multicultural metropolis that raises up more than its share of beloved artists, from indie to hip-hop to the unclassifiable. His unique approach is to zoom in on the rooms where it's happened – the live venues that come and too frequently go – as well as on the people who've devoted their lives and labours to collective creativity in a city that sometimes seems like it'd rather stick to banking. For locals, fans, and urban arts denizens anywhere, the essential *Any Night of the Week* is full of inspiration, discoveries, and cautionary tales.'

– Carl Wilson, *Slate* music critic and author of *Let's Talk About Love: A Journey to the End of Taste*, one of Billboard's '100 Greatest Music Books of All Time'

ANY NIGHT OF THE WEEK

A D.I.Y. HISTORY OF TORONTO MUSIC, 1957–2001

JONNY DOVERCOURT

COACH HOUSE BOOKS, TORONTO

copyright © Jonny Dovercourt, 2020

first edition

 Canada Council Conseil des Arts
for the Arts du Canada

 ONTARIO ARTS COUNCIL
CONSEIL DES ARTS DE L'ONTARIO
an Ontario government agency
un organisme du gouvernement de l'Ontario

Canadä

Published with the generous assistance of the Canada Council for the Arts and the Ontario Arts Council. Coach House Books also acknowledges the support of the Government of Canada through the Canada Book Fund and the Government of Ontario through the Ontario Book Publishing Tax Credit.

LIBRARY AND ARCHIVES CANADA CATALOGUING IN PUBLICATION

Title: Any night of the week : a DIY history of Toronto music / Jonny Dovercourt
Names: Dovercourt, Jonny.
Identifiers: Canadiana (print) 20190146907 | Canadiana (ebook) 20190141492 | ISBN 9781552453964 (softcover) | ISBN 9781770566095 (PDF) | ISBN 9781770566088 (EPUB)
Subjects: LCSH: Popular music—Ontario—Toronto—History and criticism.
Classification: LCC ML3484 .8 T686 D74 2019 | DDC 781.640971354—dc23

Any Night of the Week: A DIY *History of Toronto Music, 1957–2001* is available as an ebook: ISBN 978 1 77056 608 8 (EPUB); ISBN 978 1 77056 609 5 (PDF)

Purchase of the print version of this book entitles you to a free digital copy. To claim your ebook of this title, please email sales@chbooks.com with proof of purchase. (Coach House Books reserves the right to terminate the free digital download offer at any time.)

TABLE OF CONTENTS

INTRODUCTION

A t the start of 2017, Toronto lost seven of its dedicated music venues. In the space of three months, the Silver Dollar Room, the Central, Holy Oak, Hugh's Room, the Hideout, the Hoxton, and Soybomb all closed their doors – most of them forever. The alarm bell was sounded in Toronto's local music community: panel discussions were convened, council meetings were flashmobbed. The 'Vanishing Venues' crisis was a teeth-grinding irony in a town trying to brand itself a 'Music City' – and the home of the world's most popular musical artist.

In the twenty-first century, new original music is Toronto's largest and most successful cultural export. The 2010s were the decade of Drake and the Weeknd, when hazy, melodic hip-hop and R&B became – along with Raptors basketball – proud ambassadors for Canada's largest city, the sprawling, misunderstood metropolis on the north shore of Lake Ontario. A decade earlier, in the 2000s, Toronto became a global hotspot for indie music, with tuneful, communitarian collectives like Broken Social Scene and the Hidden Cameras busting beyond the city's borders, followed by a breathtaking diversity of visionary artists from Fucked Up to Tanya Tagaq.

Considering this bounty, it's hard to believe that pre-2000 Toronto was a tough place to be if you wanted to make music. For local bands in the twentieth century, hailing from here was a handicap, if not an outright curse.

This book is about how Toronto transformed itself from an uptight provincial backwater to one of the world's musical meccas. It's the story of how Toronto found its voice in original, homegrown music, and how our current wealth was built upon the hard work of countless community architects and the geography of supportive architecture.

But 'creative cities' like Toronto – which have identified music and the arts as key economic drivers – still lack the means to sufficiently protect these supportive spaces. And just as these bricks-and-mortar sanctuaries need preservation, so too does our history. Toronto's musical history is in danger of being forgotten – and this especially holds true for the analog, pre-Internet twentieth century.

Today's endangered music venues are at risk of joining a long list of extinct species. And today's hometown heroes, who deserve every shred of success that has come their way, could not have gotten there without the trails blazed by the likes of Kensington Market, Martha and the Muffins, Michie Mee, and Do Make Say Think. Every band and venue has a lifespan, and some rest in peace for good reason. But other promising groups and spaces died tragically young. Their memory must be kept alive in order to safeguard the future.

In 2001, I found myself at ground zero of the Toronto indie-music explosion. There was a palpable sense of excitement; the old apathy was dying away, and it felt like a new day was rising. Barely a year or two earlier, such optimism would have seemed far-fetched.

I was a key instigator of a new artist-run collective called Wavelength. Everyone in attendance at our first meeting, in 1999, was a member of an active band on the local independent scene. Our various groups had been exploring the more accessible fringes of underground music – shoegaze, post-punk, art-pop, lo-fi electronica. We were mostly Toronto natives who came of age in the far-flung suburbs; as a geeky, overweight kid playing in a basement band, I had found self-confidence and belonging in the downtown indie music community, as so many of us had. We also shared a sense of frustration. There were plenty of places to play, but breaking out of the city seemed impossible. Toronto was the capital of the Canadian music industry, but there was hardly any record-label interest directed toward our corner of the music scene, despite critical acclaim and campus radio support.

Instead of complaining, it was time to *do* something about it. This led to the weekly Wavelength music series and accompanying monthly zine. We succeeded beyond anyone's wildest dreams in building community and excitement, and we were lucky to start out during a groundswell of new music, indie labels, DJ nights, and youthful institutions.

But we weren't the first.

Rent Boys Inc. were part of a vibrant DIY post-punk scene in the early eighties.

Toronto has had a massively rich popular (or semi-popular) music scene going back to the 1950s, across a variety of genres and backgrounds. It's a story that has never been comprehensively told – and this is not the book that is going to do it. Nor is this a comprehensive document of any one time period, genre, or scene. Other books have already done that incredibly well, including Nicholas Jennings's sixties timepiece *Before the Gold Rush*; Liz Worth's oral history of seventies punk rock, *Treat Me Like Dirt*; Nick Smash's eighties post-punk compendium, *Alone and Gone*; and Denise Benson's multi-decade club culture roundup, *Then and Now*. I hope one day to read comprehensive histories of Toronto hip-hop, reggae, or rave music – genres I was less immersed in but felt it was important to include. (I'm especially looking forward to Del Cowie's forthcoming *This Is a Throwdown: A Toronto Hip-Hop History*.) I've also only dipped into jazz, folk, and global music, and haven't touched classical or opera, which have all had their own fascinating parallel evolutions. And I've hardly mentioned metal.

What I wanted to do with this book was find common cause across eras and genres, and tell a 'DIY history' of independent, alternative Toronto music. Everyone in Canadian music has had to be do-it-yourself to a certain extent, as there was little domestic music industry in the early days. I wanted to explore what made this city special and what made it a struggle.

Toronto has always had a strong history of live music venues. We've also benefitted from visionary – and sometimes controversial – live music promoters and bookers. But when it comes to Toronto music on record, the city has often fallen flat. The mainstream music industry failed our greatest artists in the pre-Internet era, overlooking them entirely or screwing them over. The smartest artists learned to work around the domestic record industry. Toronto never had the taste-making indie labels of the US or UK until the twenty-first-century advent of Arts & Crafts, Buzz Records, and ovo Sound, among others. Many of our most original artistic voices were left with no choice but to release their own records. Many essential Toronto records are now long out of print, essentially erased from the cultural record. You won't find them on Spotify. Piecing together the city's sonic history involves digging through used-record bins and YouTube rips.

★

This book charts a chronology signposted by the life cycle of music venues as the scene migrated through different neighbourhoods.

As musicians and artists are often urban pioneers – and unwittingly, the first wave of gentrification – the growth of the music scene, as marked through its live venues, in many ways charted that of the city's urban form. One of Toronto's most attractive features is a walkable downtown rivalled only by New York amongst major North American cities. But what gives it an advantage is its long commercial avenues that stretch on for kilometres: New York may have Times Square, but it does not have a Yonge Street.

And it definitely does *not* have a Queen Street – arguably the most important countercultural avenue in Canada. A handful of Queen West originals have been going strong for well over three decades: the Cameron House, the Horseshoe Tavern, the Rivoli, and the Rex all still book live music most nights a week – and all are locally owned.

On any night of the week in Toronto, an eager music-goer can curate their own personal music festival just by hopping from club to club. No other city can claim to being home to so many licenced venues that regularly book original live music – more than two hundred, by most recent estimates – across a variety of musical genres. Our Great Lakes geography makes us a major tour stop for visiting acts, and combined with our vibrant local scene, this means there's a dozen great shows happening any night.

In addition to being plentiful, Toronto venues have – until recently at least – also been relatively easy to access for artists. Though it could be hard to break into the club circuit for a young band starting out, once that seal was broken, an established band could have their pick of places to play. Most Toronto venues didn't (again, until recently) charge a rental fee to book a show. The door/bar split – the bands keep the money from tickets or cover, and the venue takes the bar proceeds – has allowed the independent music scene to thrive since the mid-eighties.

I'll especially focus on the under-two-hundred-capacity clubs, coffeehouses, and do-it-yourself (DIY) halls and churches that are the crucial petri dish for local music scenes – and that give Toronto artists a stage on which to experiment and take risks, their intimate size cultivating a sense of community among musicians and fans.

There is admittedly a downtown bias at work here, due to the concentration of venues in the city centre and systemic privileging of white-male-dominated rock music – one that marginalized people and genres have had to work harder to overcome. It's still embarrassing that Toronto has no dedicated hip-hop venue and that reggae hasn't had a regular home downtown since the BamBoo closed in 2002.

Dispersed throughout the book are profiles that dig deeper into the lives of artists and scene-builders I viewed as pioneers who helped push the art

Parts Unknown were among the circle of indie bands that co-founded Wavelength in the mid- to late nineties.

form forward. Few of these artists have been welcomed into the Can-rock canon, and I hope their music can be discovered by a new generation. The fact that these architects are unjustly forgotten or overlooked also explains the book's timeline. Twenty-first-century artists benefitted from the rise of the Internet, allowing them to communicate directly with their fans, who could find them with a few clicks. The accomplishments of these pre-2001 artists are thus less well-known, and more in need of being heard. (Please note that the pull-quotes spread throughout the book are taken from original interviews with the subjects, except in cases where a source is noted.)

Toronto can be a strange place to call home. I've lived here my whole life, and I'm still trying to understand what makes it tick. It's a cosmopolitan, multicultural megacity – the fourth-largest in North America – but oddly invisible to the rest of the world, and resented by the rest of Canada. This has resulted in a well-documented inferiority complex that can make it feel like a giant small town. For complex reasons of geography and economics, it's hard to leave here once you put down roots – and easy to feel trapped and resentful. I've seen the Toronto music scene go through several cycles of boom and bust in morale. But our status as a big, clumsy underdog makes us easy to root for: *this* is going to be the time we finally get it together. It's through our music that we've come to know ourselves – and become known. The impact of Toronto music is written into the city's streets, its airwaves, and our consciousness. The city's most successful musical artist of all time, Drake, was able to rename the town. The '6ix God' was the first artist to create an identity around the city's mythology and export that into multi-national success. That's a big change from the icons of the sixties: Joni Mitchell, Neil Young, and the Band all had to flee the city and jump the US border to make it big. This book is not their story.

This is the story of those that didn't 'make it' by the conventional music-business definition of success. Instead, they collectively made something much more valuable: they built a community. This is the story of how Toronto did it ourselves.

YONGE STREET
1957–65

Rock'n'roll, R&B, calypso, and jazz populate the city's first strip of licenced venues – but imported nighttime entertainment has yet to become a homegrown art form.

My Saturday-afternoon ritual as a Scarborough kid was to head downtown and walk south along Yonge Street. Record shopping was my lifeline to a wider world. It was like a retail version of a rock show: local opener the Vinyl Museum, followed by deep-cut mid-billed act the Record Peddler, wrapping up with big-name co-headliners A&A and Sam the Record Man.

The Yonge Street strip was seedy in the late eighties, but never threatening. Even at its sleaziest, Toronto felt safe. The Yonge Street strip was garish, and gloriously so. The record stores, head shops, strip clubs, and porn theatres stood alongside video arcades, burger joints, and the World's Biggest Jean Store.

Today, that strip retains little of that underbelly charm. Yonge-Dundas Square now anchors it, a gleaming, dystopian monument to corporate consumerism. The porn theatres have long since closed. The only record shop left is Sunrise, which somehow survived the music-retail holocaust of streaming. Even the titanic HMV Superstore was felled in 2017, one month before the closing of the Hard Rock Café. This marked the end of Yonge Street as a destination for live music, a whimper of an ending to a history that began sixty years earlier.

In June 1958, twenty-three-year-old Ronnie Hawkins pulled up his sister's Chevy outside Le Coq d'Or, at 333 Yonge Street – thirty-three years before the address became home to HMV. He and his band marvelled at the cursive, Vegas-style neon sign and the blinking advertisements for Bar-B-Q Chicken and Steaks. They had driven 1,400 miles north from Arkansas – and come off a week's stand playing their first gigs across the border, in Hamilton, Ontario. But that was just a warm-up: Yonge Street was where Hawkins and his band, the Hawks, would make it big – or at least big-fish-in-a-small-pond – in what Hawkins would dub his 'promised land.' Toronto would have its introduction to the raw, rollicking sound of early rock'n'roll through 'Rompin'' Ronnie Hawkins, a.k.a. the Hawk.

The band set up on the tiny stage, placed right behind a banquette with dining tables complete with place settings. This was a fancy place, and the Arkansas crew was there to rip it up. Ronnie Hawkins was a ball of energy on stage, famous for his backflips and 'camel walk.' Some say he was a better performer than singer, but he definitely had the pipes to back up his moves. More importantly, Hawkins was a natural entrepreneur who could sniff out a business opportunity from thousands of miles away.

Rock'n'roll was already in decline in its native USA, but it was still brand new in Toronto. Trends travelled more slowly back then, and by '58 the new sounds of the American south were only starting to make their way north. Toronto was at the northern end of an informal network of venues that radiated throughout the eastern United States and across the border. This was sometimes known as the Chitlin' Circuit, as it offered safe spaces in which Black artists could perform. ('R&B' may now connote the emotive sibling genre to hip-hop, popularized by Drake or Mariah Carey, but sixty years ago, 'rhythm and blues' referred to *all* African-American music, previously sold under the now-dated name 'race music.')

Geographical distance and demographic difference – the GTA was then overwhelmingly white – slowed the migration of R&B and rock'n'roll to Southern Ontario. This delay worked to Hawk's advantage. Though the band was all white, their brand of rockabilly swung hard with the influence of Southern R&B. Toronto audiences had a huge hunger for this new music, which Hawkins was happy to sate. The band mostly played covers – creative interpretations of songs by Chuck Berry, Bo Diddley, and others. Rock'n'roll in fifties Toronto was still more imported entertainment than homegrown art form, beholden to trends from elsewhere.

★

In the late fifties, Toronto was only waking up to being a big city. The Le Coq d'Or was one of a handful of licenced bars – almost all located along the east side of Yonge Street between Queen and Gerrard – that booked live music. With larger halls Maple Leaf Gardens and Massey Hall nearby, this was the city's first concentrated zone for music venues, setting the template for Toronto's future success in other downtown neighbourhoods. And Yonge Street succeeded when the city was finally allowed – after decades of temperance – to provide another main attraction: alcohol.

The Yonge Street strip was racier and more garish than anywhere else in Toronto, but the club was much nicer than what Ronnie Hawkins & the Hawks were used to down south. Unlike the rough-and-tumble juke joints of Arkansas or Tennessee, the Le Coq was a country-and-western-themed cocktail bar with a dress code. (In a peculiarity of Canadian English, much like the El Mocambo, it was always called 'the' Le Coq d'Or.)

Ronnie Hawkins: *It was such a beautiful club, and shit, at that time you had to dress properly to get into a bar. They wouldn't let Neil Young in there! The places I'd been playing in the south, you'd have to show a razor or puke twice before they'd let you in. Evel Knievel would have been afraid to go to some of those places I played.*

Show-going in Toronto was a more orderly experience in the fifties and sixties. Due to restrictive liquor laws, the Le Coq was a seated dining lounge – you couldn't move tables with a drink in hand. Bands like the Hawks played week-long residencies with multiple sets a night. More work, of course, meant more money – another thing Hawkins liked about coming north. Liquor laws also mandated union pay scale for musicians performing in licenced bars. Ronnie Hawkins may be the only musician in history to express fondness for Ontario's notoriously strict rules around alcohol consumption. Cocktail bars had only been legalized in Ontario in 1947.

It's hard to believe in our secular modern age, but the Christian church held sway over all aspects of the city's public life, and the stentorian Blue Laws barred almost everything besides praying on the Lord's Day, Sunday. Playground swings were locked up. Ball games were banned. And Sunday shopping would remain against the law until 1992, the year the Blue Jays won their first World Series.

In response to the rampant alcoholism of the nineteenth century, Ontario began its crackdown on liquor consumption in the early twentieth, with church-based temperance movements driving entire districts of the city dry. West-end Toronto neighbourhood the Junction wouldn't serve a drop for almost a century, finally turning the taps back on in 1997. Prohibition reigned in Ontario starting in 1916, four years before the US – Canada became a haven for liquor smuggling only in the later days of US Prohibition. The creation of the Liquor Control Board of Ontario began the slow process of liberalization, but citizens had to acquire a permit to buy take-home alcohol, and the creepy LCBO had invasive powers to enter private residences to monitor consumption.

Public drinking in taverns was legalized in 1934, but these could only serve beer and wine. After the end of World War II, with Toronto starting to feel the swing of liberation in its hips, premier George Drew began to loosen liquor laws. He was rewarded with a vicious backlash from the temperance league, losing his own seat in the following year's provincial election. But the right to enjoy a mixed drink in public would stand alongside the Yonge Street subway, the 401 expressway, and poured-concrete architecture as one of the modern marvels bestowed upon postwar Toronto.

The city's very first cocktail bar was the Silver Rail, at Yonge and Shuter. Later in '47, the Colonial Tavern opened a few doors down as the strip's first live music club. At a time when one of the first American-born forms of musical expression was entering one of its many golden ages, the Colonial became Canada's premier venue for jazz.

In its 1950s and '60s heyday, the club would book the likes of Miles Davis, Ella Fitzgerald, Thelonious Monk, and Sarah Vaughan, but in its early years, the Colonial made history by booking all-Black swing band Cy McLean and the Rhythm Rompers, the first Black musicians booked on Yonge Street. One of Toronto's original jazz musicians, McLean had been playing in the city since the mid-thirties. In 1950, Colonial Tavern manager Tommy Newton led efforts among the city's bar owners to begin hiring homegrown Canadian talent.

Next door to the Le Coq was the Edison Hotel, which booked jazz and country music, but it jumped on the rock'n'roll and R&B train earlier, booking Bill Haley and Bo Diddley. On the northeast corner of Yonge and Dundas sat the massive Brown Derby Tavern, which claimed the longest bar in Canada and booked jazz, country, *and* rock'n'roll. Steele's Tavern, opened by Greek immigrant Steele Basil, booked a variety of then-exotic sounds, including the 'captivating Hawaiian sounds' of the Paradise Islanders. And across the street, live R&B found a dedicated home at Club Bluenote, an after-hours dance hall that opened its doors in 1959.

By the late fifties, the Yonge Street strip had become a major tourist attraction, drawing weekenders from across the province who would drive their cars up and down the strip to gawk at the lights and the locals. Liquor laws were still archaically segregated along gender lines, with bars divided between sections for men and 'ladies and escorts.' Taverns were not a place for women to socialize alone or in groups.

The drinking age was twenty-one, and age was perceived differently in those days: long before today's extended youth culture, at twenty-one you were an *adult*. Hotel bars like the Edison became popular with working men, who would come in from smaller Ontario towns to spend the weekend. Though Ronnie Hawkins found placid Canada safer than Arkansas or Tennessee, Yonge Street could still be rough. There are stories of civilians carrying their own concealed nightsticks when hitting the strip.

They may have been the first to play Southern rockabilly in Southern Ontario, but by the time the Hawks played on Yonge, there was already a burgeoning DIY teen scene of young upstart rock'n'roll bands in the growing suburbs, turned on by a spark lit elsewhere.

On April 2, 1957, Elvis Presley played two concerts at Maple Leaf Gardens, Toronto's hockey palace. It was Elvis's first and only appearance outside the US. Members of the Metropolitan Toronto Police Force kept the crowd of 23,000 in line. In a *Footloose*-level display of Puritanism, the cops ensured the kids remained *seated*.

Among the teenage garage bands fired up by the early blast of rock'n'roll was the Rhythm Chords, formed in 1957 by Robbie Robertson, a thirteen-year-old Scarborough guitarist of Mohawk/Cayuga and Jewish heritage. On bass was Pete 'Thumper' Traynor, a name familiar to anyone who's played in a rock band in Canada: in the mid-sixties, he founded the Traynor amplifier line, a notoriously loud, tough, and affordable make of guitar amp.

The Rhythm Chords became Thumper and the Trambones, or sometimes Robbie and the Robots, after Traynor drilled some holes in Robertson's Harmony guitar and installed antennae to make it resemble Robbie the Robot from *Forbidden Planet*. Fifties Toronto's teen scene was fluid, with bands switching and trading members and identities. Robertson and Traynor looked up to one really solid band called the Gems, fronted by another high schooler, Black vocalist Bobby Dean Blackburn.

Robertson also briefly played with Little Caesar and the Consuls, which formed in '56 and became Canada's longest-running rock'n'roll band. What set the Consuls apart is that they didn't just play covers; they began to add their own compositions to their set lists.

Tommy Wilson (Little Caesar and the Consuls): *One thing you can say about Caesar is, we were a dance band. And once we started playing, the people*

just didn't sit down until we stopped playing. Especially at the teen dances we played – those were made for dancing, whereas the Yonge Street clubs, it was a blue-collar crowd, who came down to drink and party. They wouldn't dance – unless they got too drunk!

Little Caesar & the Consuls: a rock'n'roll dance band.

With the demand for live rock'n'roll quickly outstripping the capacity of Canada's then-non-existent music industry – and the time constraints of the bands who had to manage themselves – young entrepreneurs stepped in to fill the void. Ron Scribner booked teen dances at his high school when he was just eighteen and began representing local bands, including Little Caesar & the Consuls and Robbie Lane & the Disciples. In the mid-sixties, Scribner would become Canada's first rock booking agent, establishing the Bigland Booking Agency and laying the groundwork for a domestic music industry.

More was happening on Yonge Street than just rock'n'roll – and not all the clubs were licenced. The R&B scene around Club Bluenote kept growing through the sixties. The leading stars of the burgeoning US soul scene – Stevie Wonder, the Supremes, Jackie Wilson – began to drop in and jam after playing their sets at bigger venues.

Bobby Dean and the Gems were the first house band at the Bluenote; in October 1960, their spot was taken over by Kay Taylor & the Regents, a band of white male instrumentalists fronted by a Black female singer. Playing hits like 'The Twist,' Taylor & the Regents developed a fast, danceable R&B style. Other Black women vocalists that came out of the Bluenote included Shawne Jackson, of the Silhouettes and the Majestics; and Shirley Matthews, who had a local pop hit, 'Big Town Boy.'

Jackie Shane had a local chart hit in 1963, with 'Any Other Way,'

Jackie Shane: '60s soul star.

an affecting soul ballad by William Bell. Originally from Nashville, Shane was an incredible vocalist and a striking, captivating performer with a flamboyant fashion sense. She was also Black and transgender, at a time when the latter identity was misunderstood at best. Shane presented as a crossdressing man and delighted in keeping audiences guessing if she was gay or straight, a man or a woman.

Shane joined trumpeter Frank Motley and His Motley Crew as vocalist, and they relocated to Toronto in 1961, first performing at the Holiday Tavern at Queen and Bathurst, which much later became the Big Bop. They then moved up to Yonge Street, playing the Brass Rail and later to the Saphire Tavern.

Toronto became Jackie Shane's adopted hometown. Even though the city was openly homophobic in the 1960s, Shane's status as an entertainer provided some protection, and she provoked more curiosity than hatred. She was able to shut down hecklers with sassy stage banter while openly using gay slang like 'chicken' in her songs. Vanishing from the public eye in 1971, Shane's career and story were rediscovered by a new generation of music fans in the 2010s. Now an LGBTQ+ icon, Jackie Shane is included in the music mural on Yonge Street.

Another unlicenced Yonge Street club was the Music Room, above the King Koin Laundromat. Run by singer/songwriter Sara Ellen Dunlop from 1962 to '66, it was one of the city's first gay and lesbian clubs, running drag shows and dance nights when queer identity was still deeply underground.

There were other after-hours clubs on the strip. In 1960, members of Toronto's small but growing Caribbean community opened the Calypso Club at 267 Yonge, which capitalized on the fifties calypso craze. Though the audience was mostly white Canadians seeking a taste of 'the Islands' – with all the problematic exoticization that entails – the performers were primarily Caribbean immigrants, such as Trinidadian steel band the Tropitones, and Jamaican-born calypso singer Lord Power. Similar spots opened up, including the Caribbean Club and Little Trinidad, until a police crackdown on after-hour clubs put an end to most of them. But they marked the start of a space for Caribbean music to be heard in Toronto, which continued at venues aimed at the Black community, such as the WIF (West Indies Federation) Club, which opened at Brunswick and College in '62.

Jazz music wasn't going to get squeezed out by any of these new trends. Jazz had had a foothold in Toronto since the 1920s, with bands playing at a strip of venues along the western Lakeshore, including Sunnyside Pavilion, Club Top Hat, and the Silver Slipper. Bert Niosi, 'Canada's King of Swing,' played boathouse/dancehall the Palais Royale innumerable times through the thirties and forties. Duke Ellington and Count Basie played there too. Refurbished in 2006, the Palais remains a Jazz Age jewel.

The Colonial remained the premier jazz club downtown, but it had competition from the Town Tavern, at Queen and Yonge, which opened in 1949 and became a jazz club in '55 at the suggestion of Montreal pianist Oscar Peterson, who later recorded a well-regarded live album at the club.

Then there was George's Jazz Room, which booked jazz five nights a week inside George's Spaghetti House, a ways off the strip at Dundas and Sherbourne. It might have been Toronto's first music venue booked by a musician, Moe Koffman, who had a surprise pop hit in the US with jazz-flute 'Swinging Shepherd Blues.' George's owner Doug Cole later opened Bourbon Street on Queen Street West.

These clubs became the home of Toronto's mainstream jazz establishment – solid, dependable, and entirely stuck in the bebop era in which they opened.

★

Those early years of playing the teen dance circuit shaped Robbie Robertson into a shit-hot guitarist. After his band the Suedes opened up for the Hawks at a gig at the Dixie Arena in Mississauga, he was pulled into Hawkins's orbit – and flung on a whole new trajectory.

Robbie Robertson: *The first time I saw Ronnie and the Hawks perform, it was a revelation. After that night, I would look at music in a whole different light. It was the most violent, dynamic, primitive rock'n'roll I had ever witnessed, and it was addictive.* (*Testimony*, 2016)

The ever-opportunistic Hawkins drafted whiz-kid Robertson, first to write songs for him and then to play bass for the band – which involved a life-altering pilgrimage down to Arkansas. The rest, as they say, is overly documented history. The kind of history that Toronto schoolkids should be able to recite by heart but that instead remains the purview of the record-collector set: Robbie Robertson joined Arkansan drummer Levon Helm as part of Ronnie Hawkins's hard-working backing band, rehearsing all day and all night.

Eventually, the other original band members would be replaced one by one by Canadians from all over Southwestern Ontario: Rick Danko, from Simcoe, on bass; Garth Hudson, from London, on organ; Richard Manuel, from Stratford, on piano. Robertson moved to his rightful spot on guitar; his gnarly sound and style, assisted by speaker-slashing tricks he picked up from Pete Traynor, made him a guitar god to the next generation of Toronto bands.

Eventually, the Hawks would tire of their boss's dictatorship and go their own way. In 1965, Mary Martin, a Torontonian working for Albert Grossman's management in New York City, would recommend the Hawks as the backing band for Bob Dylan. They toured the world backing up the American folk icon, enduring astonishing abuse from purists aghast at Dylan going electric.

And eventually the band would go their own way once more, moving south to Woodstock, New York, in 1967, and becoming the Band. With the release of *Music from Big Pink* and their self-titled follow-up album in '68 and '69 respectively, the Band would become one of the defining acts of the later hippie era and of the 'Americana' sound, despite being four-fifths Canadian in membership.

Back at the start of the sixties, the spoils of Yonge Street were too much for Ronnie Hawkins to resist. His attempts at a US recording career were stalled, his biggest hit, 1959's 'Mary Lou,' peaking at a modest number twenty-six on Billboard. The lineup of the Hawks that became the Band solidified by late '61, and in March of '62, Hawkins married a young Canadian, Wanda Nagurski, whom he had met at one of the band's teen dances at the Concord Tavern (a.k.a. Club Concord), in the west end at 925 Bloor, near Ossington – an address now well known as the downtown location of Long & McQuade. A Heritage Toronto plaque marks the site.

The Hawks became the house band at the Le Coq d'Or, dominating the Yonge Street strip with their raucous rockabilly sound through the sixties. Hawkins became a father and a Canadian citizen, finally calling his 'promised land' his permanent home. He even bought the club above the Le Coq, turning it into his own teen-dance moneymaker, dubbing it the Hawk's Nest.

By late '63, Levon & the Hawks were playing their own gigs a block south at Friar's Tavern, a new addition to the new strip that had opened a block south at the eventual location of the Hard Rock Café. It was at Friar's that Dylan heard the Hawks play, in September '65, and where he jammed with them to build the bold new sound of folk-rock. The fusion of folk music and rock'n'roll would dominate the second half of the tumultuous sixties, but back at the decade's dawn, they couldn't be further apart – and in Toronto, they were also separated by geography.

YORKVILLE
1960-68

An all-ages youth-focused bohemian community brings focus to politics and creativity, marking the beginnings of homegrown original songwriting.

I f Yonge Street is Toronto's answer to Times Square, then Yorkville is our Fifth Avenue, home to high-end luxury boutiques, hotels, fancy restaurants, and a few commercial galleries. Unlike Yonge Street, it's not a place of which I have any fond formative memories. For most of my youth, I had no idea that, decades earlier, Torontonians of my parents' generation had literally filled the streets of Yorkville as wayward hippie flower children.

By the time my parents moved here from England in 1970, that crucial cultural moment in the city's evolution had already passed. It's hard to believe now, but if you look closely at the storefronts of Yorkville Avenue and Cumberland Street, you can see the bones of the old Victorian row houses that made Yorkville of the sixties a quaint bohemian village and one of North America's key 'urban utopias' for the youth counterculture, alongside New York's Greenwich Village and San Francisco's Haight-Ashbury.

Yorkville is probably the civic music-history lesson most likely to be taught in Toronto schools. But the common knowledge of its heyday usually relates to its famous exports – Neil Young and Joni Mitchell – neither of whom spent all that much time there. The story of Yorkville's rise and fall as a preserve for music venues during this crucial period of cultural change is less widely known.

As 1959 ticked over into the brand-new decade, the next of many new youth revolutions was underway. If Yonge Street's bars were home to rock-'n'roll and R&B, Yorkville's coffeehouses made space for jazz and folk. The folk music revival started by American acts like Pete Seeger and the Kingston Trio became the chosen music of earnest, politicized college kids who viewed rock'n'roll as teenybopper garbage. Unlike Yonge Street's bars, Yorkville's coffeehouses didn't serve alcohol, creating a new public space for people under twenty-one to congregate. An all-ages scene!

Saskatchewan-born Cree singer/songwriter Buffy Sainte-Marie made Yorkville a second home.

Buffy Sainte-Marie: *Coffeehouses offered an atmosphere for young people to be together and have a safe place to go and hear music that was actually about themselves and their peers – that was us, the songwriters. People who are sitting in a coffeehouse drinking coffee and talking, they're thinking, not boozing. They're sharing political and artistic perspectives, and it was quite beautiful.* (Andrea Warner, *Buffy Sainte-Marie: The Authorized Biography*, 2018)

Espresso was another new import to Toronto in the fifties, and Continental-flavour coffeehouses sprouted up all over Yorkville Village in 1960: among the first were the Half Beat, the Purple Onion, and the 71 Club. Above these cafés, on the second floors of the narrow old houses, were cheap and plentiful rental apartments, soon populated by youthful, disaffected artists.

Between Yonge Street and Yorkville, both geographically and historically, was the Bohemian Embassy, a coffeehouse opened by poet/actor Don Cullen in 1960, near Yonge and Wellesley. The Beat scene was another late arrival from the States, and the Bohemian Embassy marked the beginning of Toronto's beatnik-inspired bohemia, hosting readings by members of the city's emerging literary scene, including Margaret Atwood and Gwendolyn MacEwen. It also booked folk singers.

A nineteen-year-old artist named Sylvia Fricker (later Tyson) made her debut at the Bohemian Embassy in early 1960. She had just moved to the big city from small-town Chatham, Ontario, three hours southwest.

Sylvia Tyson: *I was sort of comedy relief between the terribly intense young poets from the University of Toronto who used to come in and read their poetry,* *swearing at their mothers and all that.* (John Einarson with Ian Tyson and Sylvia Tyson, *Four Strong Winds*, 2011)

Soon, she began performing in a duo with singer/guitarist Ian Tyson, a real-life cowboy and B.C. native, who had hitchhiked east from Vancouver in the summer of '58, around the same time Ronnie Hawkins made his first pilgrimage north.

A talented graphic artist, Tyson supplemented his performance income on the nascent coffeehouse circuit by painting decals on tumbler glasses, and he was introduced to Fricker by his boss. Ian & Sylvia quickly gained a local following for their beautiful harmonizing and striking looks.

Ian & Sylvia would become the first Yorkville success story. The Village's coffeehouses, with their small stages and rapt audiences, made the area a breeding ground for a new species: the singer/songwriter. Twenty-one-year-old country singer Gordon Lightfoot left his hometown of Orillia, Ontario, for Toronto in 1960, discovering folk music after seeing Ian & Sylvia play the Village Corner.

The folk revivalists wanted their music to be taken seriously as an *art form*. In August 1961, the first Mariposa Folk Festival was held in Orillia, an hour and a half north of the city in bucolic cottage country. Modelled on Rhode Island's Newport Folk Festival, Mariposa featured an all-Canadian lineup, unheard of at the time; Ian & Sylvia were one of its first headlining acts.

Not long after, the duo travelled to New York City and dove into the burgeoning Greenwich Village folk scene, befriending folk sensation Bob Dylan (legend has it Ian was the first to get him high) and signing with his notoriously hard-nosed manager, Albert Grossman, who made them big names on the US college circuit. Inspired by Dylan, in 1963 Tyson and Fricker began writing their own songs, including Tyson's 'Four Strong Winds,' which years later, in 2005, was ranked the greatest Canadian song of all time by CBC listeners.

In the early sixties, Canadian identity was such a nascent thing that even mentioning a Canadian place name (the province of Alberta) in a song was revolutionary. CBC host Peter Gzowski once called 'Four Strong Winds' the 'alternative national anthem.' Ian & Sylvia married in 1964, their marriage and creative partnership lasting until '75, by which time they were Canadian music royalty.

ARTISTS, JAZZ, & THE ISAACS GALLERY

When Avrom Isaacs opened his namesake gallery in Yorkville (832 Yonge St.) in 1961, it was a big deal in the Canadian art world. Isaacs was already an established art dealer, working with some of the nation's most exciting modern artists, and the gorgeous custom-designed space was the perfect place to view contemporary art. Isaacs envisioned his gallery as a hub for experimentation across the arts, hosting film screenings, readings, and more – revolutionary for the early sixties.

The gallery became the rehearsal space and performance venue for the Artists' Jazz Band, a collective of untrained musicians and visual artists. The core sextet was joined by various guests, most notably Michael Snow, who in addition to being one of Canada's hottest up-and-coming painters, was also a jazz pianist.

Together with Snow, the AJB helped establish free improvisation in Canada. One step beyond free jazz, free improv players in the US, UK, and Europe received respect and acclaim, but in Toronto's mainstream jazz clubs, the audience reaction was one of deep indifference.

By the end of 1964, Yorkville's coffeehouse circuit was solidified with the opening of the 120-seat Riverboat. Folk music had grown strong enough to support a larger venue. While most Village coffeehouses had a thrift-store aesthetic, owner Bernie Fiedler envisioned the Riverboat as a classier step up. Rival coffeehouse owners, envious of the German-born Fiedler's success, snarkily referred to the basement space as 'the U-boat.'

Bernie Fiedler: *As far as I'm concerned, a club with a name has an awful lot to do with making a star. The Riverboat is the ultimate place for a folk artist to play in Canada. Artists say if you play the Riverboat, you're ready for O'Keefe Centre and Massey Hall. After that – well, you're at the top.* (Marilyn Beker, *Globe and Mail*, March 9, 1968)

Gordon Lightfoot, having gotten his start at more rough-and-tumble Steele's Tavern, was popular enough to become a headlining act at the Riverboat by

Much stronger was the reaction in the press to the Mixed Media Concerts presented at Isaacs Gallery from 1965 to '67 by Udo Kasemets, at which the Artists' Jazz Band performed. The *Globe* called the series a 'hoax,' the *Star* called it 'grotesque.' An Estonian-born classical-music polymath, Kasemets was one of Toronto's earliest followers of John Cage. Inspired by Cage's multi-media 'Happenings,' Kasemets sought to create open-format, non-seated concerts where the audience could drift in and out at their leisure – as much installation as performance.

Other performers at Kasemets's series included London, Ontario, noise-music pioneers the Nihilist Spasm Band, two future members of Syrinx, and poet John Giorno. In the fall of '65, Michael Snow screened his film *New York Eye and Ear Control*, which featured a free-jazz soundtrack by hot NYC players and images of his recurring 'Walking Woman' figure – edited with no reference to one another.

By then, Snow had moved to New York with his wife, artist Joyce Wieland, and delved into the brave new world of experimental filmmaking. In 1967, he made Wavelength, one long forty-five-minute zoom-in that reinvented cinema the same way Cage did music. Michael Snow is now one of Canada's most celebrated artists, but most people forget he makes music.

early '65. Joni Anderson, an aspiring folk singer who had moved east from Saskatchewan, tried to get booked there, but as legend has it, she was offered a job as a dishwasher instead. Without a union card, Anderson played gigs at 'scab clubs' before marrying American Chuck Mitchell, taking his surname – though the marriage would be short-lived – and moving to Detroit, then New York, then California. As Joni Mitchell, she invented her own open tunings, rejecting the traditionalism of the folk revival and digging deep to become one of the twentieth century's most original songwriters.

Indigenous poet and painter Duke Redbird was Mitchell's across-the-hall neighbour on Huron Street when she first moved to Toronto. He heard her working on some of her earliest songs, her high, operatic voice travelling through the walls. At the time, Redbird was reading his own 'performance poetry' alongside folk singers at the Purple Onion. He had been drawn to Yorkville from Saugeen First Nation by the Village's promise of artistic freedom.

Psychedelic rockers the Paupers hypnotize the Flick Coffee House in Yorkville, 1967

Duke Redbird: *Yorkville was where the artists were. And that's where my generation was. We were the beginning of the Baby Boomers, we were in the majority, and the world seemed to be our oyster. We were going to claim it as artists, poets, songwriters, and entrepreneurs.*

Though Canada was comparatively free of the turmoil south of the border in the mid-sixties, Yorkville's cauldron of countercultural engagement inspired songwriters to take aim at militarism, imperialism, and white supremacy. Cree singer/songwriter Buffy Sainte-Marie was a fellow Saskatchewan-born artist and an inspiration to Anderson, who had headed east in part to see Sainte-Marie play the 1964 Mariposa Folk Festival. Though not based in Toronto, Sainte-Marie regularly played Yorkville venues, motivating the growing anti–Vietnam War movement with her song 'Universal Soldier,' which she wrote during set breaks at the Purple Onion. Sainte-Marie also experimented sonically, becoming one of the very first folk singers to make use of brand-new electronic synthesizers.

But folk music's monopoly on the Village was soon challenged by the resurgence of rock'n'roll. In January 1964, an after-hours club named Brave New

World opened on Davenport, the first venue in the area to book rock or rhythm'n'blues. The acts booked there by CKEY DJ Duff included David Clayton-Thomas, who later fronted Blood, Sweat & Tears.

The British Invasion and Beatlemania sparked renewed excitement around electrified 'big beat' sounds, and young men began wearing their hair long. A wave of Brit-band soundalikes began popping up in Toronto, blatantly waving the Union Jack with names like Jack London & the Sparrows, the Liverpool Set, and the British Modbeats – an example of Toronto's oddly obsessive Anglophilia. This new wave of rock groups found a Yorkville home in coffeehouse Jacques' Place.

Toronto had always been a private, behind-closed-doors place. Yorkville changed all that. By the spring of '65, the Village streets had become a full-on outdoor hangout zone for aimless baby-boomer youth looking for fun. The promise of cheap housing and easy, endless good times attracted young people from across the country – as well as an increasing population of young Americans evading the Vietnam War draft. Open use of marijuana and stronger hallucinogens became common, and a moral panic set in amongst the elder generation. Suburbanites would read about far-out hippie fashion in the daily papers and drive downtown on weekends to watch the freak show. Yorkville Avenue turned into a slow-moving parade of gas guzzlers and gawkers.

But to the artists living inside that panopticon, it was a dreamland.

Neil Young: *The Yorkville scene. I'd never seen anything like it. Music was everywhere. Two years before the Summer of Love. It was this big deal, Toronto in '65. I was just growin' up. It was a great experience. I loved it. It was freedom.* (Jimmy McDonough, *Shakey*, 2002)

Come 1966, Yorkville reached its peak of venue saturation: music historian Nicholas Jennings, author of the essential scene history *Before the Gold Rush*, estimates no fewer than forty clubs and coffeehouses were booking live music. Not only were they getting more plentiful, the venues were getting weirder. The Mynah Bird capitalized on the more lurid side of the sixties sexual revolution, garnering inches of column ink by featuring topless go-go dancers, body painting, and a nude (male) chef. Owner Colin Kerr originally opened the coffeehouse to help promote a band he was managing, also named the Mynah Birds.

The frontman of the Mynah Birds was a teenaged Black American draft dodger from Buffalo named Rick James – the very same Rick James who recorded the eighties funk hit 'Super Freak' and was later immortalized in a Dave Chapelle catchphrase. To maintain his cover, James renamed himself Rickie Matthews, at the suggestion of local soul singer Shirley Matthews, who also let him pretend to be her son. The Mynah Birds went through countless membership switches through their two years of existence, and the final lineup featured a long-haired lead guitarist named Neil Young. A Toronto native who had been living in Winnipeg and playing in bands like the Squires, Young made his way to the big city seeking fame, but Yorkville was not good to him. His first band in Toronto, Four to Go, couldn't even get a gig, and he was stuck on the bottom rung of the folk circuit.

If you ever wanted to know what a band with Rick James and Neil Young might sound like, the Mynah Birds were a perfect missing link between British Invasion rock and American R&B/soul. This unique approach made them the first mixed-race group signed to Motown Records. But fate derailed the Detroit sessions for their first album: discovering that James had deserted from the navy, Motown execs convinced him to turn himself in. That was the end of the Mynah Birds.

Yorkville may have been a happening scene, but that wasn't enough for Neil Young. As the legend goes, he and fellow bandmate Bruce Palmer played a game of chess while high on LSD in Yorkville's Cellar club in March 1966, during which they hatched a scheme. The pair hopped in a Buick hearse and drove south and west without looking back. They soon ended up in Los Angeles, stuck in a traffic jam, where their Ontario plates announced their presence to American musicians they'd previously crossed paths with, Stephen Stills and Richie Furay. Together, they formed Buffalo Springfield, immediately becoming one of the biggest groups of the California psychedelic rock era. For Neil, splitting town was a smart career move.

Young: *I thought that if I made in Toronto, it would be easier to make it in L.A. So I went to Toronto and I couldn't make it. So I said, 'Fuck Toronto – I'll go to L.A. and make it. If I make it in Toronto, all I am is big in Toronto. If I go to L.A. and make it big, then I'm big in the fuckin' WORLD.' (Shakey)*

★

In late '66, the Yorkville scene entered a fertile period of creativity. Folk and rock were no longer worlds apart, and R&B was becoming increasingly amplified. The bands that stayed home began to find their own voice, leaving behind colonial imitation in favour of artistic experimentation.

Thrilling new sounds arose from crossover between the Yonge Street and Yorkville scenes. R&B band the Five Rogues, once the house band at the Bluenote on Yonge, became Mandala, amplifying their explosive soul-rock sound with psychedelic light shows incorporating disorienting strobes – and fourth-wall-breaking antics by vocalist George Olliver. A few years before Iggy Pop, Olliver began wading into the crowd, held back from their adoring clutches by a menacing, black-clad 'security guard' – who was really part of the show – in some kind of bizarre proto-punk James Brown routine.

The Ugly Ducklings, meanwhile, started off as a Rolling Stones clone band, but then the Scarborough youth started writing their own songs, such as the incredibly catchy 'Nothin',' which became a local hit on CHUM radio. While the Ducklings electrified tiny Charlie Brown's, Luke & the Apostles blew the roof off the Purple Onion with their psychedelic blues. The folkier side of psych-rock was no less dynamic. The Paupers, driven by the thunderous drums of Skip Prokop – and the managerial prowess of industry upstart Bernie Finkelstein – became one of the most popular bands in the Village, quickly outgrowing El Patio Cafe.

The nascent domestic music industry and media were keen to celebrate this emerging local music scene. The Ugly Ducklings, Luke & the Apostles, and the Paupers all participated in 'The Toronto Sound,' a day-long, fourteen-band festival held on September 24, 1966 at Maple Leaf Gardens, sponsored by CHUM radio and the *Toronto Telegram*. No one could really decide what 'the Toronto Sound' actually sounded like, though most of the bands shared a frenetic energy, combining raunchy, distorted guitars with danceable R&B rhythms. The show drew some US industry attention northward, and a few of these bands broke into the American market – but with ultimately mixed results.

By the summer of 1967, Yorkville Villagers were tired of the unwanted attention from the rest of the city. An increased police presence in the neighbourhood led to harassment of youth perceived as 'loitering.' An activist group named the Diggers, led by charismatic, guitar-toting, media-savvy David DePoe, pressured City Hall to crack down on automobiles instead of people.

Following an unsuccessful meeting with mayor William Dennison and controller Allan Lamport to convince them to pedestrianize the Village, DePoe and the Diggers organized a 'sit-in' in the middle of Yorkville Avenue on August 20, 1967.

Chanting 'Close Our Streets!,' an estimated thousand Villagers participated in the peaceful protest. Police violently broke it up, arresting forty-six people, including middle-aged journalist/activist June Callwood. The Summer of Love ended with a bummer. It was a far cry from May, when thousands of flower children had streamed into Queen's Park for a love-in featuring performances by Buffy Sainte-Marie and Leonard Cohen.

The City's elders had decided: the hippies had to go. Ontario MPP Syl Apps called Yorkville 'a festering sore in the middle of the city,' while Lamport deemed it a 'cancer.' Yorkville, as they saw it, was dirty, depraved, and diseased. The hippies' desire to drop out of society represented sloth and immaturity, not social progress. These Greatest Generation gappers thought the area would serve much better as a shopping centre.

Throughout the fifties and sixties, pro-development 'boosters' – developers, business interests, and their supporters at City Hall – had big plans to modernize the city. Charming old residential neighbourhoods and grand stone commercial buildings needed to go, clearing a path for a business-friendly metropolis at the service of the automobile. Much of Toronto's historic downtown core was demolished.

By 1968, things got worse for Yorkville: biker gang the Vagabonds infiltrated, ostensibly offering the Villagers protection from the cops but instead sexually assaulting women and getting hippies hooked on harder, nastier drugs. Reports of an outbreak of 'Hippie Hepatitis' incited further horror in the media. Only a tiny number of cases were actually confirmed, but the impression of an infectious 'epidemic' was enough to turn the Village into a ghost town. The Riverboat lost $15,000 in the space of just six weeks.

The opening of Rochdale College in the fall of '68 further encouraged the hippie exodus. Located a few blocks west on the edge of the University of Toronto campus, Rochdale was a free, experimental co-op university. The imposing concrete tower that housed it fulfilled the City fathers' wishes by hoovering hippies off the street, offering them year-round sanctuary from the prying eyes of the public. Though Rochdale was home to a recording studio, it didn't host much in the way of live music beyond impromptu jam sessions in its apartments. Others who didn't migrate to Rochdale instead fled the city for communes in rural Ontario. The free Village of Yorkville had effectively fallen.

One by one the coffeehouses closed their doors in '68/'69. City Hall sped up the domino-fall by making their business licences harder to renew. The Yorkville of the sixties was effectively erased by one of Toronto's earliest examples of gentrification. Developers began buying up area properties to demolish or convert them. The transformation of Yorkville from hippie haven into luxury shopping district concluded with the opening of Hazelton Lanes mall in 1975.

The Riverboat was the last of the original Yorkville music venues standing, making it all the way to 1978. The lowering of the drinking age from twenty-one to eighteen in 1971 was one of the final nails, as unlicenced coffeehouses could no longer compete with bars. New owner Ron Carlyle, to whom Bernie Fielder had handed the keys seven months earlier, blamed disco and Ontario Place. The Riverboat's final night, featuring performances by seventies folk singers Dan Hill and Murray McLauchlan, was a tribute to a bygone era. It's unlikely Yorkville will ever recapture its bohemian glory days. The Village's organic creation and shamefully intentional destruction should serve as a cautionary tale for how a city can support its culture – or not.

JAMAICA TO TORONTO
1967-75

The birth of Canadian reggae in Toronto – and Mississauga.

August 13, 1967, was a record-breaking day for the Toronto Island Ferries. Thirty-five thousand people made the journey across the inner harbour to attend the final day of a brand-new festival called Caribana. Nine months in planning, the week-long festival, modelled on Trinidad and Tobago's Carnival, was Toronto's growing Caribbean community's contribution to Canada's centennial celebrations. Montreal might have had the futuristic marvels of Expo 67, but we had a *real* party: calypso steel bands, sunshine, dancing, spicy food, colourful costumes, and, of course, a parade. It was a success beyond all expectations, and Caribana '67 started an annual tradition that has defined the August long weekend in Toronto ever since.

Live music at the first Caribana included Trinidadian calypso titans Lord Kitchener and the Mighty Sparrow, as well as a local band, the Cougars, fronted by Jay Douglas, who had moved to Toronto from Montego Bay, Jamaica, in '63. They were one of several bands with members who'd been 'drafted' to come play in Toronto's proliferating Jamaican clubs. Though at first these groups played Black American–style R&B to appeal to the expectations of Toronto audiences, they started to slip in some of the new sounds emanating from the studios and sound systems of Jamaica.

Canada had become an attractive destination for many Jamaicans fleeing political violence and economic uncertainty. Racist immigration policies started to become a thing of the past in the mid-fifties, at first to allow more Caribbean women to come to Canada as domestic workers. The 1962 Immigration Act, which focused on skills and education over race, helped liberalize entry, as did the point system, adopted in '67. Prime minister Pierre Trudeau's policy of official multiculturalism made the country look progressive and welcoming. People steered clear of the US to avoid the draft. And there was work here, especially for musicians.

Karl Mullings was one of the organizers of Caribana '67 and the booker of the WIF (West Indies Federation Club) at Brunswick and College. He was also a talent scout and manager who coaxed Jamaican musicians to make the flight north to Toronto. The Cougars were the WIF house band, while the Sheiks held it steady at Club Jamaica on Yonge Street.

Reggae, ska, and rocksteady were almost completely unfamiliar to white Canadian audiences. Little did Torontonians know they were in the presence of greatness: this exodus included some of the real innovators of the Jamaican sound.

Jackie Mittoo was a musical genius, an astonishingly talented keyboardist and organist who had been a member of the Skatalites and the musical director at groundbreaking Studio One, the label/studio considered the 'Motown of Jamaica.' In 1969, he moved to Toronto. Despite his accomplishments in his native land, he worked some pretty thankless gigs. He was a solo entertainer at Fran's Restaurant in the early seventies, performing seven hours a day (!) all by himself. Later on, he moved over to Dr. Livingstone's lounge at the Bristol Place Hotel, out by the airport. But he also got to open for Barry White at Massey Hall.

Another talented Jamaican musician didn't have such a happy experience. Wayne McGhie was a singer/guitarist and, unlike many of his contemporaries, also a songwriter. In 1969, with the help of many of his Jamaican friends, he

The Cougars played a Jamaican-Canadian spin on American R&B.

JoJo Bennett and Bobby Gaynair.

recorded an incredible album of stirring soul music that may be Canada's finest contribution to the genre. *Wayne McGhie & The Sounds of Joy* was released the following year by Scarborough-based Birchmount Records, but it was poorly promoted and didn't make much impact on its release. To make matters worse, a warehouse fire destroyed all of the remaining copies.

Beset by mental health challenges, McGhie dropped out of music and out of sight, ultimately cared for by his sister. Meanwhile, *Sounds of Joy* became coveted by crate-diggers and hip-hop artists. In 2004, it was reissued by Seattle record label Light in the Attic as part of a series called 'Jamaica to Toronto.' In 2006, the series made waves with the titular compilation, *Jamaica to Toronto: Soul, Funk & Reggae 1967–74.*

Reggae music in Toronto was crucially DIY, driven by the passion of its creators and fans, who had to build much of the industry infrastructure themselves. By the early eighties, Jamaican-Canadian music was one of the city's most important forms of musical expression, and reggae's influence on everything from post-punk to hip-hop can't be overstated. And it began in just a few clubs, booked by Jamaican musicians, who booked Jamaican musicians.

In 1974, Jamaican-Canadian music would get its first studio, the first Black-owned studio in the country. Reggae fan Jerry Brown moved to Toronto in 1968 and got a job in an auto body shop. He bought a house out near the airport, amidst the sterile sprawl of Mississauga. And he built a studio in the basement. His wife suggested the name Summer Sounds.

A community of musicians developed around Summer. People liked the vibe, that you could smoke weed inside, that Brown wasn't afraid to push his gear into the red to get that big bass sound. Jackie Mittoo became Summer's unofficial musical director, and a house band developed, named Earth, Roots and Water. Like Studio One, it became a label as well. The first Summer Records release was a roots-reggae single by Johnny Osbourne in 1974. Brown sold it by taking it around to the several Jamaican-owned record shops that had begun to crop up on Bathurst and Eglinton West, a district becoming known as Little Jamaica.

But people weren't that interested in Canadian-made reggae. To get the records to sell, he had to add a sticker that said 'Made in Jamaica.'

AFTERMATH: CANCON AND BACK TO THE STRIP
1968–75

Pop/rock gets taken seriously as art and moves into bigger halls, but smaller bands have nowhere to go but cover-band bars on increasingly sleazy Yonge Street.

A s Yorkville began its collapse, it also produced one of its greatest bands. Kensington Market were discovered by manager Bernie Finkelstein after debuting at the Night Owl café, and he quickly recognized their original voice, which combined British folk with hazy psychedelia to create textures previously unheard in pop music. Guitarist Luke Gibson joined their ranks after the dissolution of Luke & the Apostles in mid-'67, and a later addition, John Mills-Cockell, took their sound to an otherworldly new level with his Moog synthesizer. The band used local references in both its band name and the title of its first album, *Avenue Road* – the name of the main thoroughfare on Yorkville's western border.

Carole Pope (Rough Trade): *Kensington Market were my favourite band, because they were so far ahead of their time. I kind of think the Beatles ripped them off.*

The late sixties saw rock grow up and confidently declare itself Art for Adults. But groups like Kensington Market couldn't discount commerce entirely. Though their two albums reached great artistic heights, they failed to deliver sales-wise, despite the support of Warner Brothers in the US and a hotshot producer, Felix Pappalardi, who'd made his name with Eric Clapton's Cream.

Most of their Yorkville counterparts who still called Canada home suffered the same fate. Phil Spector's stamp of approval and a deal with Ahmet Ertegun's Atlantic Records couldn't save Mandala, who managed only a handful of singles and one album, *Soul Crusade*, before combusting in '69. The Paupers' early New York buzz led to representation by Albert Grossman and an appearance at the Monterey Pop Festival alongside Joplin and Hendrix in June '67, but they played a disastrous set, from which they never really recovered. Their debut album, *Magic People*, wasn't the hoped-for psychedelic *Sgt. Pepper*-goes-to-Canada masterpiece, and the band was done before its follow-up was released. And the Ugly Ducklings never became more than regionally renowned, though their legend in the global garage-rock community grew after their '69 breakup, through numerous re-releases and comp appearances.

While Toronto's homegrown rock bands seemed dogged by bad luck, the city's audiences were blessed with an increasing frequency of larger events, such as 1969's Toronto Pop Festival at Varsity Stadium. The lineup included Sly & the Family Stone, the Velvet Underground, the Band, Steppenwolf (who had gotten their start in Yorkville before relocating to L.A.), and, playing one of their final shows, Kensington Market. The same promoter, John Brower, would stage the Toronto Rock and Roll Revival festival later that year at the same arena, famously featuring John Lennon and Yoko Ono.

Larger, more ambitious venues were also a part of Toronto's post-Yorkville rock scene. The Rock Pile, at 888 Yonge Street, on the northeastern edge of Yorkville, was housed in a massive old building – Toronto's Masonic Temple, opened by freemasons in 1918. Earlier in the sixties, it had booked R&B concerts as Club 888. With its 1,200-person capacity, the Rock Pile was Toronto's answer to big US rock halls like the Fillmore. Led Zeppelin performed their first Canadian show there on February 2, 1969. The Rock Pile's reign was short-lived – its owners ran out of money in August '69. The Masonic Temple was used for a variety of purposes throughout the seventies, including a big-band revival in 1973, before coming back to life as the Concert Hall in the eighties. The last act to play the Rock Pile was McKenna Mendelson Mainline, a gnarly electric blues band so popular they did a four-night stand.

The Electric Circus, 38,000-square-foot, seven-room club on Queen Street just east of Yonge, featured mostly local rock bands alongside strobe-light shows and a mirror-laden Infinity Room, a 'total environment' designed for full-on freakout. Beyond the novelty of the space, it never really took off as a music venue: numerous visiting bands cancelled gigs, and kids thought the four-dollar cover charge was too steep. The club declared bankruptcy, closing in mid-1970. Two years later, City-TV, the scrappy local channel opened by Moses Znaimer, set up shop in the building. Much later, in 1988, *Electric Circus* was revived – in name only – as City's legendary dance-music program.

With the Rock Pile and the Electric Circus gone, the big rock show action moved up the street to the more staid Massey Hall, the storied Victorian-era soft-seater that had been the country's pre-eminent concert hall since 1894. Though more renowned as the home of the Toronto Symphony Orchestra and famous jazz concerts like 1953's summit of Charlie Parker, Dizzy Gillespie, Charles Mingus, Bud Powell, and Max Roach, Massey couldn't ignore the youthquake. In 1965, it was where Levon Helm quit Dylan and the Hawks after the booing from electrically offended folkies became too much.

Gordon Lightfoot began his annual series of concerts at Massey in '67, now a five-decade-long tradition. In 1971, Neil Young performed two sold-out solo acoustic concerts at the hall, released thirty-six years later in an astonishingly crystal-clear live recording. Young had returned to Toronto a hero five years after splitting the apathetic scene, now an American recording star with a gold-selling album, *After the Gold Rush*, under his belt. The home-town audience let out a hearty cheer when Young mentioned that 'town in North Ontario' in 'Helpless.'

There was a newfound pride in homegrown music in 1971. The new decade had produced Canada's first pop superstars. Winnipeg's the Guess Who topped the US charts with 'American Woman.' Joni Mitchell released her masterpiece *Blue* that year, the most beautiful exploration of depression ever recorded. Though she wrote the song that made the music-fest mythical, Mitchell didn't play Woodstock, but the Band did – and the quintet continued to play to massive crowds while touring albums like *Stage Fright*. Lightfoot, meanwhile, had his first international hit in '71 with 'If You Could Read My Mind.' He maintained his home base in Toronto, buying a mansion in uptown Rosedale.

Lightfoot's northern-stronghold strategy would later become the norm, especially once arts funding opened up to pop artists. Meanwhile, a group of frustrated musicians, writers, and aspiring record industry members came together to build a wider audience for homegrown music. In fine Canadian social-democratic style, they decided to lobby the government to intervene. And it worked! Part of the blame for the obstacles faced by Canadian artists was laid on unsupportive domestic radio stations, and in January 1971, the CRTC's Canadian Content ('Cancon') regulations became law. Reluctant broadcasters were suddenly required by law to dedicate 25 per cent of their airtime to music determined to be Canadian in origin, through a delightfully patriotic system called MAPL (Music, Artist, Performance, Lyrics).

The architects of Cancon included music journalists Stan Klees and Walter Grealis of trade mag *RPM*, and musician Skip Prokop, formerly of the Paupers, who in 1969 had debuted an ambitious new band at the Rock Pile. Lighthouse were a thirteen-member classical/rock orchestra with an airy, optimistic sound. They immediately became beneficiaries of increased airplay, resulting in huge record sales – though primarily within Canada, beginning a trend for domestic groups that continues to this day.

By 1973, Lighthouse were huge enough to play for tens of thousands at free concerts at Nathan Phillips Square, outside Toronto's City Hall, and get introduced by the City's new progressive 'reform' mayor, David Crombie – a sign that, post-Yorkville, rock music had been accepted by the mainstream. Rock and pop were now considered art, worthy of the concert hall and the public square.

But where did smaller, scrappier bands play in the early seventies? There weren't a lot of options. New Yonge Street bars like the Gasworks began to fill the void with hard-rock bookings, but otherwise the strip was taking its nickname a bit too literally. The Bermuda and the Brown Derby booked topless dancers, and the Brass Rail and the Zanzibar became Yonge's longest-running strip clubs – with strip shows sometimes taking place alongside live bands.

The music scene's move away from cafés and into clubs in the seventies was partly spurred by long-overdue liberalization of those Presbyterian liquor laws. In 1969, bars' Saturday-night closing time was extended from 11:30 p.m. to 1:00 a.m. – in recognition of the God-given right to be hungover in church. The following year, the gender segregation of beverage rooms was outlawed. Bars became a place for heterosexual singles to meet and mingle. And in 1971, both the voting and drinking age were lowered from twenty-one to eighteen.

The Gasworks, at Yonge and Wellesley, happily catered to the mixed and youthful beer-drinking crowd, booking folk singers and cover bands. Upstairs, the same management ran hard-rock club the Chimney. Another new rock venue, the Nickelodeon, was upstairs from Friar's, still going strong into the seventies. It was there that Ronnie Hawkins, indestructible survivor of the fifties *and* the sixties, staged another comeback in 1972. Meanwhile, the long-running Colonial Tavern began to book hard rock alongside its blues and jazz offerings, with bands like A Foot in Coldwater, who may have written the world's first power ballad with '(Make Me Do) Anything You Want.' The Piccadilly Tube booked bands like Moxy, who later in the seventies shaped the commercial Canadian rock sound of groups like Loverboy.

Two bands that got their start in Yonge Street clubs in '73/'74 went on to become Toronto's best-loved hard-rock exports.

Rush played their first show in a church basement in North York in September '68, over the next years playing the high school dance circuit and bars like the Penthouse Motor Inn in east Scarborough. A Zeppelin-influenced boogie-rock trio at the time, they played the Piccadilly Tube and the Colonial frequently in '73/'74. Garnering zero label interest, Rush (with the help of long-time manager Ray Danniels) released their first single and self-titled album on their own label, Moon Records. Their DIY era didn't last long: the blue-collar anthem 'Working Man' got heavily played by DJ Donna Halper at Cleveland radio station WMMS, and the band signed with Mercury Records in the States. By the end of 1974, they could headline Massey Hall.

Original drummer John Rutsey wasn't up for big-time touring and was replaced by virtuosic Neil Peart, who brought his love of Tolkien and sci-fi into the mix as he became the band's chief lyricist. The '75 album *Fly by Night* incorporated prog-rock and metal influences in songs like the multi-section epic 'By-Tor & the Snow-Dog.' (If it hasn't already happened, someone should write a master's thesis on the significance of Toronto's two biggest rock-band exports being steeped in nerd culture: Rush and the Barenaked Ladies.)

Often considered Rush's 'little brother band,' Max Webster originally formed in Sarnia, Ontario. They too got their start at the Gasworks and the Piccadilly Tube, playing there and nearby Larry's Hideaway from '73 through '76. Max Webster displayed a more overt sense of humour than Rush – from songs like 'High Class in Borrowed Shoes' to their outlandish dress sense: beanpole frontman Kim Mitchell had a thing for mesh onesies.

Though hard-rock clubs mostly catered to a straight crowd, the Yonge Street strip was also beginning to create safer spaces for people of non-mainstream orientations. Up the street, the all-ages after-hours dance club the Manatee was aimed at a gay male crowd. In 1975, the same block hosted bi-gender disco Club David's, renowned for its drag shows (and later a key Toronto punk venue). This marked the beginnings of Toronto's gay village, now centred at Church and Wellesley.

By the late seventies, Yonge Street's long, slow decline had begun. The dream of an outdoor, pedestrianized Yonge Street died with the 1977 opening of the Eaton Centre, which hastened the chain-store suburbanization of the strip. The same year, the city was shaken by the tragic murder of Emanuel Jaques, an eleven-year-old shoeshine boy, drowned in the sink of a Yonge Street massage parlour. With three gay men convicted of the crime, homophobia fuelled the public outcry to clean up the 'sleaze' on the strip.

First-wave '77 punk band the Curse wrote the song 'Shoeshine Boy,' provocatively making light of Jaques's killing, and further stoking fury. This new wave of rock bands were also making a mockery of the Yonge Street strip itself, with its musicians'-union-controlled bars and big-haired cover bands. By the time of the Gasworks' hair-metal heyday of the late eighties / early nineties – as memorialized by Scarborough's Mike Myers in *Wayne's World* – the hard-rockin' strip had devolved into Spinal Tap self-parody.

Intersystems.

INTERSYSTEMS + SYRINX
Acid, Synths, & Chance
1967–72

One of the most far-out happenings of Toronto's psychedelic era happened not in the streets of Yorkville but within the hallowed halls of academia. In February 1967, a student council at the University of Toronto hosted its second annual arts festival, Perception 67. Inspired by growing mainstream awareness of hallucinogenic drugs, the symposium featured a who's who of the counterculture, including Beat poet Allen Ginsberg. Timothy Leary was the slated keynote speaker, but the Canadian government barred him from the country. Organizers travelled to the border to receive a pre-recorded tape of his 'sermon.' New York absurdist rockers the Fugs played at Convocation Hall – a gorgeous, domed amphitheatre – for a capacity crowd of 2,000. The openers, Torontonian Stu Broomer's free-jazz Kinetic Ensemble, were booed off the stage – and bombarded by paper airplanes.

The most unanimously well-received component of the weekend was the Mind Excursion. Multimedia artist Michael Hayden converted a drab basement cafeteria into a walk-through art installation intended to simulate an acid trip. Visitors took off their shoes and walked over gravel, cotton wool, and popcorn, amid mirrored walls, stroboscopic lights, film loops, and live dancers. The soundtrack was electronic *musique concrète*. Five thousand people lined up to journey through the Mind Excursion – and another three thousand had to be turned away. The Mind Excursion marked the debut of a new art collective: Intersystems. The four-man partnership saw Hayden joined by poet Blake Parker, architect Dik Zander, and composer John Mills-Cockell – all just twenty-three years of age.

Michael Hayden was a buzzy visual artist who exhibited work at Toronto galleries starting in '64. As a teen, he'd hitchhiked across the States, hung out with the Beats in San Francisco and first dropped acid in New York, where he met Leary and the Fugs. A charismatic motivator, he convinced local businesses to donate $24,000 worth of materials – from aluminum foil to Christmas lights to bubble wrap – to build the Mind Excursion.

Intersystems' electro-sonic visionary, John Mills-Cockell, was inspired as a teenager by an encounter with the work of Canadian composer Hugh Le Caine. Canada is unfairly forgotten for its contributions to early electronic music (which at the time was essentially an R&D wing of classical music), and Le Caine, a nuclear physicist by profession, invented one of the world's first synthesizers. Mills-Cockell's U of T music prof, Myron Schaeffer, invited him to check out his new electronic music studio, inspiring the young composer to buy a pair of used tape decks and an editing block and perform his own pieces at the Mixed Media Concerts organized by Udo Kasemets. After he left U of T to study at the Royal Conservatory of Music, his composition teacher, Dr. Samuel Dolin, asked him and classmate Ann Southam – who would become one of Canada's foremost minimalist composers – to set up an electronic music lab there. Three of the eight students at their first class would go on to become JMC's collaborators: Michael Hayden, Blake Parker, and Alan Wells.

Blake Parker's father, Harley, was a painter and research associate of philosopher Marshall McLuhan, whose theories about electronic media and their impact upon society and communication fascinated these young artists.

Intersystems didn't play concerts, they made 'Presentations.' Some took the form of art installations, including a coin-operated light-and-sound sculpture containing fluorescent liquids that was the star attraction at the Sculpture '67 event in Nathan Phillips Square that summer. Following the City Hall premiere, the collective threw an all-night party at which 1,600 people passed through the Intersystems loft on Adelaide East and danced to psych-rock band the City Muffin Boys.

Intersystems built their own musical instrument, the 'Coffin' – a giant electric stringed instrument encased in a six-foot-long mirrorized box. But

Mills-Cockell desired a greater sonic range than the electronic gear of the time could afford. The group had struck up a friendship with Robert Moog, who had pioneered the world's first compact, commercial synthesizer, controlled by two keyboards in addition to the knobs and cables of its predecessors. They drove their Day-Glo vw camper van to the Moog factory in Trumansburg, New York, to buy a Mark II synth – acquiring theirs the same day as Wendy Carlos, who would popularize the sound of analog synthesis with the best-selling album *Switched-On Bach*.

In March 1968, Intersystems performed the world's first live synthesizer concert, performing inside a two-storey aluminum structure built within the Art Gallery of Ontario's Print Room. Afterwards, they ran across town to witness John Cage and Marcel Duchamp play a musical chess match on a specially designed, responsive game board. Cage lost. The historic occasion marked Duchamp's last public appearance. Later that same month, they premiered an even more ambitious Presentation. *Network* was a 'game' piece – possibly inspired by the chess match – that took over a large room at the American College Editors' Conference in Washington, D.C.

John Mills-Cockell: The game consisted of thirty-three telephones and thirteen televisions. There were thirty-some players that were sitting at eleven desks, and they would be watching the televisions, randomly switching from channel to channel, each one independently. And they would call the person next to them and tell them what it was they saw on their channel on TV.

Network was witnessed by systems theorist Buckminster Fuller, whose geodesic dome had graced Expo 67 the previous summer, and who was sufficiently enthralled to invite the group to remount it a month later at Southern Illinois University. This time, their arts performance found them caught in the crossfire of the anti-war movement.

JMC: There was a riot outside the room where we were doing our concert. The protestors broke through the doors and took over the room. The dean said, 'Okay, you've got to stop playing now. Turn the lights on. Turn the sound off.' We went and pleaded with him to let us continue. Gradually everybody calmed down and started sitting on the floor. Blake and I started playing this slow mantric chant. And everybody was just hypnotized by it.

Intersystems' prolific output – they were together just two years – can be credited to their insane work ethic - they worked fifteen hours a day, seven

Syrinx.

days a week; though LSD may have helped as a stimulant. Incredibly, they also had time to record and release three albums' worth of music. These are difficult listening – abstract and dissonant, and Parker's declamations are often unnerving — but far ahead of their time. The self-released 1968's *Free Psychedelic Poster Inside* – which had nothing 'inside,' just a manila envelope containing the record – was the companion piece to their most ambitious Presentation of all.

In the summer of 1968, Intersystems took over the second floor of an industrial building in Montreal. The Mind Excursion Centre, created with the help of a financial backer, was intended to be a more permanent iteration of the piece that got it all started at Perception 67. This 'total environment' consisted of eleven chambers, including a Kaleidoscope Room, a Floating Room, and a Mirror Maze. By early winter '68, struggling to cover costs, they closed up shop – and the group began to wind down.

In late '68, Mills-Cockell had a visit from his friends Bernie Finkelstein, who managed Kensington Market, and Eugene Martynec, the band's lead guitarist and pianist. Looking for something to set their sound apart, they 'seconded' JMC and his Moog for the recording of their second album. He hauled the massive electronic rig on stage for a handful of gigs at the Rock Pile, starting in March of '69. It proved challenging, however, as the Moog had a mind of its own and often refused to stay in tune. Other factors caused Kensington Market to disintegrate shortly after the album's release.

JMC: Intersystems had pretty much run its course, so it was no surprise when I said I wanted to go with Kensington Market. Michael was getting other commissions and I'm not sure what happened to Blake. I think he was probably the most upset by the breakup. It was hard.

Mills-Cockell moved to the West Coast and began work on a solo record. His new synthesizer compositions embraced classical virtues of melody and harmony; some of them featured Alan Wells, his former Royal Conservatory student, on conga. Upon completion of these sessions, JMC returned to the capital of the Canadian music business.

JMC: I traded a Crown amp for a bag of peyote buttons and took the train across the country. Bart Schoales met me at the train station and took me up to this restaurant called Meat and Potatoes. The owner said, 'Do you want to start playing here tonight?' And so I did. And who should show up but Doug Pringle with his soprano sax. He said, 'Do you mind if I sit in?'

Meat and Potatoes was a 'hip boite' (according to the *Globe*) feeding jazz and inexpensive grub to U of T students, its decor including inflatable sculptures by Michael Hayden. JMC and Pringle began improvising together, and the novelty of the synth/sax combo caused a stir. Meanwhile, Bernie Finkelstein had started up his own record label dedicated to championing Canadian talent. True North Records' first release, in 1970, was the debut by folk singer Bruce Cockburn. The second was slated to be John Mills-Cockell's solo debut, but they added Pringle's sax to a few tracks from the Vancouver sessions – and then Alan Wells resurfaced in Toronto. The new trio was christened Syrinx – the name of a nymph from Greek mythology, as well as a Debussy piece, among other esoteric meanings.

Syrinx's music seems frozen in time yet peculiarly timeless. Their instrumentals are calm and unhurried, minimalist but unrepetitive. At times the melodies are almost medieval. Released in late 1970, Syrinx's self-titled debut wouldn't sound out of place alongside modern ambient or post-rock.

Syrinx immediately began attracting high-art attention. The National Ballet of Canada commissioned them to score works for young performers, including a nineteen-year-old Karen Kain. Classical conductor Milton Barnes commissioned new pieces for his Toronto Repertory Ensemble; the resulting Syrinx/orchestra mash-up was captured on a suite called *Stringspace*. They were also asked to create the theme song for a current affairs TV show called *Here Come the Seventies*. It became a surprise hit single.

JMC: We were rehearsing in a third-storey walkup loft on King West. Right across the street was the Diamond Taxi dispatch centre, with a loudspeaker outside calling the cabs. And we had the window open, and Doug said 'Holy shit, come here, listen.' They were playing 'Tillicum' on the taxi dispatch speaker. We hadn't even heard it before. We didn't know it had been mastered for a single!

Bigger engagements followed, including opening for Miles Davis at Massey Hall and Ravi Shankar in Montreal, but the good fortune of 'Tillicum' coincided with tragedy. On March 3, 1971, a fire raged through a warehouse next to the old Bohemian Embassy location, destroying the studio where Syrinx had been recording. They lost all their equipment, including the Moog Mark II, and the master tapes for their second album. A day-long benefit concert on April 4, 1971, at the St. Lawrence Centre – featuring, among others, Beverley Glenn Copeland, Bruce Cockburn, and Murray McLauchlan – helped replace Syrinx's lost gear.

By 1972, Syrinx were stalled. Though still providing music for theatre and dance, they also found themselves playing week-long stints at small Toronto venues like Grumbles Coffeehouse and the Dovercourt Tavern.

JMC: I just decided that I'd done enough of it. And I probably didn't handle it very well. Alan was especially really broken up about it. And I'm not sure he ever really recovered from that. He moved out west almost instantly.

John Mills-Cockell began a long career writing music for film and television, concurrently releasing a series of solo albums, including 1973's *Heartbeat*. In 1977, Doug Pringle was part of Toronto's first wave of punk rock, playing synth in the Poles.

Intersystems and Syrinx were rediscovered in the twenty-first century when they appeared in the 2014 documentary *I Dream of Wires*. The Intersystems discography was reissued by Italian label Alga Marghen in 2015, followed by the Syrinx retrospective *Tumblers from the Vault*, released on Brooklyn label RVNG Intl. This surge of rediscovery culminated in a Syrinx reunion performance at Moogfest in Durham, North Carolina, in 2017.

START SPADINA
1971–77

With rock music becoming increasingly corporate, and progressive Toronto occupied by city-building, a short-lived bohemian scene on Spadina Avenue lays the groundwork for a new spirit of audacious originality.

O n October 27, 1973, an out-of-town band with an outrageous new look and sound played the Victory Burlesque Theatre, west of Yonge at the corner of Spadina and Dundas. The New York Dolls bridged the gap between glam rock in the UK – David Bowie, T. Rex, Gary Glitter – and what would become punk rock. The local opening act was that proggy blues-rock trio from Willowdale, Rush. A few months later, the Victory would host another Toronto punk first, when Detroit's Iggy and the Stooges, on the verge of heroin-fuelled collapse, played there in January 1974.

Toronto's strip clubs weren't limited to Yonge Street. Originally a Yiddish theatre called the Standard that opened in 1921, the Victory Burlesque had been pushing Toronto the Good's buttons since the early sixties. A large hall, the Victory was broken in as a rock venue by Mainline, the blues trio formerly known as McKenna Mendelson Mainline.

In 1972, they staged a live show called the Mainline Bump 'n' Grind Revue, in which the band played in drag alongside four strippers. Sex sells, and the live album they recorded became a cult hit; Moses Znaimer filmed the show to broadcast late at night on City-TV alongside softcore porn. But the building was sold in 1975, becoming the Chinese-community-oriented Golden Harvest Cinema.

The Victory was the southern anchor of a string of music venues along Spadina, another north-south strip that began to rival Yonge Street in density. Spadina's early twentieth-century Jewish garment businesses had given way

Downchild Blues Band helped make neighbourhood bar Grossman's Tavern into a happening music venue.

to the new Asian eateries and grocery stores, following the expropriation of the Ward (the original Chinatown) to make way for New City Hall, and an influx of immigration in the late sixties. Its multi-ethnic, working-class charm and plentiful, affordable housing attracted bohemian artists in search of a new Yorkville.

At the corner of Spadina and Cecil, in a Victorian house, Grossman's Tavern sits on the edge of Kensington Market. Since Al Grossman opened it as the city's first kosher cafeteria in 1948, Grossman's has been a watering hole for various immigrant communities: Jewish, Hungarian, Caribbean, Chinese, and in the post-Yorkville seventies, hippies, who gratefully quaffed down the twenty-five-cent pints. Grossman's regulars in the first half of the seventies included Kid Bastien's New Orleans–style Camellia Jazz Band and the Downchild Blues Band, who convinced the owner to start booking live music.

Richard Flohil (veteran publicist): *The Downchild Blues Band were the first band that played there outside of Hungarian accordion duos. The band called me because I had this spurious rep as the blues maven, and said, 'Would you consider working for us?' So I went to Grossman's and I didn't get served. I said, 'What does it take to get a beer around here?' This huge waiter said, 'You sarcastic fuck, you're out.' And they kicked me out! On the way out, Al, this*

diminutive little guy said, [whispers] 'Come back tomorrow, it'll be all right.'
So I did. And I worked with Downchild for thirty-nine years.

Folk singer/songwriter Murray McLauchlan hung out at Grossman's, immortalizing Kensington Market in his '74 civic anthem 'Down by the Henry Moore,' its title celebrating the landmark piece by the British sculptor outside City Hall. (Since McLauchlan's travelogue says he went 'skating in the Square,' we must assume he wasn't talking about the better-known Moore outside the Art Gallery of Ontario.) The tavern's regular groups would get booked into 'Grossman's Presents' concerts for the square elite at the swanky St. Lawrence Centre for the Arts. Though it's clearly seen better days, in 2020 grimy Grossman's still hosts blues jams and Dixieland jazz matinees.

Gary Cormier (concert promoter): *Grossman's was a cool place. I took my parents there on Saturday afternoons to hear jazz. It was mostly Dixieland jazz, but there'd be more adventurous stuff. Bands didn't get paid a lot of money. But if you wanted a gig, you could go and ask them and they would probably give you a gig. Which is the way it should be. There were hookers, artists covered in tattered jeans and paint, and older gentlemen in natty tweed jackets with elbow badges who probably had a British accent, listening to fancy jazz. And everything in between.*

Further north, at the corner of College and Spadina, sat the Silver Dollar Room, nestled next to the run-down Waverley Hotel and Scott Mission. Opened in 1958, the 'Dollar,' as it was affectionately known, had already been through numerous lives by the mid-seventies: blues bar, jazz club, country and western joint, strip club. This would continue over the next four decades, with more progressive-minded indie bookers including Elliott Lefko in the late eighties and Dan Burke in the 2000s, though Gary Kendall of Downchild's bookings would brand the Silver Dollar Toronto's unofficial home of the blues.

Not far down Spadina is another landmark with which Dan Burke would become associated: the El Mocambo. But is it the club that's the landmark, or is it the huge neon palm tree that hangs out front, fetishized as a historic signifier of a lost Toronto of cheap draft and easy good times? Fun didn't come so easy when the El Mocambo opened in 1948, among the first wave of cocktail bars. Its name roughly translates as 'the roadhouse' in Spanish; its original owners likely jumped on the postwar tiki fad. There was live music in the romantic dining lounge, but troubadors Gus Mauro & His Gay Caballeros were barred by the liquor board from strolling while playing, and had to remain seated like the patrons. The fifties and sixties passed the club by, its older clientele immune to the counterculture.

In 1972, the building was bought by Mike Baird and Tom Kristenbrun, a former Toronto Argonauts football player. They decided to get the El Mo caught up with the times and cash in on its proximity to the U of T campus – and the lowered drinking age. They kept the neon palm sign but gutted the interior, painted it black, and made it into a workmanlike rock club with two live rooms. The main floor bar catered to up-and-coming acts, while the larger upstairs space was a mini concert hall for bigger-name groups. A Foot in Coldwater played the opening night, and early bookings included jazz-rock band Dr. Music, heavy rockers Crowbar, and Spadina's ubiquitous blues bands Downchild and Mainline.

The El Mo's surefire booking policy would keep the beer taps flowing through the seventies. Talent buyer Neill Dixon – who would go on to found the Canadian Music Week conference – brought in old-time bluesmen like Muddy Waters and Howlin' Wolf. Jazz greats Hugh Masekela and Charles Mingus took the stage, as did up-and-comer Tom Waits, who opened for local bluegrass heroes the Good Brothers.

But in March 1977, the event that would forever define the El Mo took place. Billed alongside April Wine as 'the Cockroaches,' the Rolling Stones played two secret shows, their first club shows in fourteen years, with the aim of recording a live album. The subsequent media circus focused on the salacious presence of Margaret Trudeau who, instead of celebrating her sixth wedding anniversary to PM Pierre, was partying with Mick Jagger and Ron Wood. Four of the tracks recorded there ended up on the album *Love You Live*.

The Stones gigs made the El Mocambo the city's highest-profile rock club for a while, and the increasingly corporate branch-plant music industry used it to showcase acts they hoped would break big. Blondie, Devo, and Elvis Costello played there in 1978; a fresh-faced U2 in 1980. But a younger generation of bands built a new community further south on Queen Street West – to the first-wave punk rockers, the El Mocambo was the land of the dinosaurs.

The El Mo went through many changes in relevance and ownership through the next two decades, reaching a latter-day heyday in the late nineties with Elvis Mondays godfather William New and notorious promoter Dan Burke at the booking helm. The club's most recent saviour is venture capitalist and *Dragon's Den* TV star Michael Wekerle, who sank millions into a years-long reno to restore it to former glory. It's hard to tell if the latest incarnation of the El Mocambo will be more concert venue or classic rock museum. But if nothing else, Wekerle has rebuilt the iconic Neon Palm tree sign hanging over the Spadina sidewalk.

But back in the seventies, the El Mocambo gave Spadina Avenue a cultural moment as the city's live music centre, in the wake of the demise of Yorkville and Yonge Street's slide into sleaze. This era been somewhat forgotten; the chasm between the hippie and punk eras amounts to cultural 'lost years,' not greatly understood today outside of nostalgia for bell-bottoms and Afros.

One could speculate that the youthful post-hippie boomers became more focused on social activism than music in the seventies, as the live music scene became increasingly soaked in booze. The Jane Jacobs–educated urbanists who tried in vain to pedestrianize Yorkville in the Summer of Love turned their attention to a bigger automotive threat: the proposed multi-lane Spadina Expressway that would have razed parts of the Annex and Forest Hill neighbourhoods and sent massive amounts of car traffic down Spadina. A civic apocalypse.

Making common cause between Rosedale elites and leftie progressives, the 'Stop Spadina' citizens' movement – with high-profile supporters including Jacobs, Marshall McLuhan, and newly elected allies on city council, including future mayor John Sewell – succeeded in blocking the expressway's construction. It's thanks to these activists that the strollable Spadina we know and love exists today.

After Stop Spadina, early-seventies Toronto was in the glow of civic optimism. The Eberhard Zeidler–designed Ontario Place opened in 1971, providing children with a futuristic play space and concert audiences with a nifty 360-degree rotating stage at the park's beloved open-air venue, the Forum. The post-Stonewall birth of the gay village in the Church and Wellesley area began to make Toronto a beacon for tolerance. And in 1973, construction started on Toronto's ultimate futurist symbol, the CN Tower.

Some of the most interesting Toronto music of the early seventies came from the intersections of folk and jazz suggested by the music of Joni Mitchell. In 1970, a Black singer/songwriter named Beverly Glenn-Copeland released two gorgeous self-titled albums. Originally from Philadelphia, Glenn-Copeland came to Canada to study composition at McGill in Montreal, and ended up living in Toronto for a few years. Then living as a woman, Glenn-Copeland opened for Syrinx at the St. Lawrence Hall and performed alongside jazz guitar icon Lenny Breau at Global Village, a theatre located in an old warehouse on St. Nicholas Street. Glenn-Copeland, who transitioned as male in the nineties, experienced a later-life renaissance with the 2016 rediscovery of his 1986 album *Keyboard Fantasies*.

Glenn-Copeland also contributed vocals to albums by Bruce Cockburn, the Ottawa artist who in some ways led the folk movement out of its post-Yorkville exodus with his bucolic self-titled debut album in 1970, also the first release for True North Records. Launched by Bernie Finkelstein, True North aimed to support Canadian music exclusively. Cockburn and his friend and labelmate Murray McLauchlan were popular enough to headline the Riverboat – and by '74, both could sell out Massey Hall. But they were the exceptions among homegrown artists.

Gradually, the folk scene spread to other parts of the city. New coffeehouses included the Nervous Breakdown, in Cabbagetown; Grumbles, at Jarvis and Adelaide; Egerton's Restaurant, at Gerrard and Church; the Fiddler's Green, at Eglinton and Mt. Pleasant; Shier's, in suburban Don Mills. Eventually, the folk and singer/songwriter community moved west to its longest-running venue home, the Free Times Café, opening in 1980 on College Street, just west of Spadina.

A short drive down the highway, in Hamilton, a garage band called Simply Saucer cranked up their amps and droned on a hypnotic Velvet Underground frequency, tuned to the cosmic waves of Sun Ra and Can. Their proto-punk sound, too far-out for its time and place, was little heard beyond their home rehearsal space and a few surreal high school dances. A '74 demo recording session with Bob Lanois, brother of future superstar producer Daniel, and a live recording at Hamilton's Jackson Square, were eventually released as the album *Cyborgs Revisited* – fifteen years later. Simply Saucer are now recognized as true pioneers of Canadian underground DIY rock, and one of the key missing links between psychedelia and punk rock.

Back on the Spadina circuit, another group stood with stilettoed heels on either side of the coming revolution. Rough Trade played some of their earliest gigs at Grossman's in 1975, and Carole Pope and Kevan Staples's band mashed up funk/R&B with swaggering glam rock. Having started out as teens in Yorkville in the acoustic project O, they were one of the few acts whose career bridged the hippie and punk eras.

Like Patti Smith in New York, Pope spoke to the disillusioned idealists of the sixties and influenced the disaffected youth who kickstarted the punk movement. Rough Trade's confrontational stage presence served Toronto notice that something new was on the way, waiting to slap them in the face.

ROUGH TRADE
Pleasures of the Flesh
1974–86

Carole Pope was one of the first women in pop music to use sexuality to express herself, fuck with the male gaze, and incite the attention of the authorities. At Rough Trade's early mid-seventies gigs at Grossman's Tavern, she dressed up in bondage gear and whipped audience members with a riding crop. She grabbed her crotch on air at the 1980 Juno Awards, causing heads to roll at the CBC but also inspiring a young k.d. lang, watching at home in Edmonton, to consider that she might one day be able to express her own sexuality in music. Where the band was really perverse was in their approach to the music business; if there was a correct way of doing things, these contrarians enjoyed doing the opposite.

Though their biggest hit came out in 1980, the band's roots date back to the late sixties. In an era when youth was prized, they didn't hit the big time until they were on the far side of thirty. Carole Pope was a product of the hippie counterculture who became a feminist foremother to the punk/new-wave generation. At a time when bar bands were expected to play covers, they insisted on performing their own songs – and became one of the biggest draws on the Toronto club scene, graduating from Grossman's to Yonge Street venues like the Chimney and the prestigious Colonial Tavern.

And though Rough Trade anticipated punk when it came to confrontation, originality, and fashion sense, musically they had one foot firmly stuck in the classic-rock tar pits. In 1977, while their punk progeny were Crashing 'n' Burning, Rough Trade were at Massey Hall, creating a burlesque musical called *Restless Underwear* with Baltimore drag performer Divine. It was universally panned. The band's sexual satire often went over people's heads; they honed their sense of humour through their friendship with Second City comedians like Dan Aykroyd and Catherine O'Hara.

Bizarre celebrity encounters followed them: everyone from Maggie Trudeau to Elton John to 'Happy Hooker' Xaviera Hollander came to see them play in the early days. Martin Short opened for them with a stand-up set and had beer sprayed all over him. Pope was romantically linked to UK soul star Dusty Springfield. Initially a heterosexual couple, Pope and co-founder/guitarist Kevan Staples became platonic collaborators as she came to terms with her orientation.

Rough Trade are now recognized for making the first song with lesbian lyrics to hit the pop charts anywhere. Inspired by Pope's teen years attending Cedarbrae Collegiate Institute in Scarborough, 'High School Confidential' is Pope's finest moment, her uber-confident delivery an expression of lust toward a blonde, statuesque young woman – the embodiment of the fifties 'Sex Bomb' archetype. Though, in typical Rough Trade fashion, you can't really tell if it's autobiographical or camp storytelling.

I sat down with Carole Pope over coffee to try and unwrap some of the contradictions of the Rough Trade story.

What was it like hanging out in Yorkville as a teen?
It was really amazing, because there was this whole music scene going on. I eventually left home and moved there. I saw my first drag queen sashaying down the street. I saw Joni Mitchell at the Riverboat. I saw bands like Kensington Market and the Ugly Ducklings, who actually went to my high school. And I remember seeing Brian Wilson drive down the street in a limo. And Mitch Mitchell and Noel Redding from Jimi Hendrix's band just hanging out in a café.

So you met Kevan Staples at an audition for another band, is that right?
Yeah, I knew this crazy violin player and this other guy who played the keyboard. They were starting a band and I went and auditioned and then

Kevan showed up. He was not really a guitar player, but he was playing guitar with sitar picks on his fingers. We hit it off right away. And that band didn't happen. We were madly attracted to each other – we fell in love and would just lie around and listen to music and smoke pot.

Did it take a while before you started making your own music?
I think lying around smoking pot kind of wastes a lot of time. I would never do that again – I hate pot now! It took me a long time to get into it and I was like, 'Oh my God, all that time I wasted.' Although it did make me appreciate music more. But I loved LSD. That was the drug that really opened me up. I had a vivid imagination anyway. I remember listening to the same song for eight hours.

O was your and Kevan's first band, an acoustic duo, around 1968/69. Did you play live at all?
I'm not even sure if we did any gigs in front of anybody, but people used to come to our rehearsals. We may have done one or two gigs. We did play on top of a psychedelic bus, but I don't know why!

After that, there was a bit of a break and you changed your name to the Bullwhip Brothers. What were you up to in the years leading up to Rough Trade?
There was a performance space that we played called Global Village. And that's when we met Danny Aykroyd and Valri Bromfield. We used to go to Second City all the time and smoke a lot of pot. We were trying to figure out what we were doing. We thought that maybe (a) we should get another band name, and (b) actually get a band. I came up with Rough Trade because I was obsessed with male homosexuals. Everything about them. Lesbians didn't have that much profile, but gay men had leather and lube.

What were Rough Trade's early musical inspirations?
All the funk and R&B, and of course the Beatles and the Stones and Hendrix. There was a lot of seventies music I hated. I liked disco for a while. When it first started it was kind of raw, and then it became really insipid. And that I found really depressing. But then punk started and I was like, yeah – I was all about that.

Was Second City an influence on your performance style?

It was just so inspirational to see everybody improvise and it was so brilliant. We played Grossman's Tavern a lot, and they would come and see us – and we would go see them. Margaret Trudeau showed up at Grossman's. We were trying to be really cool and not freak out that Margaret Trudeau was in the audience.

What was the scene like at Grossman's?
It was really happening. There was always a lineup to see us, and that's where we met General Idea. There was Granada Gazelle, Flakey Rose Hip, all these insane artists. We just really bonded with them and always hung out together. We ended up in *FILE* magazine and then they did most of our album covers.

What do you think attracted them to Rough Trade?
Just because we did what made us happy and there weren't that many people doing original material. And not that many people were doing sexual stuff. I ultimately ended up wearing a bondage suit and whipping people in the audience. And certainly using a riding crop.

Was Toronto an easy place to shock people then?
I guess. I mean, to us it was all a parody, but some people took it really, really seriously. The cops used to come and see us, because I was grabbing my crotch. Apparently that was offensive. But there were punk bands who were bloodletting and stuff, and that was not offensive.

Was Toronto more uptight than other big cities?
I think so, yeah, absolutely.

Do you think you helped Toronto loosen up?
I do, because we just didn't care. And I think the audience picked up on that. And I mean, people came out because of Rough Trade, or people got inspired to start their own bands.

Did you feel you were making a statement being an original band in the seventies?
We got real joy in writing songs and putting them out there. People said, 'Oh you can't do original material, nobody wants to hear that.' We said, 'Well, there's lineups down the street, you're full of shit.'

In those days, you were allowed to make a bunch of albums and come into your own and develop as an artist, unlike now. I think the world caught up with us, but I think we were always trying to expand as artists. I also think that I was very threatening and I'm going to say 'androgynous.' I love that term and I wish people still used it now, because now it's so political – the way people identify, I mean. 'Androgynous' to me was a lot sexier, and not political. I'm probably going to offend a lot of people by saying that!

★

Though Rough Trade spent the 1970s as one of Toronto's best live bands, by the time the eighties came around, they embarked on a more straightforward career as recording artists. Their '76 *Live!* album had been a one-off for Jack Richardson's Nimbus 9 subsidiary Umbrella, and they were still without a label until Bernie Finkelstein wandered backstage after a show at the Music Hall on Danforth in the summer of 1980. The next day, Rough Trade signed to True North Records.

With Pope and Staples backed up by the solid rhythm section of Terry Wilkins and Bucky Berger, and producer Eugene Martynec at the console, their 'proper' debut *Avoid Freud* was released that fall. It still hasn't been topped as Toronto's best-ever album title.

The album's hard-rock production, combined with the band's austere, leather-clad, shoulder-padded fashion sense – as captured by General Idea on the stunning cover – launched it immediately onto the charts. But it was Rough Trade's smart, ironic sex appeal that got Torontonians talking, especially when it came to 'High School Confidential.' Lesbian love was still a decade or two away from mainstream acceptance, and many listeners assumed Pope was a man (though her voice is quite clearly a woman's), or told themselves she was speaking from the perspective of one. But the line 'I wanna cream my jeans when she comes my way' was deemed too risqué, and the song was initially banned by local radio stations.

Making up for their leisurely pace in the seventies, Rough Trade released three albums over the next two years, starting in late '81 with *For Those Who Think Young* (think: Jung). Continuing the new-wave rock sound of *Avoid Freud*, it marked their commercial peak, as single 'All Touch' saw them break into the US market.

In September 1983, Rough Trade were invited to open for David Bowie at the CNE Grandstand as part of his Serious Moonlight tour. Following the unexpected mass success of Bowie's *Let's Dance*, the Torontonians played to

100,000 people over two nights. Bowie watched their set from the side of the stage and liked the band so much he added them to more Canadian dates. According to Pope's memoir, they were asked to continue on with Bowie to California, but their US label refused to give them tour support.

That disappointment was the beginning of the end for Rough Trade. After releasing a few flat records, Pope and Staples dissolved the band in January 1986. Taking their breakup with a fitting smirk, they embarked on a farewell tour, Deep Six in '86, playing their last local gig at RPM. The Clichettes opened, the feminist performance-art trio lip-synching to male cock-rock – complete with dangling fake phalluses – anticipating later gender-provocateurs from Peaches to Vag Halen, the ultimate spawn of Rough Trade. Pope began a solo career, moving to Los Angeles, while Toronto-bound Staples began composing for film and TV, but Rough Trade will remain their biggest, boldest statement.

THE GARYS
Please Welcome ...
1976-93

In all the Toronto music histories that have been written so far, no one is more universally beloved than the Garys. More than mere concert promoters, the two men named Gary curated creative experiences that put art and artists first — often at their own expense — and were critical scene-builders.

The Garys brought the Ramones to Toronto in 1976 to play the New Yorker Theatre, inspiring the first wave of punk rock in Canada. They remade the Horseshoe Tavern in their own image and hosted the first of punk's many funerals with the Last Pogo (1978). At the Edge, they created the perfect post-punk/new-wave club in an old Victorian house (1978–81). And with the Police Picnics (1981–83), they staged some of Toronto's most successful outdoor music festivals. Their list of booking firsts reads like the best Spotify playlist you could stumble upon.

Growing up in the Forest Hill neighbourhood of Toronto, Gary Topp went with his parents to see what is considered to be the first rock'n'roll concert in Toronto: Bill Haley & His Comets at Maple Leaf Gardens in 1956. As a teen, he hung out in sixties Yorkville, checking out folk, blues, and jazz acts and soaking up the counterculture. After college, he wrote for a film trade magazine, and in his mid-twenties started a distribution company called Toppsoil Films. Their early titles included a Jimi Hendrix concert film.

Gary Topp: But nobody would show it because it was only fifty minutes long. So I said, 'Well, let's find a movie theatre and show it ourselves!'

An early exemplar of the scrappy, entrepreneurial, DIY spirit, Gary Topp took over a dilapidated old cinema in Toronto's quiet east end.

GT: We found the Roxy Theatre on Danforth at Greenwood. It was a pigsty, and hadn't been used for about a year. Everybody said, 'Why are you going out there?' I didn't know where the fuck Greenwood and Danforth was, but I knew it was on a subway line. And we turned that into a major successful cinema showing two different movies every night for ninety-nine cents. And I started booking bands there on the stage, which *might* have been a yard deep.

Rebranding it the Original 99-Cent Roxy, in 1972 Topp began screening cult films like John Waters's *Pink Flamingos* alongside the occasional live band, such as Rough Trade, who played their very first show there. Bands had to line up in a row to perform on the narrow lip of the stage in front of the screen.

GT: The thing about the Roxy was, it was a real scene. It was probably the biggest scene Toronto ever had, other than the Rock Pile. We would do seven hundred to a thousand people a night. You could walk in and hear Roxy Music or Frank Zappa blasting through the speakers with trailers running on silent. In those days, you could smoke cigarettes in theatres, so everybody's doing pot and hash and whatever drugs. It was a really crazy wild place, but it was also a club for people who were discovering all these filmmakers and movies and music. I've never seen anywhere like it. It really was a breeding ground for the Toronto punk-rock-slash-new-wave-whatever-new-music scene.

In 1975, experimental violinist Nash the Slash played his first gig at the Roxy, accompanying a live score to Luis Bunuel's 1929 silent film classic *Un Chien Andalou*. But live music was still mostly a side venture for Topp in the Roxy days. The following year, Topp got into a dispute with the Roxy's landlord, and he jumped ship. He and business partner Jeff Silverman relocated downtown, to Yonge Street arthouse cinema the New Yorker Theatre. It was there that Topp struck upon a cultural moment.

GT: We took over the New Yorker and continued the same policy, except it was a $1.99 admission. I started running a movie there called *The Blank Generation*, which [documented] all the bands that were playing at CBGB and Max's. And I was showing that at midnight, and one night I was just sitting there watching it and having a joint. I thought, I've run every movie I ever wanted to show. I gotta do something new, get into something else. Let's build a stage in front of the screen and bring *these* bands in, because these bands struck me the same way as people like Sun Ra and John Coltrane struck me in jazz in the sixties. They were doing something completely different from everything else that was out there.

Television, Blondie, Talking Heads, Patti Smith, Richard Hell ... a group of idealistic young musicians, poets, and artists were in the process of revolutionizing the pop music world with a raw, direct, back-to-basics approach – just a day's drive away, on the bleak, bankrupt streets of Manhattan.

GT: I never thought I'd be a music promoter. But I decided to build a stage. And I had no idea about anything. I went to David 'Blue' Bluestein, the major booking agent at the time, and said, 'I want to book a band.' He says, 'What band do you want?' I said, 'You ever hear of the Ramones?' And he said, 'No, but I'll see if I can find them.'

The Ramones' Toronto debut in fall '76 was a watershed moment for the local music scene, with members of the soon-to-form Viletones and Diodes in attendance. This put our Gary at ground zero of a subcultural explosion. But by then, there were two Garys.

GT: I met Gary Cormier because we needed a new candy counter built at the theatre. He had been a music agent but got fed up with the business and just became a carpenter. He really knew how to book bands. I didn't, I was more of a fan. I knew what I wanted, and I knew how to run a night at a theatre, but I didn't really know anything about the music business.

Born in Montreal and raised in Whitby, high school dropout Gary Cormier sang in R&B bands as a sixties teen before training as a carpenter, then going to work for a booking agency. He was living in a loft on King Street West when he discovered Rough Trade. Offering to manage the hot new group, Cormier took them from grimy Grossman's to the fancier Colonial. He was well attuned to the culture storm brewing on the horizon.

Gary Cormier: I could feel it coming. The culture was shifting away from having to do somebody else's material, to a time when the emphasis was on, 'What have *you* got to say?'

Reggae band Earth, Roots & Water opened for the Police at the Horseshoe Tavern in 1978.

GT: Everybody thinks we were punk rock, but we booked Ali Akbar Khan, Cecil Taylor, John Cale, Carla Bley, Lewis Furey, Lightnin' Hopkins, and Tom Waits. We were booking out of our record collections. We weren't like every other booker that just booked from *Billboard*. We were music lovers and we were booking what we wanted.

The Garys booked concerts at the New Yorker for about eighteen months. In early '78, they received an attractive offer to move shop to the Horseshoe Tavern, where they brought the best of the new wave down to Queen West. During their brief but illustrious Horseshoe run, the Garys booked the cream of the cross-the-pond crop, but no gig is more fabled than November 2, 1978: the Canadian debut of reggae-inspired new-wave power trio the Police. Local support was supplied by roots reggae crew Earth, Roots and Water. Only fifteen people were there. The Police were so taken with their opening act that they wanted to take Earth, Roots and Water on their North American tour the following year, but by then the group was sadly no more.

Their booking run at the 'Shoe was brief but action-packed, concluding with the dramatic double-whammy of the Last Pogo and the Last Bound-Up concerts in December 1978.

GT: We didn't last long at the Horseshoe. It was hard to make money there because everything we did was so off the wall. I'd always say the scene was probably about a thousand people, bands and audience combined. Half the people were in bands – and they don't have money. Only the people who knew the music cared about the Horseshoe. The industry didn't give a shit.

The record company mafia were afraid of that kind of music and they didn't know anything about it. They didn't do their homework. They didn't have ears, they didn't have eyes, and they were just fucking dumb. And we didn't have carpeting, like the El Mocambo.

The Garys' next venue promised to be a more permanent home for the new wave. Starting on New Year's Eve 1978/79, they took over the Edge, where their booking tenure lasted two and a half years. It was their last full-time venue home. At 11:30 p.m. on June 6, 1981 the Garys learned the club was closing suddenly. They hosted a surprise wake until five a.m.

GT: We did great stuff at the Edge. It was an old building, there was hardly any insulation. If you had minus twenty degrees outside, it got cold in there. Bands would have to wear gloves to play. The plumbing would break often and water from the men's washroom would pour down in front of the stage. My favourite moment was one time Jonathan Richman played there, just acoustic at the time. He just stood back and let the water run. I was doing the lights and it looked like Niagara Falls.

Meanwhile, the Garys were building on their relationship with the Police. While booking the Edge, they started branching out and promoting larger concerts. The Police's fanbase had grown exponentially in the two years since they debuted at the Horseshoe, and by November 1980, they could fill the 2,700-seat Massey Hall.

Though the competing new-wave Heatwave festival had been a dismal financial disaster in the summer of 1980, losing over a million dollars for promoter John Brower, the Garys were unfazed and decided to stage their own sunshine show.

GT: When we first saw the Police at the Horseshoe, we looked at each other, [Cormier] was at the soundboard, I was doing lights, and said, 'These guys would be great outdoors.' In '81, we needed to do a bigger show with them. Some guys had rights to a farmer's field in Oakville and were bugging us to put on a big outdoor show there.

The Garys called it the Police Picnic, a cheeky trolling of the Metro Police, who had hosted their own fundraising event with the same name on Toronto Island for many years. Twenty-five thousand people attended the first Police Picnic, held August 23, 1981. With the Police anchoring the bill, the rest of the lineup included Iggy Pop, the Specials, the Go-Gos, Oingo Boingo, Killing Joke, and John Otway, with Nash the Slash the only local. The already stacked lineup could have included Prince – a booking blocked by the Police's management, according to Topp.

GT: We put a great package together, but think how much greater it would have been with Prince. I understand why they didn't want to do it, though. I was DJing that show before the Police came on. I was playing reggae and stuff, and then I played 'Celebrate' by Kool and the Gang. The band's manager came up and said, 'You've got to take this off!' In those days, it wasn't cool to play disco.

Two more Police Picnics took place, and in 1982–83, the Garys took the party into the city, taking over Exhibition Place. Ugly grey tarpaulin protected the Astroturf as new wavers semi-covertly sipped on smuggled-in booze. Musical highlights included James Brown, Talking Heads, Peter Tosh, Joan Jett & the Blackhearts, and King Sunny Adé, with Ready Records repping Toronto via Blue Peter and the Spoons.

After the closure of the Edge, the Garys had become roving presenters, focusing on larger concerts at a suite of venues, remaining Toronto's foremost promoters of what became known as alternative music. They made use of venues like the Music Hall on the Danforth, the Palais Royale, and one historic space they would help revive: the Concert Hall, in the Masonic Temple on Yonge Street, former home of Club 888 and the Rock Pile.

GC: The people who ran the Masonic Temple wouldn't rent it out for concerts. They had a lot of bad memories from the Rock Pile days. The building had really been put through the wringer. After the last Rock Pile show, people were seen going down Yonge Street carrying brass railings and stuff like that. But we kept on sending them newspaper clippings of different shows we'd been doing. We'd phone them every time we needed a room for a certain date. They said, 'No, but check with us next month.' And eventually they conceded to let us do a show there. We ended up doing two or three hundred shows in that room.

Later in the eighties, they booked shows at Larry's Hideaway – boldly presenting free-jazzman Ornette Coleman at the grungy punk club – as well as RPM, the Diamond, and the Siboney. But by the time the nineties hit, booking bigger and bigger gigs was pushing the Garys toward burnout.

GC: Enough is enough, you know? It became such a chore, and dealing with tour managers was the least desirable part of it all. People have these demands for what's in the dressing room and it's all for their own fucking ego. Like, 'My rider's twenty-five pages!' 'Oh, mine's forty-five pages!' You know, it's like a fucking dick-measuring contest.

Gary Cormier and Gary Topp ended their partnership in 1993 and remain close friends, but continue to work in different facets of the live music business. In 1995, they were the first promoters to win a Toronto Arts Award.

PUNK CRASHES, BURNS, INVENTS QUEEN WEST 1976–78

A back-to-basics musical mentality, combined with a modern art aesthetic and alternative sexuality, marks the start of the DIY sensibility – and the early beginnings of the Queen West countercultural strip.

Punk rock was my gateway beyond pop radio as a kid. When the Minutemen said 'punk rock changed our lives,' I could definitely relate. I spent most of Grade 9 listening to *Never Mind the Bollocks, Here's the Sex Pistols*. When I was finishing high school, MuchMusic aired a short documentary series on the fifteenth anniversary of punk, which contained a few eye-opening exposés on Canada's contributions to anarchy. Though I dug Vancouver-area acts like NoMeansNo and Art Bergmann, I knew nothing about Toronto punk, and it blew my mind to learn that in 1977, my hometown had – by some estimations – the world's third-biggest punk scene, after London and New York. (Though Los Angeles might disagree with that.)

Bands like the Viletones and the Diodes became urban legends. Few of the first wave of Toronto punk bands released more than one record. The air of mystery was enhanced by the tidbits of local lore I could pick up: the Diodes didn't like playing regular bars, so they started their own. The Viletones spray-painted their band name all over town. Teenage Head started a riot at Ontario Place.

Thankfully, much light was shed on the reality of Toronto punk with the 2009–13 publishing of a wealth of literature – books by Liz Worth, Don Pyle, and Sam Sutherland, plus Colin Brunton and Kire Paputts's film *The Last Pogo Jumps Again* – which made the scene's struggles and accomplishments even more impressive.

Though they received plenty of *local* media coverage at the time, the T.O. punk bands didn't attract enough attention from international music press like the NME or *Trouser Press* to spread their notoriety beyond the city. With no influential independent labels to champion them, they were either left in the hands of big, indifferent record companies or forced to release their own records when DIY was still a brand-new approach. Without classic albums to memorialize the scene, Toronto punk rock left its mark in other ways. It helped establish the most stable foothold for live, original music in Toronto: Queen Street West.

The stretch of Queen between University and Spadina – 'Classic Queen West' – has gradually gentrified into an outdoor shopping mall over the last thirty years. But Queen West was a very different place in 1976, a dull, forgotten, near-derelict commercial strip of used bookstores and textile outlets. Second-floor apartments above these shops were cheap, plentiful, and spacious. The four-storey Neo-Gothic terracotta edifice that's now CTV/Much-Music headquarters was then just an empty warehouse. Across the street was a chicken slaughterhouse.

Mark Gane (Martha and the Muffins): *It was really down and out. The rents were low, so that's why artists lived there. I remember a lot of dusty storefronts with passed-out drunks. It was* dead *on the weekends. And as Johnny McLeod [of Johnny and the G-Rays] said, the bands, meaning the collective scene, we made that area cool.*

Right next door to the slaughterhouse sat an unsuspecting old-man bar. The Beverley Tavern was a working-class watering hole, but without the *joie de vivre* of Grossman's. A few country and western bands played there, but they couldn't compete with the Horseshoe Tavern, the big hall down the street, where a punk icon of sorts, outspoken country patriot Stompin' Tom Connors, had stomped out his name.

A block up the street, on McCaul, was OCA – the Ontario College of Art (now OCAD). The 'Bev' became the unofficial OCA 'cafeteria,' where students and faculty would gather after class to quaff ninety-cent quarts of Black Label. A band made up of OCA students asked the owners if they could play the Beverley's small upstairs room; thankfully, the owners would book *anyone*.

The Dishes began a weekly residency at the Bev in February 1976. In an era overpopulated by long-haired, bluesy hard-rock cover bands, The Dishes stood out: not only did they wear their hair short; they played short, sharp, angular, art-rock inspired by glam heroes David Bowie, Roxy Music, and Sparks. The lack of musicians' union rules at the Bev meant they played what they wanted, and they began to develop an original sound.

The Dishes courted a new hip, fashionable audience. A vibrant contemporary arts scene had emerged in Toronto during the first half of the seventies, through the emergence of the artist-run centres: institutions like A Space Gallery and Art Metropole, the latter opened by the influential Toronto-based conceptual art collective General Idea. Mostly started by artists' collectives as spaces to create and exhibit challenging, contemporary work, the ARCs helped make Toronto a world leader in progressive art.

General Idea were known for subverting elements of pop culture, from beauty pageants to TV talk shows, and publishing their own satirical lifestyle magazine, *FILE*. GI became some of the Dishes' biggest fans and supporters and later designed their two record covers. Both collectives were also gay-identified (though the Dishes were more ambiguous), and along with Carole Pope and Rough Trade, queer artists had a huge influence on Toronto punk and new wave.

Arty proto-punk band the Dishes, at the Hart House Quadrangle, University of Toronto, 1977.

The bemused outsider perspective of being both gay and Canadian informed General Idea's work, as did a rock'n'roll sensibility. The trio of AA Bronson, Felix Partz, and Jorge Zontal were more like a band themselves, inserting themselves into their own artwork as if staging their own campy

CCMC HANGS MUSIC IN A GALLERY

Just steps away from the Beverley and the OCA, another group of artists decided they wanted their own clubhouse. On the cold night of January 25, 1976, the members of free-jazz improvising group CCMC unlocked the front door to the warehouse space at 30 St. Patrick Street that they had all been pitching in to renovate. Drummer Larry Dubin hung up a sign that said, 'No Tunes Allowed.' No one came to the show. The band played anyway.

Michael Snow had moved back to Toronto in 1972. He'd become an art star during his near-decade away but never lost his love for music, especially jazz and improvisation. Circa '74, he began playing with some new cats, a mix of trained players from York University and self-taught blasters from the Artists' Jazz Band. The CCMC was

born. They never publicly stated what the acronym stood for – it could change from show to show (e.g., 'Craven Cowards Muttering Curses') – but it was quietly, officially, the 'Canadian Creative Music Collective.'

The fall of '75 saw renewed activity in the local free-jazz scene. One night, the band called a meeting. After brainstorming, they decided to apply for a Canada Council for the

promo photo shoots. They anticipated the utopian/dystopian science-fiction aesthetic of punk with multi-year conceptual projects like *The Miss General Idea Pavilion 1984*, which dated back to 1971 and continued beyond its titular, Orwellian year.

Though GI was based out of a studio on Yonge Street, their social tentacles extended into Queen West. They included punk scenesters in their artwork, including model/singer Anya Varda and restauranteur Sandy Stagg, whose greasy spoon Peter Pan, at the corner of Queen and Peter, was a hangout for new wave art hipsters – Dishes frontman Murray Ball worked there as a cook. But what General Idea really imprinted on the punk movement was the DIY sensibility.

Arts grant to open a place of their own. Jazz music was just starting to get recognized as an art form by government funding bodies, and CCMC asked for a hundred grand. They got twenty – plus another six from the Ontario Arts Council. It was enough to run their whole first year.

CCMC played every Tuesday and Friday night at the new venue, which they named the Music Gallery. Their shows were equally rehearsal and performance; for free improvisers, there is really no distinction. There may or may not be an audience. CCMC's music is by turns wonderful, maddening, surprising, cacophonous, and even tuneful. It's not for everyone, and it may not be for anyone.

They began presenting a proper 'concert season' featuring groups such as Arraymusic, the Glass Orchestra, and the Canadian Electronic Ensemble, expanding their programming to include contemporary classical, electro-acoustic, and various world musics. The Music Gallery also launched its own in-house record label, Music Gallery Editions; among its more intriguing early releases was *Whalescapes* by Interspecies Music, a human-voice imitation of whale songs.

CCMC were just as punk as punk rock, hermetically sealed from trends, fashion, and marketability. And unlike any other venue in Toronto, the Music Gallery was adaptably movable; 30 St. Patrick was the first of now five different locations for Toronto's first artist-run centre for music and sound. (I worked at Music Gallery from 2002 to '11, after the CCMC ended its affiliation, doing almost every job there from publicist to general manager to artistic director to bartender to impromptu sound tech.)

As the first band to put up photocopied flyers on telephone poles to promote their gigs – ads in the daily papers being too expensive – the Dishes changed the streetscape of Queen West. By repurposing the Beverley as a performance space, they laid the groundwork for a new venue network that valued independence, creativity, and community.

Punk rock exploded on Queen West, but the fuse was lit back on Yonge Street. New York's Ramones played the New Yorker Theatre at a show booked by the Garys on September 24, 1976, exactly ten years to the day

Brilliant self-publicist Steven Leckie fronted the Viletones, vicious rivals to the Diodes.

after the 'Toronto Sound' concert at Maple Leaf Gardens. The first wave of Toronto punk bands formed within weeks. And the first two became the city's best known.

While the Viletones were tough, streetwise kids fronted by a brilliant, self-educated self-publicist named Steven Leckie, a.k.a. Nazi Dog (an offensive moniker he later dropped), the Diodes were art students with music-biz aspirations. Forming at OCA, the power-poppy Diodes began playing gigs in the college's auditorium, including opening for New York's Talking Heads in January '77, and a seminal show entitled '3D' alongside the Dishes and another OCA band, the Doncasters.

The Viletones, meanwhile, played their first gig in April '77 at the Colonial Underground and immediately served notice that Toronto punk rock had touched down, with their vicious back-to-basics sound, Leckie's self-mutilating antics, and a provocative typewritten manifesto that began: 'Don't even think about groups from England or the States. Just think about Toronto groups' – though, it should be noted, the missive also disparaged fellow Toronto groups, including Rough Trade and Goddo.

Leckie's advance publicity tactics – much of which involved intimidating rival bands at their own gigs while advertising his band's name on the back of his leather jacket – meant the Viletones' debut was packed to the rafters. 'Not them! Not here!' was the horrified headline in the *Globe and Mail*, with journalists fearing/hoping the media firestorm created by the Sex Pistols had jumped the pond.

First-wave Toronto punk band the Diodes on stage at Crash 'n' Burn, the DIY venue they ran, 1977.

Steven Leckie (the Viletones): *We were really into promoting this apocalypse to come, and it came. It came. We did it.* (to Liz Worth, *Treat Me Like Dirt*, 2009)

The Diodes didn't feel the same rebellious glory when they played the Colonial. After ignoring requests to turn down the volume, the band were brutally attacked by the club's bouncers at a gig a few weeks later. That effectively ended the Colonial's brief run as a punk club, and the Diodes' interest in the bar circuit. At the start of summer '77, the band set about creating a safe space for punk rock in Toronto – which would become one of the most mythologized sites in the city's music history: the Crash 'n' Burn.

Located on the punk-friendly stomping grounds near OCA and the Beverley, the Crash 'n' Burn existed for just two brief yet explosive *months* in the basement of a building on Duncan Street, three blocks south of Queen. Now the heart of the Entertainment District, in 1977 the area was virtually uninhabited. Toronto's original DIY venue didn't have to worry about noise complaints.

In contrast with the fussy puritanism of today's DIY spaces, where self-reliance is often fetishized, the Crash 'n' Burn was supported by an arts patron: CEAC (the Centre for Experimental Art and Communication) were more politicized, leftist rivals to General Idea, also led by gay men. CEAC's Bruce Eves and Amerigo Marras were excited by the revolutionary possibilities of punk and had already lent the Diodes their basement as a rehearsal space. A series of weekly gigs was the next step.

Much like the Music Gallery, the Crash 'n' Burn was a venue programmed by musicians simply as a space where new music could be heard outside of the commercial considerations of selling booze. The Diodes and their manager, Ralph Alfonso, used two old doors as a bar, dutifully filling out Special Occasion Permits with the provincial liquor authorities. They built a small stage and brought in a basic PA and lights. The bare, white-walled basement space made punk shows more like performance art. Outside of the archaic seating rules of licenced bars, the space in front of the stage was wide open for new-school pogoing and old-school shimmying. In Ross McLaren's ground-zero punk doc, *Crash 'n' Burn*, the crowd appears to be evenly co-ed.

Toronto punk made space for women, and among the first-wavers that played at CNB were the Poles, fronted by visual-artist-turned-vocalist Michaele Jordana, alongside partner Douglas Pringle, formerly of Syrinx, on synth. The Curse, one of the world's first all-female punk bands, picked up their instruments only weeks before playing the Crash 'n' Burn.

The Toronto scene also included Hamilton's all-male Teenage Head, who had been together two years at that point and blew everyone away with their tightness and streamlined fifties rock'n'roll vibe.

The Diodes picked all the talent, repping the cream of the Toronto punk scene and saving their own CNB gigs for opening slots for out-of-towners. It could get hot and sweaty in that basement, and the club's rep as a powderkeg quickly spread.

Ralph Alfonso (manager, the Diodes): *In a way, you just tried to feed more into the media to get more press. For Steve Leckie and the Viletones, it was exactly what they wanted – that was their image. At the Crash 'n' Burn, it seemed to exacerbate the violence and the negativity, because all these people looking to get into a fight started coming out.* (Worth, 2009)

By the end, the Crash 'n' Burn was attracting hundreds of people a night, and suburban weekenders had discovered the freak show that was punk. CEAC's main-floor tenants, the Liberal Party of Ontario, got tired of the noise, mess, fights, and capacity violations and asked their landlords to find new downstairs occupants. Ross McLaren took over the basement space and turned it into the experimental film-screening room the Funnel. The Diodes returned their focus to their own career.

A year later, a bigger political scandal wracked CEAC when the *Toronto Sun* revealed their grants were being used to publish a periodical, STRIKE, that supported leftist Italian terror group the Red Brigades. Spooked arts councils cut the funding, and CEAC sold the building.

With mainstream media coverage of the punk movement either lurid or condescending, the community had to get the word out and document itself, by itself. Fanzines became people's presses. London had *Sniffin' Glue*, and Toronto had the *Pig Paper*. Started by Gary 'Pig' Gold in 1975 as a fanzine dedicated to the Who, the *Pig Paper* began covering punk in the summer of '77, with typewritten write-ups of Ramones and the Saints alongside locals the Viletones and the Curse, and the famed 'Pigossip' column. There was also *Shades*, a larger-format newsprint zine that started up in '77 and continued for another six years, Toronto's first real alternative-culture tabloid and the predecessor to *Now*, *Nerve*, *Eye*, and *Exclaim!*

After the Crash 'n' Burn, the only place the first-wave punk bands could get booked was Club David's, a gay disco located near Yonge and Wellesley. Gays and punks shared a feeling of marginalization and persecution – both were feared and misunderstood by the mainstream. Though not to the same brutal degree as gay-bashing, punks were regularly attacked on the street in the seventies. David's was short-lived as the new home for punk, lasting only

The Curse were among the world's first all-women punk bands.

through the fall of '77, until the club burned down in a suspicious fire following a New Year's Eve show. Its owner, Sandy LeBlanc, was murdered a year later.

At the start of 1978, punk was briefly homeless again, though some shows did happen at the Shock Theatre in Little Italy. Yet the first wave had expanded, with new bands including the Ugly, the B-Girls, Cardboard Brains, Scenics, and the Mods. Hamilton proto-punks Simply Saucer got swept up in the Toronto tsunami as well, as did the Demics, from London, Ontario.

Though the live show is the peak experience of punk rock, recordings are still the movement's legacy. And many of the great Toronto punk bands had spotty recorded output. Toronto punk on record is best represented by a handful of amazing singles – the Viletones' 'Screaming Fist,' the Poles' 'CN Tower,' the Diodes' 'Tired of Waking Up Tired,' to name three. If someone got the rights to put them all together on vinyl, you'd have a kick-ass period comp.

But producing a *great album* – now the primary document of rock music culture – evaded most of the Toronto bands. The best first-wave Toronto album might be *Underneath the Door* by the Scenics, who stylistically were more proto-punk, jammy and jangly in a Velvet Underground/Feelies fashion.

Gary Topp: *If you listen to bands from the Horseshoe era or Crash 'n' Burn era today, they're better than fucking bands in L.A. They're as good as most bands in New York, better than most bands in England. We were lucky, in Toronto, because we had connections to New York and to England, and we had variety in our music. It was an amazing variety and an amazing development of talent and musicianship. It was the life and blood of all of these kids. And when you hear their records now, they stand up to anything. Better than anything that's out there now touring at the Horseshoe every night.*

In March of '78, the Garys packed up shop at the New Yorker Theatre, moving down from Yonge to give Queen West the kick in the ass it needed. The canny promoters took over the Horseshoe and gave it a makeover as a 'concert club,' upping the capacity and ushering in a golden age for new music shows in Toronto.

The Garys built a new stage, moving it from the side of the room, where it had been in Stompin' Tom's day, to its current location at the back. Country wasn't shown the door entirely, but its thirty-year dominance at the 'Shoe was at an end. After the retirement of original owner Jack Starr in '76, the club had needed to reinvent itself.

By '78, punk was in the process of getting rebranded – or expanded in definition – as new wave. Though we now associate the term with swoopy hair and synths of the eighties, in the late seventies, 'the new wave' referred to *all* the new music that was rising up from the underground to slay the dinosaurs of corporate rock. Punk rock was just part of the new wave, but so were reggae, free-jazz, art-rock, power-pop, and more. The Garys brought their finely tuned curatorial vision to the Horseshoe's booking, and for nine glorious months, the corner of Queen and Spadina was home to Canada's equivalent to CBGB.

The more out-there side of American new wave – what was starting to be called post-punk – must have freaked out the regulars: the Contortions, Pere Ubu, Richard Hell and the Voidoids, and Suicide, alongside more accessible US imports like the B-52s and Talking Heads. Avant-garde jazz visitors included Carla Bley and Sun Ra, while live reggae was repped by Torontonians Ishan Band; Leroy Sibbles; Earth, Roots, and Water; and the I Threes. The new wave wasn't all 'new' – the Garys also brought back sixties rockers Sam the Sham and the Troggs, and R&B legend Etta James. Most of the first-wave Toronto punks played the 'Shoe in '78, along with an OCA-bred new-wave band fronted by two women with the same name – Martha and the Muffins, graduating from the Beverley Tavern. Another beloved Beverley band, the Biffs (featuring Carole Pope's younger brother Howard) played way-ahead-of-its-time dance-punk-pop at the 'Shoe, but sadly the group split before they could commit a single to wax.

By the fall, the Horseshoe's owners informed the Garys they were sick of the chaos brought in by the punk crowd and that their tenure as bookers was coming to an end at the start of December. Pissed off, Cormier and Topp decided to book a two-night blowout. A tongue-in-cheek nod to *The Last Waltz*, the Band's pompous Boomer farewell concert of two years earlier, the Garys' final night at the 'Shoe was entitled the Last Bound-Up in honour of its bondage-loving headliners, Rough Trade, while the penultimate night was a mini-fest featuring a round-up of Toronto's first-wave punk elite: the Last Pogo.

Friday, December 1, 1978, marked the most infamous concert in Toronto music history. The Last Pogo not only marked the end of new wave at the Horseshoe, it also marked end of punk rock as a secret society in T.O. – the original scenesters were becoming outnumbered by suburban voyeurs. Well over capacity, with the club packed literally to the rafters, audience members standing on tables, beer taps running dry, and a gleefully destructive eviction-party atmosphere, the Last Pogo was primed to be a non-metaphorical riot. But who played? The Scenics, the Cardboard Brains, the Secrets, the Mods, the Ugly, the Viletones, and headliners Teenage Head. In an incredible moment of unscripted rock'n'roll theatre, a group of undercover cops, who had been drinking at the bar all night, decided the over-cap crowd was getting unruly and took to the stage to shut down the show as Teenage Head set up to play.

A mustachioed plainclothes officer and bassist Steve Mahon got into a heated exchange, pointing fingers in each other's face. Eventually, the cops let the band play one song – 'Picture My Face' – to pacify the crowd, before Topp got on the mic to tell everyone to go home. Audience members began smashing wooden tables and chairs.

Yellow police cruisers lined up outside to disperse the crowd. But beyond some anti-hippie violence provoked by Steven Leckie and his thuggish enforcers the Blake Street Boys, the atmosphere seemed mostly mischievous, more riotous fun than full-on riot, as evidenced in Colin Brunton's film of the night. A live concert album followed in '79, and in 2013 Brunton released a three-hour documentary version was issued, covering the entire first wave of T.O. punk.

All this recorded evidence certainly contributed to the Last Pogo's mythologized status. After all, there is no record of what, if anything, happened the following night at the Last Bound-Up. (According to the Garys, not much beyond a good show.) The Last Pogo made the front page of the *Toronto Star* the next day, but Peter Goddard's review didn't even mention the violence; it read more like an epitaph for the fad that was punk. Two nights later, the Horseshoe returned to its country and western roots with the premiere of a stage play, *Hank Williams: The Show He Never Gave*.

If anything, the 'Last' shows marked the end of Queen West's first, abortive era as a creative music district. It wouldn't be until the early eighties that the now-familiar venue network would begin to take shape. The Horseshoe entered into a short period of decline that would last a half decade. Until then, the new music would venture back to more well-travelled parts of the city.

MARTHA AND THE MUFFINS
Far Away in Time
1977–

'Echo Beach' is the biggest hit and most enduring anthem of the Toronto new-wave era, making the top ten in the UK, South Africa, and particularly Australia, where it still gets used in Pepsi commercials. Echo Beach, as a place, did not exist in real life. Mark Gane, guitarist/vocalist for Martha and the Muffins, wrote it after spending a summer's night gazing back at the city from Sunnyside Beach, just west of Ontario Place.

Martha and the Muffins' music and aesthetic was deeply rooted in Toronto's geography. Their cover of their 1980 debut album, *Metro Music*, consisted of a map of the city and its shoreline. But the song's lyrics, a meditation on daily drudgery and the desire to escape to a better place, make it universal: 'From nine to five I have to spend my time at work / My job is very boring, I'm an office clerk.'

'Echo Beach' remains an incredible, timeless song, from Gane's amazing opening guitar figure to Andy Haas's soaring sax solo to the irresistible, transportive chorus: 'Echo Beach / far away in time.' In 2011 it lent its name to an outdoor waterfront concert space, located, appropriately enough, at Ontario Place. Echo Beach, the place, now exists. Forty years after it was written, the song still inspires the fictional to become real.

Mark Gane (guitar/vocals): There's a youth hostel in Australia called Eco Beach because it's all running on green power. There was an English dramatic series called *Echo Beach*. There's a German label called Echo Beach that put out a tribute album that was all remixed versions of the song. There's a beach in Bali, a boutique hotel in Zanzibar. There was an Irish jumping horse named Echo Beach, and an iris flower, and an end-of-the-world science-fiction story based on it ... It's crazy.

'Echo Beach' was only the third song the band ever played, as self-taught Mark Gane muddled through constructing a pop tune.

MG: It was the DIY thing ... there's no chorus until the very end! I didn't know what I was doing.

Martha and the Muffins were no one-hit wonder, though, nor were they a one-song band. Arguably, they went on to imprint Toronto's most consistently strong discography of the 1980s. They stayed ahead of trends, constantly innovating in sound and instrumentation. Their approach to pop music was rooted in their backgrounds in art school and avant-garde, experimental music.

MG: In 1977, I was going to OCA, and there was a fellow student named David Millar. And we were both monitors in the Sound Lab for experimental music. David had been in a lot of bands before, like Oh Those Pants! And he just said, 'Do you want to start a band?' We had already collaborated a bit earlier at the old Music Gallery on St. Patrick. I played guitar, not particularly well, but I thought, 'A band, that would be really cool!'

Martha Johnson (vocals/keyboards): You had one rehearsal before I joined. I had just been guest-appearing in Oh Those Pants!, which was a big band – ten or twelve guys from OCA who sort of played instruments. But it was mostly a party band that got paid in beer. I was the only girl in the band and I had the Ace Tone organ I had bought about a year before. David asked me to join Mark and himself, and that was the beginning.

First assembling in the spring of '77, the new band spent the summer of Crash 'n' Burn holed up in a practice space a block away that they shared with Johnny & the G-Rays. Their debut show was the OCA Halloween party that October. Johnson had been part of an early-seventies 'broken social scene' of creative teens from suburban Thornhill that included Steven Davey of the Dishes. At twenty-seven, she was something of a scene vet, having performed with Oh Those Pants! and the Doncasters.

Intentionally choosing a cuddly, retro band name in reaction to the cartoon-violent monikers of their punk peers, Martha and the Muffins excelled at the tuneful, danceable, but vaguely robotic sound of early new wave. With founding guitarist Millar leaving in February '78, the band established their 'classic' six-piece lineup with the addition of Andy Haas on saxophone and a second Martha, vocalist/keyboardist, Martha Ladly. The band's lyrics were questing, intellectual, existential meditations on modern alienation.

In June '78 at a studio in Scarborough, they recorded their first single, 'Insect Love'/ 'Suburban Dream,' released in January '79 on their own Muffin Music label. They performed regularly at the Beverley and then the Horseshoe throughout 1978, quickly becoming the go-to 'house band' of Queen West's burgeoning visual arts scene.

Their early Beverley gigs attracted the attention of the daily papers, with positive notices in the *Star* from their pal Steven Davey (also a writer as well as a drummer for the Dishes) and Peter Goddard. There were very few mixed-gender bands back then – decades before Arcade Fire or July Talk – and having two women up front garnered additional interest, often sexist and condescending.

The Muffins soon attracted attention from much further afield.

MG: We did that five-song recording, and Andy [Haas] – he didn't tell anybody he was going to do this, he just did it – mailed it to Glenn O'Brien, the music critic at *Interview* magazine in New York. I still have the postcard. I'm paraphrasing, but he said, 'I love this. Can I do anything? And by the way, Robert Fripp likes it too.'

The Torontonians' minds were blown to hear the King Crimson guitarist was a fan of theirs. The same tape made its way to Virgin Records, who wanted to hear the band live. In March '79, they drove to New York to play Hurrah, the 'rock disco' that booked many a visiting UK new-wave act.

MG: Robert Fripp was there, standing twenty feet off the stage in his little suit and tie. And I'm just going, 'Holy shit, this is my biggest guitar hero!' Meanwhile, my backup guitar was a rented right-hand strung upside-down, as we could only bring down a minimal amount of gear. But that started the whole thing. Within a matter of months, if not weeks, DinDisc/Virgin offered to sign us.

MJ: To a very bad deal.

MG: It was the kind of deal that Richard Branson made his early fortune on, because it ripped off artists. But at the time, we all thought Virgin Records was a really cool label. Interestingly, when we were talking to Fripp right after the show, we told him that Virgin was interested and all he said was, 'I'm not sure that would be the right label for you.'

DinDisc was a brand-new Virgin subsidiary dedicated to the new wave. In August '79, Martha and the Muffins were flown across the pond to record at Branson's Manor Studio, where they tracked the songs that made up *Metro Music*. Little of the rest of their debut album reached the heights of 'Echo Beach,' but *MM* still had some fine songs, such as 'Paint by Number Heart' and 'Saigon.' The band were darlings of the fickle British press throughout the first half of 1980, performing on *Top of the Pops* and opening a few dates for glam-rock pioneers Roxy Music. But despite the success of 'Echo Beach' in Britain and its colonies, the single didn't make a dent in the US, which the band blames on Virgin's acquisition by Atlantic.

The pressures of their relative overnight success put a lot of strain on the band, negatively impacting their relationships with each other, with their producer, and especially with their label.

MJ: It was success that ended the band because there were all these differences of opinion and there were things to do with the money. With Mark being the writer of 'Echo Beach,' it was starting to become weighted, a lot of people felt, unfairly. Success always brings a lot of troubles.

The original lineup began to disintegrate midway through 1980. Martha Ladly left the band first, after her romantic relationship with Mark Gane ended, and she stayed behind in the UK, launching a brief but glorious solo singing career. After painting the cover art for the second Muffins album,

Ladly focused on her graphic design work, heading up Peter Gabriel's Real World Design. Dr. Ladly is now a professor of design at OCAD, where her journey began four decades earlier.

★

DinDisc put a lot of pressure on the band to follow up 'Echo Beach' with another hit. Their sophomore-jinx album, *Trance and Dance*, was rushed onto the record racks before the end of 1980, and it sounds like it. The band even sounds like they are playing faster, trying frantically to outdo the B-52's. The album did not contain another 'Echo Beach,' and the label wasn't happy. The feeling was mutual.

DinDisc wanted the band to continue with both Marthas for the sake of marketability, but the remaining Muffins refused. They returned home to make their third record free of label interference and the threat of commercial compromises. The winter of 1980–81 was a sad one for Mark Gane, and the new material he was writing reflected this sombreness. But spring was around the corner.

Not long after, Gane and Johnson, who had begun a romantic relationship, decided to solidify their creative partnership, establishing themselves as the band's leadership. They found a talented new bassist, Jocelyne Lanois, with a dubwise style. Her brothers, Daniel and Bob, ran a studio in Hamilton called Grant Avenue, where they had recorded seminal proto-punk tracks with Simply Saucer. More recently, Dan had recorded a single for Toronto's new-wave funk crew Time Twins. In Virgin's eyes, he was a 'no-name' producer, and the label cut the budget for the Muffins' third album, but they went ahead and worked with Daniel Lanois anyways. (A few years later, Lanois would collaborate with Brian Eno to co-produce U2's *The Unforgettable Fire*, becoming one of the world's biggest record producers.)

The result, released in October 1981, may be one of the greatest Canadian albums of all time. You can go ahead and delete 'Canadian' from that statement. *This Is the Ice Age* was a gorgeous meditation on time, place, and transition. The band did away with commercial accommodations and made a purely artful statement. Gane indulged in his electro-acoustic and *musique concrète* background, creating lush ambient soundscapes.

But *Ice Age* was still song-based, and they were memorable, engaging songs. Many were drumless, dropping the beat in favour of space, sound, and lyricism. When a beat did drop, it often showed the influence of Afrobeat and dub reggae. Some elements were well ahead of the times – songs like 'Swimming' showed off the vocal interplay that would be deployed years later by UK band Stereolab, as pointed out by American academic and Muffins expert Leonard Nevarez.

MG: *Ice Age* was just basically all about the trauma of the previous year.

MJ: And your breakup with Martha.

MG: And my breakup with the other Martha. The whole thing just came into that album, and there was no record company to tell me what to do. Finally, I could approach an album on an intuitive, experimental, let's-see-what-happens level. And Dan was the guy. I'd say, 'I want an emotional feeling of things falling apart, can we try pushing cardboard boxes down the stairs and slowing that down three octaves?' And he'd already be out there setting the mics up.

Ice Age was the best thing. I remember we were recording the bed tracks at Nimbus 9 in Yorkville and I was living on Bloor Street and I could walk there every morning and it was spring. I was just thinking, this is the best thing I've ever experienced. We would go in there and just do stuff with this guy who is totally into it. And I felt so liberated.

MJ: We were writing together and getting together romantically too. It's like a soap opera!

This Is the Ice Age didn't contain another 'Echo Beach.' But it was still warmly received, garnering rave reviews in the UK and decent CFNY play. It also gave MatM their first shot at significant touring in the United States, where they developed a cult following.

MG: We got a good review in the *NME*, but it was a very mixed reaction overall ... some people went, 'Man, they just killed their career. The second album was a bomb and now they put *this* out.' And other people went, 'Well, this is a huge step up.'

The band finally severed the toxic relationship with DinDisc/Virgin, jumping ship to a new Toronto-based label, Current Records, run by their new manager, Gerry Young. In early '82, another membership upheaval left Mark Gane and Martha Johnson the only remaining members from the original lineup. The band savoured their newfound artistic freedom in a *Now* cover story, but former member Andy Haas publicly aired his grievances in a biting Letter to the Editor published the following week, accusing Gane and Johnson of careerism and hypocrisy. The remaining Muffins chose not to respond. The wound still stings thirty-five years later.

MG: I think the fractures were just so getting so deep with Andy.

MJ: He left before he left.

MG: During *Ice Age* he did a lot of great stuff on that album – not conventional sax things, a lot of really interesting textures. He's one of the people I have the most respect for as a player, of all the people we've had in the band.

The pair would have no further contact with the saxophonist, a silence that would last for decades. Haas relocated to New York City, where he became an active participant in the downtown creative-music scene. He maintains a musical connection with Toronto as a member of the sprawling space-jazz ensemble the Cosmic Range, who record for T.O. label Idée Fixe. (He declined to be interviewed for this book.)

On their fourth album, 1983's *Danseparc*, it sounded like the band had been reanimated. The speedy tempos and African polyrhythms make it a close second to *Ice Age* as the band's best.

In 1984, Johnson and Gane renamed themselves M+M for the release of *Mystery Walk*, recorded in New York at Nile Rodgers's Power Station studio, with Daniel Lanois back at the helm. As far as reinventions go, it doesn't get much better than 'Black Stations / White Stations' – the title a not-so-subtle call-out of the segregation of commercial radio at the time (and the non-existence of non-white radio in Canada). Audiences responded with their feet – 'Black Stations / White Stations' went to number two on the US Billboard dance charts. The brand confusion of the name change ultimately didn't serve them well, though, as fans didn't realize the band behind 'Black Stations' was also responsible for 'Echo Beach,' and they'd never again reach such heights of popularity.

The late eighties marked the start of a quiet period for Gane and Johnson, during which they moved to Bath, England, and began work on their seventh album. Returning to Toronto, they released *Modern Lullaby* in 1992, though their new label, Intrepid Records, went bankrupt shortly thereafter. The record's atmospheric pop made only minimal impact, mostly within Canada. Following the birth of their daughter the same year *Lullaby* was released, Johnson focused on making children's music through the mid-nineties. In 2010, Martha and the Muffins released the more folk/funk-rock-oriented *Delicate*, their first album in eighteen years, and played reunion shows at the Music Gallery.

Original members of the six-piece Martha and the Muffins – the lineup that recorded 'Echo Beach' forty years ago – are now communicating in their efforts to get back their US copyrights lost in the original Virgin deal, and the question of a reunion is starting to get raised – delicately.

MG: It would be nice if everybody could make amends. Andy's the only one we haven't really seen from that first band. I don't know how he feels about it. We've always been drawn toward fairly intense, eccentric people, and it can go off the rails really easily. But it was all a long time ago, and all I think you can hope for is peace, right? Globally, culturally, sociologically ... with people you had battles with. Who needs that, man? It's a waste of time.

THE GOVERNMENT
The Band Was A Good Band
1977-83

The Government are likely the first, and still the best-known, Toronto band that can be called post-punk, though singer/guitarist Andrew J. Paterson would probably disagree with that reductive assessment. Like Devo, they got swept up in the frenzy of '77, their herky-jerky, robotic playing style fitting in with the futurism of new wave. What they also shared in common with the Akron, Ohio, devolutionists was the idea of being more of an art project than a traditional 'band.'

Paterson also didn't have the usual band background. Getting into experimental theatre and performance art while attending U of T's University College, he was a member of the VideoCabaret multi-media theatre collective, along with playwrights Michael Hollingsworth, Marion Lewis, and Deanne Taylor. VideoCabaret created the first-ever theatre productions to integrate cameras, tapes, stacks of blinking TV sets, and a live rock band. Its house band, Flivva, included guitarist Michael Brook, later an Eno/Fripp collaborator and inventor of the 'Infinite Guitar.'

Flivva left VideoCab to become a stand-alone band, though bandleader/pianist/vocalist Phillip Schreibman recorded an album with the VideoCab lineup, released in 1977 as *Sympathetic Ear* by 'The Name Is Schreibman.'

Paterson severed from Flivva and moved from bass to guitar, his minimalist style falling in line with the spirit of '77.

Andrew J. Paterson: After the Flivva thing, they needed another band, so I formed what became the Government. Robert Stewart came on. I knew him socially and liked him. He'd played with, of all things, the fucking Buttered Knives [punk band Battered Wives].

With Stewart on bass and Patrice Desbiens on drums – the latter soon replaced by Ed Boyd – the trio provided 'wallpaper music,' as Paterson calls it, for VideoCab productions. Usually starring the Hummer Sisters – the performance quartet of Marion Lewis, Deanne Taylor, Janet Burke, and Bobbe Besold – VideoCab shows sent up pop culture with titles like *Nympho Warrior* and *The Patty Rehearst Story*.

Mary Dickie (music journalist): A really amazing groundbreaking show was the Hummer Sisters' *The Bible As Told to Karen Ann Quinlan*. It might have been the first Hummers/VideoCabaret production, it was hilarious and amazing and thrillingly female-driven and the Government provided the soundtrack.

The Government also played regular rock shows, gigging at the Horseshoe, the Edge, and the brand-new Cabana Room, in the historic Spadina Hotel. They included video in their own shows as well, long before it became *de rigueur* for bands to enhance their visual appeal with 'projections.' Despite the much-ballyhooed crossover between the music and visual/performance art scenes in Toronto in the seventies, Paterson felt there was more of a divide than anything.

AJP: There was tension between the art crowd and the music crowd. We got blamed for bringing the music geeks into the Cabana and ruining the vibe. It was actually VideoCabaret who made up the name 'the Government,' and at first I resisted it, because we were working with people who were getting government money. I've always thought within the art world there's a schism between people who are in governmental granting systems and people who are completely outside: they feel inhibited by them, or they're anarchists who want nothing to do with them, or they're entrepreneurs who don't believe in them.

In 1979, the Government split with VideoCabaret and went their own way as a stand-alone band – sort of. That year, they issued their first single, 'Hemingway (Hated Disco Music)' and an EP, $33^{1/3}$, which contained 'Flat Tire,' a song that received moderate airplay on CFNY. Their deadpan sense of humour helped gain them new curious listeners, but 'Flat Tire' risked becoming a novelty song.

AJP: 'Flat Tire' is a terrible record, because I tried to play a Chuck Berry lick ironically and that doesn't work beyond twenty people. So it sounded like just another stupid punk record. I was trying to do an inversion of all those macho blues songs with the car as a sexual metaphor. But it was a metaphor for being asexual and disinterested in all of that. [pause] I hate that record.

Their 1980 full-length, *Guest List*, is a bit more serious and harder to crack, but still contains fun, satirical songs. The label, Jackal Records, barely promoted it, and this furthered the modernist post-punks' disenchantment with the music business – and the whole business of 'being in a band.'

AJP: We didn't want to be a traditional band. I mean, *I* didn't. We felt like, 'Oh, I guess that's what we've become.' Maybe I have pretensions to being more than that intellectually. So the band went out and played. The band was a good band. People liked it. But a traditional band, to me, has all been done. And all the punks were the same old shit, regurgitated.

The Government played often at the Cameron House after it opened in fall '81. With numerous artist-run centres, including A Space Gallery, Mercer Union, and YYZ, having moved into the Queen/Spadina nexus, the friendly bar – and its upstairs rooming house – became a hub for the varied artists in the area. Paterson, who not only called the Cameron home but also tended bar there, is one of the few dedicated documentarians of this ARC history.

The Government's '81 EP *How Many Fingers?* was their last stab at being a band. 'Rock music prevents people from thinking and that's probably why I hate it,' Paterson told *Now Magazine* at the time. The record's generic yellow cover and block lettering was an intentional play on the early rap records coming out of New York.

AJP: We really got into the rap and hip-hop thing. We got very modernist. Anything too rock, throw it out!

The cover also marked what could have been an exciting, creative left turn. The band had gone in a funkier, mutant-disco direction with the addition of their third and final drummer, Billy Bryans, the Toronto scene vet whose resumé went way back to Rochdale College in the late sixties, and who would soon co-found the Parachute Club. But according to Paterson, that wasn't even the plan.

AJP: Robert and I were going to do some kind of loose funk thing with Billy, but then Robert made a poster that said 'The Government.' And I'm like, 'What!?' I didn't want to play any of those songs anymore. People wanted to hear goddamn 'Flat Tire.' I thought the Government had torpedoed, we were just flogging a dead horse.

The band continued playing through 1982. The title *How Many Fingers?* was inspired by the passage in Orwell's *1984* where the Party official holds up four fingers yet convinces the broken protagonist, Winston Smith, that it is in fact *five*. The Government's refusal to break, to give in to the music industry's broken logic of diminishing returns, resulted in the only logical decision: to break up. They played their last gig in June '83 – at the Cameron House, naturally – a show they entitled 'Performing Prince Andrew's Greatest Hits.'

Andy Paterson quit music but remains active as a media artist and writer, recognized with a Governor General's Award in 2019. He does play in an electronic band called Derwatt, along with his friends Kevin Dowler and Lewis Kaye. And to this day, he does not know the whereabouts of Government bassist Robert Stewart, who disappeared from the Toronto scene. His last known mailing address was in Honduras in the early 2000s.

AJP: I think about him a lot. I'll probably go to my own grave with it unresolved. It would be great if actually he was alive somewhere having another existence … but I have my doubts.

LAST CALL FOR DOWNTOWN DIVES
1979-86

New music makes a brief return to the city centre
as new wave, punk, and hardcore give down-on-their-luck
bars a renewed sense of purpose.

I t wasn't much larger than your living room, it opened for breakfast at
seven thirty, and the toilets leaked. It could have been your decrepit local
diner, but instead it was one of the best live music venues on the continent
during its thirty months in existence. The Edge was located at Gerrard and
Church, on the main floor of a three-storey Victorian house, and from the
start of '79 to the summer of '81, it was the place Toronto's punk and new-
wave communities called home.

The Garys didn't waste much time after the Last Pogo. Ron Chapman,
co-owner of struggling Egerton's Restaurant, had attended some of their
concerts that fall of '78. The folk singers he and dishwasher-turned-promoter
Derek Andrews were booking didn't pull in the student dollars anymore,
and Egerton's needed to move with the times. The team quickly made over
the space, painting it black and expanding the stage. On December 31, 1978,
a scant four weeks after the Garys were thrown out of the Horseshoe, the
Edge opened its doors. The headliners that New Year's Eve were Martha
and the Muffins.

The Garys built upon their booking policy at the Horseshoe, bringing
in so many UK acts they made the Edge a virtual British High Commission
for new music. Its 1979–81 roll call boggles the mind: John Cale, Tom
Waits, the Police, the B-52s, Squeeze, Joan Jett, X, Gang of Four, Simple
Minds, Echo & the Bunnymen, xtc, the Cramps, Magazine, Ultravox,
Jonathan Richman, Nico, Pere Ubu, Mission of Burma, the Slits, Sun Ra
… As a sad addendum, this list does not include Joy Division: they were
booked to play there May 25, 1980, but the band never made it to North

Nash the Slash revealed his bandage-wrapped persona on stage at the Edge in 1979.

America, as singer Ian Curtis took his own life just days earlier.

Coming right after the Last Pogo, the Edge marked a shift away from straightforward punk toward the artier, more experimental sounds of post-punk – and at the same time, hitherto unseen commercial success for Toronto's new crop of bands. Martha and the Muffins spawned Canada's first international hit single of the new wave: 'Echo Beach.' The track received plenty of local support from a new FM station, CFNY 102.1, a.k.a. 'The Spirit of Radio,' which heavily boosted the British scene and select Toronto acts such as Blue Peter (on local indie Ready Records).

Though it's had a turbulent history over the last four decades – traumatic ownership and format changes, listener rebellions, beloved DJs resigning on-air – in the early days, CFNY, under the visionary direction of Dave Marsden, was a true champion of new and original music. Incredibly, it was a commercial station run out of a tiny studio in remote Brampton, with a scrappy, free-form, anything-goes sensibility. It's hard to believe that in 1994 it turned into the tightly formatted 'modern rock' 102.1 the Edge (no relation), ironically enough.

Andy Crosbie (Ready Records): CFNY *really, truly* was *the Edge. I call it the Foo Fighters channel now. Back then, it really did take chances. You could send them a new record – and they might actually play it!*

Martha and the Muffins' success began opening other doors. Nash the Slash had been performing solo with violin and electronics for four years before he played a pivotal gig at the Edge in April '79. Intending to call attention to the recent Three Mile Island nuclear disaster, Nash wrapped his face in surgical bandages. A cult hero was born. Though he had been one of Toronto's DIY innovators when it came to releasing your own records, on his label Cut-

Throat Records, Nash the Slash also signed to DinDisc and enjoyed a spell of British press hype.

Other upstart locals booked at the Edge included wiry, atonal post-punk trio the Government, ambitious roots-reggae septet Truths and Rights, and post-Dishes splinter groups Drastic Measures (who turned heads with an arch cover of the kids' tune 'The Teddy Bear's Picnic') and the Everglades. Meanwhile, the club's status as a restaurant meant it was licenced for all ages, and it began to attract high-school-aged bands from the suburbs, such as the Rheostatics, who played their first gig there in 1980, when they were all around sixteen.

Dave Bidini (Rheostatics): *My Dad drove us down to the show with all our equipment in the trunk and then we just drove straight back to Etobicoke after the show, we didn't hang out. I think it's mostly because we were fucking terrified of being downtown! That corner was pretty rough.*

Though Toronto has a rep as clean and safe, it's always had a seedy side. The Edge wasn't located far from Jarvis Street, then notorious for sex workers openly plying their trade. Assaults and drug abuse were more common downtown in the early eighties than nowadays. The first-wave punk bands, feeling less welcome at the more grown-up Edge, began to populate a handful of dive bars in the vicinity where their noise would at least be tolerated.

Down the street, on the edge of Allan Gardens, Toronto punk found one of its longest-lived homes at Larry's Hideaway, the legendarily roach-infested club located in the basement of the sleazy Prince Carlton Hotel, which had been a jazz club in the sixties. The Diodes played Larry's in November '78 before moving over to the El Mocambo, enemy territory to many punks.

While the Diodes had limited success at commercial crossover, they were eclipsed by those Hamilton heshers in Teenage Head, whose 1980 album *Frantic City* blasted into the top five on mainstream rock stations CHUM-FM and Q107. The band struck a nerve with their fifties throwback rock'n'roll, at a cultural moment that was supposed to be all about technological futurism. Their notoriety only grew after 15,000 kids rushed a free concert they headlined at the Ontario Place Forum, and a full-on riot was started by the hundreds stuck outside – one youth even swam the moat separating the lakeside park from the mainland.

Frankie Venom (Teenage Head): *We had no idea how many people were out there. We were backstage for like five hours previous, and when I walked out there, it was an unbelievable feeling. Young kids screaming, grabbing at our clothes – for about a minute I couldn't speak. Just the rush. Better than any drug, any alcohol I've ever done. We never had that again, but I'll never forget it. It was fantastic.* (to Geoff Pevere, *Gods of the Hammer*, 2014)

Larry's Hideaway became Teenage Head's home base in Toronto after hard-hustling band manager Jack Morrow recruited their original manager, Paul Kobak, to book the bands, rebranding the venue as Larry's 'Headspace' – an arrangement that lasted a few years.

Canada's economy was also in a recession, which caught up with the Edge in the spring of '81. The restaurant's daytime business was suffering as a result of all the nighttime activity. Staff paycheques began to bounce, and the owners, who had been looking to sell, suddenly pulled the plug.

In 1981, the mainstream media considered punk 'dead'– but in reality, it had just given the middle finger to the music industry and burrowed back underground. Hardcore punk shot up in cities all over North America – twice as loud, twice as fast, and infinitely angrier. In D.C., there were Bad Brains and Minor Threat; in L.A., Black Flag and Circle Jerks; in San Francisco, Dead Kennedys; and in Vancouver, DOA – credited with coining the term 'hardcore.'

Toronto's first hardcore bands were Young Lions (who also played the joke 'punk band' the Queen Haters on *SCTV*) and Youth Youth Youth, followed by legions more: Direct Action, Chronic Submission, A.P.B., Jolly Tambourine Man, and notorious punk lifers Bunchofuckingoofs. Toronto's hardcore groups didn't make as widespread an impact as those from other cities, likely because economic constraints forced them to release their music on cassette rather than more indelible vinyl.

Chris Genest (Young Lions): *That's the one piece missing from this puzzle – there was no independent record label in Toronto that put this stuff out on vinyl. If somebody would've stepped up, we'd be having a different conversation right now.* (to Derek Emerson et al., *Tomorrow Is Too Late*, 2018)

Razor-sharp hardcore crew Youth Youth Youth at an earlier incarnation of the Drake Hotel, 1982.

Larry's Hideaway and the Turning Point (run by an adorably drunk elderly couple at Bloor and Avenue) became the two most reliable venues for 'T.O. H.C.' – live footage of a dozen bands playing these clubs made up the basis of a 1984 student documentary, *Not Dead Yet* – a name later adopted by a DIY punk festival in the 2010s. Other early-eighties punk-friendly clubs in the downtown core included the Upper Lip, Igwana Lounge, Hotel Isabella, and 100 Bond Street.

With the notable exception of the razor-sharp Youth Youth Youth, the primitivism of the music in the *Not Dead Yet* film shows that Toronto hardcore bands had taken the 'back to basics' punk ethic to an extreme. At the most unapologetically crude end of the spectrum – in both senses of the word – was Bunchofuckingoofs.

Living at the most feral edges of existence in Kensington Market, which they chose for its ease of dumpster-diving and its neighbourly spirit, the BFGs turned survivalism into a kind of performance art. Their graffiti-strewn apartment on Baldwin Street became the notorious 'Fort Goof.' The Market's atmosphere of benevolent anarchy can be partially credited to the BFGS.

Crazy Steve Goof (Bunchofuckingoofs): *We're on welfare, we eat out of the garbage, we eat breakfast at the Scott Mission, we've got credit all over the fuckin' place that we can't pay. (interviewed in* Not Dead Yet, *1984)*

Alcohol was also a big factor in the band's lifestyle; Fort Goof was a twenty-four-hour boozecan. Somehow, despite countless wrecked livers, the BFGS survived into the twenty-first century as one of (if not *the*) longest-running Toronto punk bands. Steve Goof was the only constant, the grinning eye of the shitstorm.

Larry's Hideaway experienced a mid-eighties renaissance when the Garys brought in bigger shows, including the Toronto debuts of American college-rock pioneers REM and Hüsker Dü, plus thrash-metal screamers Slayer. The good times lasted until September 16, 1986, when police raided the hotel, arresting twenty-six people on narcotics, sexual assault, and weapons charges. The club tried to keep going, but the increased police presence made it untenable. The last band to play there, in December 1986, was appropriately called No Life. The hotel closed in '88, the building taken over by squatters until it burned down, reputedly by arson, in 1991. The ghost of 121 Carlton Street was absorbed into Allan Gardens park. Outlaw punks like the Bunch-ofuckingoofs must approve that it's now an off-leash dog zone.

The early eighties also marked an important moment of cultural cross-pollination in the old city centre. Forward-thinking dance clubs like Voodoo and Biorhythm on St. Joseph Street exposed new wavers to the early rap and hip-hop records coming out of New York.

Amy Hersenhoren (promoter): *It was a concentrated area of alternative culture, and it was in the middle of the city. And I think that was important because there were kids on the east side and the west side that came together. There was a whole scene of punks and mods and skids that were from the Beaches. And then there was a whole crew that were from Eglinton Station. And on Saturdays, we would all meet at Bloor, walk down Yonge Street, and go to the head shops.*

Toronto's traditional downtown core is no longer home to a single small club booking live music regularly. The city may not have been cleaned up to a New York degree, but gentrification has nonetheless driven out all the dive bars where mohawked punks and swoopy-haired new wavers once played. By the mid-eighties, the centre of creative musical gravity had moved southwest.

Blue Peter.

READY RECORDS
Architects of the World
1979–85

Chris Wardman (**Blue Peter**): Ready Records was a pioneering indie label before that was a thing. The indie/DIY spirit was here to wipe out seventies complacency and cheesy rock bands.

Though the best-known punk bands – Sex Pistols and the Clash – signed to major labels, a longer-lasting impact of the era on independent music culture was the advent of indie labels like Rough Trade, Factory, and Stiff Records in the UK. The closest Toronto had in the late seventies and early eighties was Ready Records. I remember seeing their retro-futuristic logo on the back of local albums and wondering who they were and how they got it off the ground – here, in my humble hometown.

Andy Crosbie (co-owner): Angus MacKay [co-owner] and I met at Fanshawe College in London, Ontario, in 1976. We were taking the Music Industry Arts program, the first of its kind in Canada.

In '77/'78, Crosbie and MacKay found themselves amidst a vibrant small-city punk scene. The Demics played their first gig at a loft party in downtown London in December '77. The band's MVP was vocalist Keith Whittaker, a hard-drinking, well-read Brit from Manchester who wasn't afraid to wail on a heckler mid-show.

AC: London was the perfect festering ground for punk. The Cedar Lounge had kids lined up around the block every Saturday to see the Demics. Angus and I were walking to school one day, and he said, 'We should make a record of this band.'

The pair acted as both producers and A&R, recording the Demics' debut *Talk's Cheap* over the Christmas holidays. Released in April '79, the five-song EP yielded Canadian punk's first radio hit – on CFNY, at least. 'New York City' was an atypical punk song, in that it was loud and *slow*. The song's sludgy, crashing chord changes anticipated bands like Flipper, and its head-banging quotient gave the Demics crossover appeal to hard rock fans.

Though Ready Records once made a T-shirt with the slogan 'Where art is more than just the name of the janitor,' they were still a small label at the mercy of the marketplace. Their first offices were in their cars, and they held meetings at the Pilot Tavern in Yorkville. Eventually they did get an office at a Queen Street East address where Dan Aykroyd once had a speakeasy. Though still independent, they worked out a distribution deal with a larger Canadian-owned label, Quality Records, to get their product into stores. The next band they would sign wrote an anthem of their own, 'Factory Living,' which declared: 'It's no fun starving for artistic integrity.'

AC: Blue Peter impressed the heck out of me. They had a song called 'Same Old Place' that in our estimation was as good or better as 'New York City.' And they were just great guys.

Both songs were included on the band's debut album, *Test Patterns for Living*, released later in 1979, which also received decent airplay on CFNY. Forming the previous year in the remote Toronto suburb of Markham, Blue Peter came downtown to play gigs at the Edge and Larry's Hideaway. They started as a Diodes-style power-pop/punk band, but their sound and look fell under the influence of the austere glam-pop of Roxy Music, and singer Paul Humphreys began affecting an English accent – which suited their sound but began an unfortunate trend for Canadian bands of the time. Musically, they were tight, and in guitarist/producer Chris Wardman, they had an in-house sonic visionary.

CW: Ready had great design and promotion. In 1981, we decided to go indie from our indie label and released the 45 for 'Chinese Graffiti' on our own label, AWOL Records. We soon realized we were out of our depth, and Ready took us back.

Falling (1983) featured the irresistibly danceable single 'Don't Walk Past.' Its awesome film-noir/*Blade Runner*–inspired video was the first indie video played on MTV in the US. But the hoped-for commercial breakthrough never materialized, and the band split in early '85.

AC: For the life of me, I have no idea why Blue Peter didn't obtain huge international success. They had the looks and they really cared about their craft. I really thought they would happen, and I still don't understand why they didn't.

Ready's next discovery would go even further, flying them closer to that rarefied stratosphere of worldwide stardom, as well as the artistic freedom that comes with cash flow.

AC: The Garys had moved over to the Edge, and they said, 'Hey you gotta check out this band from Burlington called Spoons.' They were exceptional musicians and [in '81] we made a record with them called *Stick Figure Neighbourhood*. Angus and I had been producing our records but the company was growing, so we had a really tough decision to make. Angus really wanted to stay in the studio and as much as my heart was there, I felt that on a practical level we had to be the record company guys. We asked former Fanshawe classmate Graham Pole to produce the album and we rented Grant Avenue studios up in Hamilton, and the engineer was a young guy named Dan Lanois.

Spoons recorded with Lanois at the same time as he was producing Martha and the Muffins' opus, *This Is the Ice Age*; the young band, meanwhile, were being managed by ex-Muffins bassist Carl Finkle, and MatM is a clear sonic influence on their debut. If the band members look like babies in their early video clips, it's because they were: keyboardist Rob Preuss was just sixteen, the others barely into their twenties. Crosbie and MacKay invested a lot of time in guiding the youthful suburbanites' career.

Gord Deppe (Spoons): In those days, a record company wasn't just business. Ready was our home base, a place to hang out. They were like family. I don't think we would have gotten the same attention from a major label.

Spoons in studio with producer Nile Rodgers.

Studious and nerdy, Spoons were more inspired by prog than punk when they started out, which explains their technical virtuosity. But their sound modernized once they heard Orchestral Manoeuvres in the Dark, and they effortlessly rode the second wave of new wave, now called synth-pop. For their second album, 1982's *Arias and Symphonies*, Larry Macrae of Quality Records connected Ready and the Spoons with a British producer, John Punter, who had worked with Roxy Music and Japan. It's unjust that the lead single, 'Nova Heart,' isn't a universally loved hit. It was little heard outside Canada, but it's one of the best singles of the era.

Arias and Symphonies went gold in Canada, and by then Spoons were popular enough to headline the Concert Hall in Toronto. Ready brokered a deal with A&M in the US, where it was hoped they would break big. They snagged a slot opening for Boy George and Culture Club on their US tour, and the New York date turned out to be pivotal.

AC: Who else was in the audience but Nile Rodgers, just coming off producing Bowie's *Let's Dance*, and he said, 'I'd like to produce this band.' So he ended up doing *Talkback* here in Toronto.

Despite the strength of Rodgers's big beat, the songs fell in an uncomfortable middle ground between the bouncy radio hits A&M were demanding and the austere, aloof sound Spoons more naturally expressed. *Talkback* was released in November '83, and again was a smash in Canada but DOA in the USA. Spoons were dropped by A&M in the States.

AC: I remember the first time I flew to L.A., the law firm I was working with sent a young guy to pick me up at the airport and he was driving me through Hollywood and saying, 'This whole studio lot was owned by so-and-so until that film bombed, and then he had to sell it.' Just like in that story, *Talkback* created a trickle-down effect that led to the label having to cease operations. We just closed the company, we just shut down. Angus and I went our separate ways, but we were always the best of friends.

It's sad that major-label economics killed off one of Toronto's most vibrant indie labels. Ready Records nonetheless left a major legacy during its six years in existence. Their roster diversified to include metal, blues, worldbeat, and reggae. They also started two spinoff labels that continued after their demise: Fringe Product, run by Ben Hoffman of record shop the Record Peddler, who licenced American hardcore records and released records and tapes by a range of local indie, punk, hardcore, and metal bands into the mid-nineties, including Youth Youth Youth, Breeding Ground, Change of Heart, and Sacrifice; and Kids' Records, run by Sharon, Lois & Bram producer Bill Usher, whose roster included Robert Munsch, Big Bird, and Oscar the Grouch. At one point, all three labels shared a PO box, which must have been interesting.

Possibly Ready's biggest legacy was the example left for the next generation as to the fragility of independent labels in Canada and their need for public support through bodies like FACTOR (which was in its infancy in providing funding to the Canadian recording industry) to survive and champion homegrown artists in this massive, spread-out country.

AC: I lobbied hard for a year, going after the Federal Business Development Bank, now the BDC. They said, 'This is designed for people that have pizza-making machines.' So I think even in our demise, I'd like to believe that we helped pave the way for other people to get proper financing.

Currently the co-owner of record label Sparks Music – a major-distributed indie whose roster includes JF Robitaille and Papermaps – Andy Crosbie looks back fondly on his formative years.

AC: We really wanted to put out music that needed to be heard. If you looked at the acts we signed and you listened to the radio at the time, you'd think, 'These guys clearly aren't doing this to make money.' But more than the music and the brief whiffs of recognition, I deeply miss my life-long friend Angus MacKay, who was a gifted and patient man. [MacKay passed away from cancer in 2010.]

Spoons lasted for two more albums, making an ill-advised foray into hard rock. The band's devoted retro-eighties fanbase has kept their back catalogue alive and fuelled countless reunion shows. In 2019, the band released their second full-length album of the twenty-first century: *New Day New World* – distributed by Andy Crosbie's Sparks Music label.

TRUTHS AND RIGHTS + MOJAH
Original Roots
1977–83

What sets Canadian reggae apart from reggae made elsewhere? Writers like Klive Walker have observed that although Toronto is the world's second-biggest centre for diasporic reggae – after London, England – awareness of Canadian reggae's existence is negligible.

One element that stands out is its basis in live bands. Jamaican reggae was all about singers, studios, and sound systems. Toronto is a live music town, packed with clubs and concert venues. After reggae hit the mainstream with the mid-seventies success of Bob Marley and the Wailers, homegrown groups had to compete with rock bands for audiences, so they presented themselves in a similar manner.

The first Toronto reggae band to release an album, Ishan People, trod the same Yonge Street club circuit as Rush and Triumph, playing the Colonial and the Chimney, as well as the El Mocambo. Their first album, *Roots* (GRT Records, 1976), was produced by David Clayton-Thomas of Blood, Sweat & Tears, one of a small handful of white Canadian musicians who championed the new sound of young Jamaica. Notably, Bruce Cockburn often collaborated with singer Leroy Sibbles, and recruited Sibbles's rhythm section to play on his '79 reggae-influenced hit, 'Wondering Where the Lions Are.' But the tension between sticking to (their) roots and crossing over broke apart Ishan People after the release of their second album, in '77.

Truths and Rights have been called the greatest reggae band ever to come out of Toronto, and though I was far too young to have seen them live, I have to agree. The few live clips that exist show them to be an astonishingly tight septet and uber-confident performers. Though they only left behind two singles to their name, their name still holds a lot of weight.

What set them apart from the other great reggae bands of the late seventies and early eighties was their originality. Sure, they were a reggae band, but they drew on plenty of other genres, from R&B to jazz to psychedelic rock. And they were a true product of Toronto – they sang about issues relating to this city, and name-checked its neighbourhoods. They blended pan-Afro-Caribbean influences – band members' roots were not only in Jamaica but also in Trinidad, Guyana, and Nova Scotia. And in singer/songwriter/guitarist Mojah, they had a charismatic and visionary bandleader.

Coming to Toronto from Trinidad as a youth in 1972, Mojah didn't find much connection with the music scene here.

Mojah: I always wanted to play music, but, you know, original music. The scene when I came here was all people doing top forty. I didn't like it, but I ended up doing cover songs. In the back of my mind, I always wanted to pursue original music. Music that I feel, music that relates to me or my environment.

He got a job installing phone lines for Northern Telecom and made friends with a co-worker, Jamaican bass player Garry Lowe, who was eager to start a band. Only problem was, Lowe couldn't actually play bass. Mojah himself was still a novice guitarist. But they didn't let that deter them.

Mojah taught Lowe what he knew, and they started jamming at his East York apartment. Their drummer was a tape recorder; they had recorded themselves tapping on a chair to make a beat. Soon, they recruited a real drummer, Abnadengel, and a vocalist, Ovid Reid. After getting bounced from house to house due to noise complaints, the young band was stuck for a practice space.

Circa 1977, salvation came via Immi-Can, a Regent Park community centre designed to help recent immigrants, especially Black youth, adjust to life in Canada.

M: Immi-Can were encouraging youths with talent to come around. And Immi-Can worked out to be the best thing that happened to Truths and Rights.

Providing them not just with a jam space but also a PA and basic equipment, Immi-Can was Truths and Rights' home base for a whole year while they developed their sound, eventually expanding to a seven-piece lineup including a keyboardist, lead guitarist, and percussionist. A Jamaican-Canadian visual artist and social worker at Immi-Can named Ato Seitu became their manager and mentor, contributing to the writing of some of their earlier songs. Mojah, Seitu, and dub poet Lillian Allen – who worked as an education coordinator at Immi-Can – collectively co-wrote what became their first single.

'Acid Rain' showed that Truths and Rights were unafraid to address social and environmental issues, especially those that hit home in Toronto. Acid rain, caused by airborne industrial pollution, became a major eco-concern in the early eighties, especially in Ontario, which sat upwind of the US Rust Belt. To Mojah, this was simply an expression of their Rastafarian beliefs.

M: When you are a Rasta man, your concern is worldwide. It's about our Earth. It's about where we live. It's about how we treat each other.

In addition to spreading a conscious message, Truths and Rights became an impressive live band. They played their first shows at community centres beyond Immi-Can, spaces frequented mostly by the Caribbean community. Promoted by flyers given out hand to hand at house parties, these shows were soon jammed.

M: We used to throw our own concerts because people wouldn't hire that kind of band with that kind of message. That helped us to build our fanbase, because we had no records, you know? And then people started following us and singing our tune although we didn't have a record.

Truths and Rights played a few larger gigs early on, including Harbourfront's Black Cultural Exposition and an Immi-Can alumni showcase of at U of T's Convocation Hall. But it was after they discovered the Edge and the new-wave scene that the band's profile started to rise. Their DIY fearlessness and thirst for original, socially relevant expression aligned them perfectly with the early post-punk era.

In the early eighties they landed bigger gigs like the opening slot for the (English) Beat at the Concert Hall and a huge Caribana party at Varsity

Stadium, supporting Jamaican greats Dennis Brown and Third World. They headlined the Horseshoe and the Palais Royale and toured out east to Quebec, where they played to huge, enthusiastic crowds.

It's mystifying that a band this hot couldn't attract the interest of a label. They had to press the 'Acid Rain' seven-inch single and its follow-up, the twelve-inch 'Metro's No. 1 Problem,' by themselves. 'Metro's No. 1 Problem' turned their lyrical focus toward social conditions, tackling racial violence and police brutality. Toronto music had never addressed the city's problems with such directness. It wasn't your typical reggae song either, starting with a Dylanesque harmonica solo, later going off into prog-rock breaks, while the upbeat verses created a vertiginous dissonance with the subject matter.

Mainstream music media attention followed: the band made the cover of *Now* in July 1982, and a year later, Peter Goddard in the *Star* declared them 'Toronto's band of the year.' The problem was, it wasn't clear if Truths and Rights was a band anymore.

Mojah thinks the band ended around '82/'83. Seitu says they never really broke up, just moved on to other projects in an 'evolutionary' way. According to Mojah, they simply weren't making enough money to cover costs.

M: Truths and Rights was a seven-piece, carrying a mixer, that brings it up to eight. It's not sustainable. The money paid to the band couldn't carry eight people.

Mojah tried making a go of it as a solo artist, releasing some singles on a few different indie labels – including one called Coach House Records (no relation to Coach House Books) – but he had trouble finding an audience. He found himself a new home, both spiritually and physically, on Queen West, at the Cameron House.

M: I used to do the Cameron one-man show. It was hard to survive. And Herbie [Tookey, owner], saw me one day and said, 'Mojah, here is a key. Here is a room. This is your room. If you could play in the back room every once in a while, that would be great. You don't have to play, but it's there for you.' Well, I utilized that room. And Herbie never took a penny from me, whether I played or didn't play. Not a dime.

In the three years he lived upstairs, Mojah became a regular fixture on the Cameron's stages and started playing with members of the Parachute Club and Rough Trade in dub-rock supergroup V. The Cameron House connection also introduced Mojah to Handsome Ned, the friendly cowboy with the sweet pipes. For the club's 1985 Christmas party, Mojah joined Ned onstage to perform a dubbed-out country version of 'Johnny Too Bad,' from *The Harder They Come* soundtrack. They called the mash-up 'rastabilly.'

M: We did one show. We should have done more. Rastabilly was a hit, man! I don't know why we were so stupid to not do another one. Ah man, I loved Ned. I loved that man's energy.

In 1990, Mojah released his long-awaited solo full-length *Broken Arrow*, on Lillian Allen's Verse to Vinyl label. Through Compass's Terry Wilkins, he met Gordie Johnson, bandleader of major-label blues-rock band Big Sugar, which Truths and Rights co-founder Garry Lowe had joined on bass. Lowe convinced Mojah to join on rhythm guitar in '99, and he got a taste of the touring life again – though the loud volume didn't agree with him.

Truths and Rights re-assembled for a handful of reunion concerts starting in 2003. It's a name that Mojah still stands by forty years later.

M: It's about speaking the truth. People normally say 'Truth' and Rights. But we deliberately put an 's' on Truths. There's one truth, but there's so many damn lies, we need to make all truth a reality. Rights – everybody fights for that. There's so much rights have been taken from all of us. Truths and Rights is a foundational name, a name that really represents us.

QUEEN WEST: THE A-LIST ASSEMBLES
1981–84

New spaces open on Queen West with the express purpose of supporting diverse, original emerging music and the grassroots arts scene, supported in turn by new community-oriented media outlets. Reggae and country music stand alongside post-punk in challenging music industry norms.

Lorraine Segato (The Parachute Club): *Even though I played all over the city, it was on Queen Street that I saw the biggest changes actually rippling out, in the effect it had on the city. You had a small-c conservative government provincially. And a small-c conservative city, too. And yet you had these waves of immigrants coming in – Caribbean, Jamaican, and West Indian immigrants. You had all of these things pushing in a confluence of energies – boom, coming from every direction. And you had the fact that artists could start inhabiting empty and derelict warehouse spaces. So that's where the culture was being born.*

Quantum Coffee makes a mean cappuccino and is one of the nicest places to work downtown – if you can snag a table. The spacious brick-and-beam backroom is usually jammed full of young techies with laptops. The third-floor mansard roof is all that remains of the historical building. Wind back a decade or so, and it was Global Village Backpackers, a grubby student hostel that briefly dallied with booking live bands in the mid-2000s. The building's garish pink, blue, and green paint job was so bright you could easily spot it from the CN Tower.

Wind back another decade to 1993 in the same space, and I'm nineteen years old, standing on the stage of the Cabana Room, on the second floor of the historic Spadina Hotel. My college rock band is playing our first gig. A handful of our friends are slumped over tables, drinking Labatt's, smoking, and hoping we won't suck. Debuting a new group or project at the Cabana became a rite of passage for young musicians through the eighties and into the nineties. Originally programmed as a multi-arts performance space by painter Robin Wall and video artist Susan Britton, the Cabana Room opened in 1979 and within a year or two moved its booking policy toward more straight-up live music gigs. Live music died there in November '95.

It was a crappy place to play, but they would book you. Bartender Jimmy Scopes did the booking – a guy from a different time, with slicked-back hair, a white button-up shirt, and a black tie. Countless new groups got their start in that tiny, beach-themed bar, thanks to Jimmy's willingness to give fresh faces a chance.

'Queen West' wasn't just about Queen Street. Though that east-west arterial hosted – and still hosts – a key handful of iconic, influential Toronto music venues, what made QSW work as an arts hub was the blocks that surrounded it. In the early eighties, the Cabana Room and the Beverley Tavern – which has never gone away – were ground zero for the next generation of independent bands. Giant empty warehouses left over from the old Garment District gave artists and entrepreneurs unexpected new playspaces. 'The street finds its own uses for things,' said author and cyberpunk pioneer William Gibson, whose novel *Neuromancer* describes a fictional military initiative, 'Operation Screaming Fist,' named after a Viletones song.

Artist-run centres like A Space Gallery, YYZ, and Mercer Union began gravitating to the area. A block south of Queen, the Assoon brothers opened the Twilight Zone on Richmond Street in 1980, booking funk and disco DJs, launching Toronto's storied warehouse party scene, and planting the seeds for the Entertainment District. In his self-published book *Alone and Gone*, musician/zinester Nick Smash tells the story of a giant loft, across the street from what's now the TIFF Bell Lightbox cinema on

Post-punk maniacs Rent Boys Inc. ruled the Queen West strip.

King, where dozens of band members lived and jammed for next to nothing, surrounded by the emptiness of parking lots and train tracks.

Brian Ruryk (the Diner's Club, Deadlines): *There was a sleeping space, or rather a place where people kind of had their bedrooms, but they were separated by a really thin piece of fabric, on a flimsy frame that divided up a larger space. And then there'd be a band practising next door when you tried to sleep! The area was really desolate. The building beside it was abandoned. It was always fun to go in there and walk around and take photos.*

There was an Edge-sized hole in the local music scene in 1981. A lack of label interest and decent venues left musicians frustrated and despondent. Many had left the city for dead – or, in a repeat of the sixties, just plain left it. Two young bands, the Hi-Fis and the Hunger Project, up and moved to New York. By the mid-eighties, they would return home and evolve into Blue Rodeo and Cowboy Junkies, respectively. The first wave of punk bands had either broken up or changed styles. Mistreated by labels and tired of the bar-band circuit, the Diodes split, half the band moving to England. Teenage Head's momentum was stalled by Gordie Lewis's injury in a car crash. And the Viletones, to everyone's surprise, went rockabilly.

The mandate of neighbourhood-bar-as-cultural-centre was picked up by a new venue that opened in October 1981. The Cameron House, Queen West survivor, has so far dodged the wrecking ball and remains awash in vibrant paint shades. Three giant fibreglass ants climb up the sides of the quaint old Victorian building. Inside, the art-festooned walls retain the same cozy, bohemian, bric-a-brac character that, for Toronto's creative community, has remained a comforting constant for thirty-plus years. 'This Is Paradise,' a sign over the bar declares, as if with a sigh of relief.

The Cameron's original owners, siblings Paul Sannella and Ann Marie Ferraro and their friend Herb Tookey, had taken over a ninety-year-old tavern with the aim of transforming it into a hub for the emerging arts and music scene. Positioned on the corner of tiny side street Cameron, the venue would commence the westward migration of the Queen Street strip beyond its previous psychological boundary of Spadina.

Ann Marie Ferraro (co-owner, Cameron House): *Over the course of some chance meetings at various parties, my brother and Herb had started discussing the possibility of purchasing a warehouse space in the area and renting to local* *artists, who were finding it more and more difficult to find a reasonably priced space in the neighbourhood. After months of looking, they came across the realtor's listing for the Cameron House. It seemed perfect. There were the rooms that they had wanted, plus a bar on the main floor.*

The Cameron had previously been a hotel, and its upper floors soon became a literal home for artists, many of whom moved into the tiny rooms above the bar – and never moved out. It would be easy to romanticize the Cameron as a northern version of New York's debauched Chelsea Hotel, but the less sexy reality is that its upper floor apartments anticipated the housing crisis that would affect the city, and especially its artist classes, in the coming decades. The owners let many artists live upstairs rent-free. The Cameron has since become deeply embedded in Toronto arts mythology. Ann Marie's musician son Cosmo Ferraro took over booking in 2010.

The Government played the Cameron's first Halloween party, in 1981. The band began to wind down the following year, having evolved from oddball art-pop into minimalist groove-funk. A new slate of younger bands had begun to emerge, defiantly independent, DIY, and opposed to the commercialization of their music as 'new wave.' Fifth Column, Rent Boys Inc., Kinetic Ideals, Vital Sines, the Dave Howard Singers, L'Étranger, Sturm Group, Breeding Ground, and Tulpa are a few of these unjustly forgotten bands. There was an amazing diversity to the Toronto post-punk groups, as they drew on influences from reggae, funk, folk, jazz, and experimental music. If there was a weakness to this scene, it was the heavy strain of Anglophilia that infected a few of the bands.

Dave Howard didn't need to affect an accent. His stage persona was that of a sardonic, occasionally demonic lounge singer, there to torment or amuse his audiences – and sometimes get them to get up and dance. After the split of his early no-wave group the Diner's Club with Brian Ruryk, who continued playing his gnarly detuned guitar along with a drum machine as Deadlines, Howard started a new band, the Dave Howard Singers. Only they weren't really a 'band' – it was just Howard, an Ace Tone organ, and a Roland Space Echo. Musically, the DHS was Burt Bacharach by the way of Suicide, but taking an apocalyptic carnival ride on primitive electronic beats and repetitive keyboard figures.

Howard's deadpan humour, audience banter, crooner vocals, and clean-cut, army-cadet-on-acid looks lent his shows at the Cameron and Beverley a surreal air – which intensified when he jumped into atonal screaming. With its childishly drawn cover, his 1982 cassette *Alone and Gone* is a lost classic of the genre later celebrated as 'outsider music.' Howard ended up moving to England two years later.

Post-punk was mostly ignored by the mainstream media; punk's shock value was old news, and the new-wave narrative was based around wacky fashion and commercial success. Self-published zines became a key source of information about artists and music-scene happenings – and a way to hear new artists. Following Fifth Column's lead with *HIDE*, zines like *Sounds from the Streets* by Dave 'Rave' MacIntosh began including tape compilations.

Dave MacIntosh: Sounds from the Streets *was named after a song by the Jam, and issue number one came out in 1981, priced fifty cents, printed very cheaply at Brampton Library due to a faulty photocopier clicker. Issue two came out a few months later, priced sixty cents. Most of the Toronto stores were happy to stock a few copies, and I would also sell them at gigs. I gave a copy to Gary Topp from the Garys, and soon after, I noticed I was let into most of his gigs, which was an exciting development.*

Other fanzines at the time included *Smash It Up* by Nick Smash, who also included cassette comps; *Schrick* and *This Tiny Donkey Looks Rather Lost*, both made by teenagers from Scarborough, including future AGO curator Jim Shedden; and hardcore zines *Cause & Effect* and *Civil Disobedience*, the latter put out by Youth Youth Youth.

With many in the zine crowd underage, in November 1981 the all-ages DJ night Start Dancing – organized by a collective of Scarborough teens – started up on Friday nights at a series of DIY rental venues downtown, including a Legion Hall on Ontario Street and the Desh Bhagat Temple on Claremont Street. Start Dancing soon added live bands, including L'Étranger, a teenaged Rheostatics, and instrumental surf rockers Mark Malibu & the Wasagas. In a booze-dominated scene, it was the first time a show series was done by the kids, for the kids.

Start Dancing lasted for over five years, surviving countless near-catastrophes, including attempted vehicular murder – after an altercation outside the temple, some asshole drove his car onto the sidewalk and through the front doors. Organizer Mark Sanders broke his arm and a few others were injured.

The *Sounds from the Street* zine also began promoting its own minifestivals, the first held at short-lived downtown club 100 Bond Street in

December '82. The SFTS fest communicated that there was an exciting new sound bubbling up from Toronto's cold sidewalks, and garnered coverage on City-TV's fine pre-Much magazine program, *The New Music*.

MacIntosh: *It's promoting what the radio is going to play in five years! This is the future of rock'n'roll ... in Toronto, anyway.* (to Daniel Richler, *The New Music*, 1983)

MacIntosh's optimistic exuberance now sounds like a long-unanswered distress call from the past. The dark dissonance of post-punk and the noisy velocity of hardcore were not where the music industry wanted to direct listeners' tastes.

Beyond loud, angry guitar bands, the Cameron House was ground zero for an explosion of diverse musical styles on Queen West. On January 9, 1982, a tall, affable young man wearing a cowboy hat and kerchief and calling himself Handsome Ned began a tradition that would last for five short but crucial years. The twenty-four-year-old singer/songwriter, born Robin David Masyk, played gritty, heartfelt country and western in the 'outlaw' style of Merle Haggard, Johnny Cash, and other icons of the fifties and sixties. Many of the punk movement's true believers – including the Viletones' Steven Leckie – were turning to the past to find authentic rebel music. Handsome Ned's weekly Saturday matinee at the Cameron united punks, new wavers, art scenesters, and country fans who missed the good old days of the Horseshoe.

Greg Keelor (Blue Rodeo, the Hi-Fis): *It was in New York that we started listening to a lot of country music. And when we got back, Toronto seemed like a bit of a ghost town musically ... Where could you play original music, especially original music that was a little different? And then we discovered Ned at the Cameron.* (interviewed in *You Left Me Blue: The Handsome Ned Story*, 2017)

Ned became a familiar presence along Queen West, with his relaxed, affable persona and Paul Newman–esque looks upon a hulking farmboy frame – a cartoonish enough appearance to be not conventionally 'handsome.' In that sense, the moniker 'Handsome Ned' could sum up Toronto – smug confidence humanized by ironic, self-deprecating modesty. The Queen West strip was developing a community 'village' feel that made it the first real successor to Yorkville.

A diverse range of other Cameron residencies soon followed. Black Canadian vocalist Molly Johnson opened new wavers' minds at her jazz night Blue Mondays and co-founded electronic soul band Alta Moda. On Sunday nights, saxophonist John Oswald led a weekly free-jazz improvisational night. Several years later, he joined CCMC, then still heard weekly at the Music Gallery.

The Queen West music and arts scene had grown big enough to accommodate a second multi-disciplinary performance venue. In February 1982, a few months after the Cameron joined the scene, the Rivoli opened its doors at 332 Queen St. West, a space that had been a vaudeville theatre and cinema going back to 1911. The Riv's back room quickly became a favourite spot for rock shows, film screenings, and theatrical performances, and a few years later it opened a front bar and restaurant that remains a Queen Street institution to this day.

The recognizable cursive Rivoli logo was created by singer/songwriter Mary Margaret O'Hara, one of a generation of arty neo-folkies that also included Jane Siberry, whose 1981 self-titled debut modernized folk music with an eccentric new wave sensibility. The Rivoli became so associated with the arty, pretentious, black-turtleneck crowd that comedian Mike Myers based his SNL character Dieter from Sprockets on one of the club's waiters.

One of the Riv's earliest bookings was buzzy enough to make it onto the cover of *Now Magazine*, the free 'alt-weekly' that launched in September '81. And this band was only playing their second-ever gig. V was a cross-genre, reggae-rock supergroup, a quintet including Mojah from Truths and Rights and Terry Wilkins from Rough Trade, along with Lorraine Segato and Billy Bryans of Mama Quilla II. The latter group came out of the lesbian women's music scene, having evolved from raunchy folk-rock into politically charged art-funk. Drummer Bryans sported a 'token male' shirt when gigging with them. To complete the loop of the QSW scene's incestuousness, he also played in the final incarnation of the Government.

Lorraine Segato: *What was interesting about V was that both Mojah and I got a lot of flak for [it] for different reasons. You had a Rasta man and a lesbian feminist coming together to sing political songs, and you had Terry's roots experience and Billy's blues background. What we did was really quite radical at* *that time – not only the music, which was this dub funk thing – but also the fact that we were singing together was a real statement to both of our communities. It was a shaking-the-rafters moment.*

Though V was short-lived – no recordings exist beyond some archival video – it was an indicator of the fertile creative breeding ground that Queen West had become, and an example of Toronto's potential for new forms of expression. Multiculturalism was firmly established as part of the city's self-identity (though the question of 'diversity' was, and still is, a complicated one in Toronto). Events like the annual Caravan Festival – where different cultural organizations set up national 'pavilions' in community centres across the city – had been going strong since the seventies, and the arts programming at Harbourfront Centre – a federally funded cultural centre on the previously neglected waterfront – exposed Torontonians to the expression of different world cultures. More than theatre, dance, or music, though, what began to bring people together at these summertime events was the *food*. WASP-dominated Toronto was only starting to discover the joys of jerk chicken, sushi, and borscht. Not to be left out, Queen West was ready for its own venue to express this new spirit of inclusivity.

The BamBoo Club opened its doors on July 11, 1983, for the record release party for a new band on the scene, the Parachute Club – a septet including V's Segato and Bryans. The BamBoo took its name from the wicker factory that had inhabited the building. Its décor was tropical, with Day-Glo pinks and blues and a courtyard patio. Owners Richard O'Brien and Patti Habib envisioned programming that encompassed funk, soul, R&B, jazz, global music – and lots of reggae: 20th Century Rebels, the Sattalites, Leroy Sibbles, and Messenjah were among its regulars.

Lorraine Segato: *I think the BamBoo is the singular most important club to come out of this city, ever, really – in relationship to world, reggae, African, and various forms of multi-rhythmic music. It birthed this whole perspective change around what was going on in Toronto.*

With the growth of the diaspora, Caribbean music became particularly popular in Toronto in the early eighties. Reggae's peaceful vibes and provocative lyrics filled both Queen West bars and larger venues like the Concert Hall and the Palais Royale.

Leroy Sibbles: *We developed a following at the BamBoo club. Every weekend we played there, it was packed. People were always looking forward to seeing us there. And we had fun. I remember that band and myself, we all became so close, so tight, so spiritual musically.*

The opening of the BamBoo coincided with the launch of Ryerson's campus radio station CKLN 88.1, an all-volunteer-run FM station that played plenty of jazz, blues, and reggae alongside a range of local underground rock bands, as well as some hard-hitting news programming, bringing a diverse sense of community and social justice to an often apolitical music scene. It also notably ran Canada's first hip-hop radio show, Ron Nelson's *Fantastic Voyage.*

Reggae singer Leroy Sibbles was a regular attraction at the BamBoo club.

David Barnard (CKLN staffer and volunteer, 1982–96): *CKLN began evolving from a primarily student-focused mandate to a more broadly defined community mandate, inviting marginalized voices to share their experiences. For the Toronto's music community, this invitation was revolutionary and timely. CFNY was becoming increasingly commercialized, and the most available and cheapest medium to record music was not considered a suitable broadcast format by most radio stations. CKLN played cassettes!*

Denise Benson (DJ/writer): *CKLN really was people speaking for and about their own communities. To me, community radio was the social media of its time. It was how you learned about shows, about artists, about activists coming together. It was a world you could tune into if you wanted to learn about your city.*

As for the band that released their debut album on that Monday night at the BamBoo, the Parachute Club became new wave Toronto's first hit-makers since Martha and the Muffins, with whom they now shared a Canadian record label, Current. The band members studied soca music in Trinidad and Tobago, which informed their percussion-heavy world-pop. Their single

'Rise Up' quickly went top ten nationally, heard everywhere from Blue Jays games to the Pride Parade, an essential sing-along for union rallies and activist marches. The song's message of liberation and equality still moves me, especially when Segato delivers the line, 'We want freedom to love who we please.'

The post-punk posse were having none of that, though.

Nick Smash (Rent Boys Inc., *Smash It Up* **zine):** *The BamBoo was the death of Queen Street, as far as I'm concerned. It was just all so polite and tame and yuppie. Everybody who went to the BamBoo to see the Parachute Club were accountants and lawyers and business people. They had their cocktails and their little Hawaiian drinks ... And we went to the Bev! Where it was five bucks for a pitcher of beer and it was the worst kind of beer you could get.*

Rent Boys Inc., the maniacal punk-funk bad boys of Queen West, were more into chaos and confrontation – while also igniting the dance floor. They gigged at an actual strip club, the Queen City Tavern, at Queen and Bathurst, and sometimes got naked themselves, a few years before the Red Hot Chili Peppers. By mid-'83, they could pack the Rivoli or the Beverley, but with zero record industry support, there was nowhere to go from there. They hatched a plan to relocate to England, which they actually pulled off, though the results were mildly disastrous. Not receiving the rapturous British reception they hoped for, the group imploded, and half the members returned home to Toronto by the end of the year, while others started new lives in the UK.

Their friends in Sturm Group developed their own rep for explosive live shows, with gigs ending in spontaneous sheet-metal percussion jams, and on one occasion, a Rivoli washroom door 'body-surfing' across the crowd. Their 1984 self-titled debut may be the best full-length to represent the Toronto post-punk era, with stunning, discordant guitar moments that now sound a decade ahead of their time.

L'Etranger, meanwhile, represented this scene's more politicized side. The trio resembled a folkier Gang of Four, with Andrew Cash's earnest, rootsy voice tackling toxic masculinity, capitalism, and militarism. Both Cash and bassist Charlie Angus later went into politics themselves, elected as NDP Members of Parliament – giving Canada a few good years of punk rock in power. But despite being able to fill clubs, L'Etranger hit a plateau by the mid-eighties, unable to expand their fanbase past the Ottawa/Montreal touring corridor - a familiar story for Toronto bands.

The second and final Sounds from the Street festival took place at the Rivoli in January of 1984, after which MacIntosh shifted his focus toward a new Ryerson-supported music magazine, *Nerve*. The remaining post-punk groups soldiered on through the eighties, with Vital Sines, Breeding Ground, and Tulpa making inroads on CFNY, City-TV, and the brand-new MuchMusic video station and maintaining a devoted following in the clubs.

By the start of 1984, Queen West's venue strip was ready to add one more A-List player. The Horseshoe Tavern had spent a whole year not being the Horseshoe Tavern. Since the Garys were turfed at the end of '78, a revolving door of managers had failed to reestablish it as a country and western hall. In December '82, the legendary Horseshoe suffered a historical indignity: it was converted into a fifties-themed restaurant named Stagger Lee's. Waiters with slicked-back hair served pub fare over checkerboard tablecloths.

New managers Ken Sprackman, Richard Crook, and Michael 'X-Ray' Macrae were brought on board. Within a decade, the Horseshoe Tavern would become the after-work headquarters of the Canadian music industry. The team rebuilt the front bar as a long, narrow, watering hole, returning the stage to its current spot on the back wall. Modernizing its bookings to reflect the changes around it, the club hosted reggae, new wave pop, and country – though in the newfangled form of Handsome Ned.

Just as important as the bands the 'Shoe booked was the way it paid them. For ages, both the musicians' union and booking agents had dictated how club booking worked. Bar owners were required to pay a flat fee set by the union to hire musicians, and then to chase the musicians down to ensure they were paid up as members – a herding-cats-level task that was pointless after punk. Sprackman cut union and agencies out of the equation, dealing with the bands directly and instituting what quickly became the industry standard for Toronto club booking: the door/bar split.

It was a brilliant new model, a win-win adaptation to the DIY era: the band promotes their own show, charging a cover and keeping the door money; the bar sells drinks and keeps all the bar revenue. An effective separation of church and state, and a more egalitarian, entrepreneurial new system – albeit one that privileged those whose friends were heavy drinkers.

Booze had made the Beverley Tavern tick since long before OCA students and the first wave of punks discovered it. As a venue, it had *never* had a cover, and bands were always paid by the bar. But musician William New dreamed up something just as revolutionary in the fall of '83. The gaunt, dreadlocked beanpole frontman of Groovy Religion, a post-punk band with a gothic, psychedelic bent, was trying to come up with a fun way to increase attendance at their regular gigs at the Bev. Following a successful three-night multi-band mini-fest at the club called the Elvis Presley Memorial Beatfest, Groovy Religion were invited to do a Monday-night residency. But rather than just make it all about his band, New dreamed up something bigger: he made it all about the community. Thus began a Toronto indie-music institution: Elvis Mondays. There wasn't a ton of significance to the name.

William New: *There are a lot of things to be learned from Elvis, he taught us how to overeat and abuse drugs.* (to *Now Magazine*, November 3, 1983)

Lofty ideals of uniting the independent music community were hidden in a Trojan Horse of tongue-in-cheek, retro rock-star worship. The first Elvis Monday, on November 7, 1983, featured Groovy Religion alongside more avant-garde acts, prog-punk quartet the Polkaholics and noise-guitar terrorist Brian Ruryk. The Elvis theme took challenging music and presented it in a fun, sometimes goofy, cabaret atmosphere.

Elvis Mondays would go on to an astounding thirty-plus year run as a rite of passage for emerging artists. The social dimension was crucial – Elvis

Rivoli regulars Sturm Group caused creative chaos onstage.

Mondays became like *Cheers* for the music scene. Long before Netflix, there was *nothing* else to do on a Monday night. This free-form curation-format-slash-social-club, on a dead night of the week, began a direct line of inspiration that led to the creation of Wavelength (of which I was a co-founder) almost two decades later.

A new generation of bands grew up around Elvis Mondays. Forming in 1982 while still in high school, Change of Heart are probably the first Toronto band that can fairly be labelled 'indie-rock,' as singer/guitarist Ian Blurton was paying attention to the noisy, melodic sounds coming from south of the border via US bands like Hüsker Dü and the Minutemen. Blurton was born in 1965, also making him this story's first member of Generation X – and Change of Heart would become leading figures in the Canadian indie-music revolution of the nineties. Through six albums over sixteen years, COH – alongside the Rheostatics and 13 Engines – would be the era's local heroes most rooted-for to cross over from DIY underground to the mainstream. With a sound ranging from punk to prog, psychedelic to pop, they were – for better or worse – often impossible to pin down, but their best songs remain civic anthems ('Ten Miles,' 'It Should Be').

Ian Blurton (Change of Heart): *There was an anything-goes attitude at the Bev. It was more or less an OCA hangout, so there was a lot of experimentation and cross-pollination. Just inventing bands on the spot, improvising a lot, and playing crazy shows with people that you'd never played with before.*

The new generation of underground rock bands associated with Elvis Mondays, including A Neon Rome, Woods Are Full of Cuckoos, and Ministry of Love, harkened back to the sixties spirit of psychedelia and the hypnotic drone-rock experiments of the Velvet Underground. Meanwhile, Rivoli regulars Shadowy Men on a Shadowy Planet brought punk intensity and a campy sense of humour to their ever more elaborate stage shows and record packaging. If anyone capitalized on the new door/split arrangement the Horseshoe brought in, it was self-publicity geniuses the Shadowy Men.

You could argue that this backward-looking trend was a reaction to the modernism of post-punk, or to the sterile plasticity of MTV and mid-eighties pop radio – or just the beginning of a twenty-year nostalgia cycle. But I'd say that by the mid-eighties, Queen West was so established as a home for the new that its young bands felt comfortable looking to the old for inspiration.

FIFTH COLUMN
We Dug a Trench
1980-95

The first time I interviewed Fifth Column, we were in a car stuck in traffic against the flow of the Santa Claus Parade, trying to get one of the members to Union Station in time to catch a train, with mere minutes to spare. The second time I interviewed them, our phone conversation ended up with Caroline Azar and G.B. Jones debating urban planning, Rob Ford, and Le Corbusier, Quebec, Robert LePage, and the value of anger in art. I got the sense that that was how their band practices ended. Kevin Hegge's *She Said Boom: The Story of Fifth Column* (2012) begins with the premise that the band loved to argue. They loved the European socialist-style debate, getting to the Truth over endless espressos, late into the night, making music until dawn.

Over their fifteen-year lifespan, Fifth Column became almost a civic institution, albeit one that often provoked fear and confusion. They remain one of Toronto's most misunderstood groups, lazily labelled 'feminist art punk.' Sure, their members were mostly women, and their music could be angry and experimental. But there's so much more to their story. They were always more art project than rock band, incorporating Super-8 films and zine-making into their practice. Musically, they drew on sixties girl groups and Lalo Schifrin spy-movie music as much as contemporary post-punk.

Fifth Column also helped spawn two subgenres. They are credited with inventing 'queercore' and significantly influencing Bikini Kill, Bratmobile, and other exponents of the Riot Grrrl movement. But these impacts were most felt beyond the city's borders, and these sexy international associations often overshadowed what the band was really about. Essentially an art collective, Fifth Column anticipated the collectivist movement that took over Canadian independent music in the early 2000s.

They are now historically identified as post-punk, which is accurate inasmuch as their music was experimental and intellectual and rejected music-industry orthodoxy.

Caroline Azar (vocals, keyboards): The punks that survived had to be thinking punks. There seemed to be a door opening where we could discuss things more taboo. Punk incited it, dug a hole — and then we went further and dug a trench.

During punk's first sonic boom, Caroline Azar was a high school student in North Toronto. At the University of Toronto, she majored in drama and appeared in an experimental film that was seen by G.B. Jones, a filmmaker and multimedia artist, at a screening at the Funnel, the avant-garde cinema that occupied the former Crash 'n' Burn basement. In 1979, Jones joined her first band, Bunny and the Lakers, alongside Peter Morgan and How'rd Pope (brother of Rough Trade's Carole). As legend has it, they only ever played one live show. Ironically, their lone album was one of Caroline Azar's favourite records, before they ever met.

At a mutual friend's insistence, in the fall of 1980, Azar went to a punk house party where Jones was playing drums with a new band, Second Unit, with bassist Kathleen Pirrie Adams and guitarist Janet Martin.

CA: I walked in, and I thought, 'Whoa, this is the first time I've seen exciting, gorgeous, young Toronto girls doing their thing.' I thought their look was impeccable, their attitude was pure, raw, and truthful, and what they played … It was a war of sound.

The band only had three songs – which they played over and over again, to Azar's delight. She was smitten with their DIY, do-it-now punk ethic: Jones had never played drums before. Azar didn't hesitate when she found out they were auditioning a new singer. The first time she met the other members was in the bathroom when the Slits played the Edge.

G.B. Jones (drums, guitar, vocals): As soon as I saw her, I was like, 'Oh my goodness, it has to be that girl. She's the coolest.' I had seen her in one of Midi Onodera's art films. I thought, 'She's an underground movie star, we have to have her in the band!'

Younger than her new bandmates, Azar also stood out style-wise – their new singer wore big sixties-style bangs and stripey sweaters. Sagely recognizing that they had a charismatic new focus for audiences' attention, the band decided to rename themselves.

Fifth Column: a contentious choice of moniker. Though no doubt the band meant to convey the idea of a group of rebels undermining an oppressive system from within, the term had a real-life fascist origin in the Spanish Civil War. The band certainly enjoyed being provocateurs.

CA: It was Kathleen and G.B. Jones who came up with the name as a metaphor. I will tell you I never liked the name. I still don't like the name, because of its connotation and its misinterpretation. What made me finally like 'Fifth Column' was when G.B. did some fanzine art. She used a quote from a convention in Michigan around fifth columnists and the art and font looked beautiful – like fifties soap opera melodrama.

The band played their first show in late 1980 at the Subway Room, in the basement of the Spadina Hotel, also home to the Cabana Room. The band immediately stood out as one of the only all-women bands on the club scene. Though groups like the Curse and the B-Girls had been part of the '77 first wave, both broke up by 1981.

But Fifth Column had no interest in being marketed as an 'all-girl band.' They were feminist at a time when the movement was experiencing backlash as well as internal dissent, during the end of its second wave. Their image was desexualized, the band members wearing multiple layers of used clothing in order to pass through the city without getting harassed. Just as they safely navigated early-eighties Toronto's rough streets and back alleys (for the most part; Jones and Azar were once randomly attacked and beaten up at the corner of Queen and Bathurst), they also navigated through different arts scenes.

A cinematic aesthetic drove Fifth Column. They started collaborating with Super-8 filmmaker John Porter, who created film loops to work as a 'moving wallpaper' backdrop to their shows. G.B. Jones shot shaky, home-movie-style images of the band hanging out in Toronto neighbourhoods, looking like they were the only residents, as if in some end-of-the-world movie.

But musically, they didn't really fit in anywhere. Early Fifth Column music is somewhere between sixties psychedelic beach-party and dissonant punk apocalypse. They aimed to be both campy and rigorously experimental – in their own untrained way.

CA: The music was influenced by soundtrack music or twentieth-century music. So even though it sounded herky-jerky and very poor and raw, we were listening to Varèse or Satie and trying to translate that onto our electric instruments and add a little rock edge. We didn't want to play regular rock-'n'roll. We found it abhorrent.

But the flipside of the Fifth Column aesthetic was a sugary sweetness that – demonstrating their subversive sense of humour – embraced a pop aesthetic still considered deeply suspicious and uncool by punks and new wavers.

GBJ: We put together this whole theory about how bands from the sixties, the bubblegum groups, that everyone just hated – we said we *loved* them, because almost all of those groups, their message was addressed to teenage girls. It was the only music you could listen to that didn't have all this really misogynist content. (to Kevin Hegge, *She Said Boom*, 2012)

The reaction to a wilful, artsy, provocative all-female band from the rest of the music scene was predictably misogynistic.

CA: It was really hostile. Even after playing one or two shows, there were all these rumours about us. We were man-haters, we were sluts, we were this or that. At that time, Toronto was really male-identified.

Fifth Column nonetheless did a lot to support the rest of the scene. In 1982, Azar and Jones and their friend Candy Parker began publishing their own photocopied zine, HIDE, which featured original artwork and band interviews – and, starting in its second issue, included home-dubbed cassette compilation tapes, featuring their own songs alongside other Toronto bands', including the Party's Over and Deadlines.

Fifth Column's first recorded material had appeared on the Urban Scorch compilation released by Scott Kerr of the Party's Over, so in some ways, they were returning the favour. The band's first proper release, the *Boy/Girl*

EP, came out in '83 on non-profit label Voicepondence Records. These early Fifth Column artifacts are all now incredibly rare collector's items.

Despite the support of Liam Lacey, pop critic at the *Globe and Mail*, their only early mainstream press champion, Fifth Column remained obscure and on the margins throughout the eighties. They played all the small clubs on the circuit – the Cabana Room, the Cameron House, Larry's Hideaway – and benefit concerts for every imaginable cause.

CA: We were always honoured when people asked us to do benefits for women's shelters. We were young and strong and could loan our bodies to that. We played for free at pro-choice rallies, all the queer events, all the campus radio stations. We even played for the Socialist Party *and* the Communist Party.

It wasn't so much that 'success' eluded them, it was more than they weren't interested. The band – and its associated art projects – was their passion, their calling, their social life. They paid their rent by working at Yorkville café Just Desserts, where they made friends with a young, gay punk rocker named Bryan Bruce. Jones renamed him Bruce LaBruce, and he soon became the band's underwear-clad go-go dancer, upending traditional gender roles and inspiring the Hidden Cameras, who offered a similar stage show almost two decades later.

In 1985, Jones and LaBruce began collaborating on a zine entitled *J.D.s* – a stencil-heavy, photocopied piece of satire that ended up securing Fifth Column's future legacy. Jones and LaBruce, disillusioned with both the lame mainstream gay scene and the homophobic, misogynistic straight punk subculture, trolled both. In *J.D.s*, they imagined a hardcore scene populated by hot, sweaty, shirtless gay boys. It was in the pages of *J.D.s* that the term 'homocore' was first coined – the subgenre was later renamed 'queercore' to be more inclusive. Queercore eventually became a real-life movement, with numerous out gay punk and hardcore bands emanating from the US in the nineties, such as Pansy Division, Team Dresch, and Limp Wrist.

The influence of punk rock crept back into Fifth Column's music, and in 1985, they self-released their debut full-length album, with the attention-grabbing title *To Sir With Hate* – perfectly combining their love of sixties pop culture with a middle finger to the patriarchy. The record's rage remains razor-sharp three decades later. The band takes on targets like schoolyard bullying and homophobia. LaBruce contributed guest vocals to 'The Fairview

Mall Story,' based on a real-life story of a police bust of gay men having sex in mall washrooms in St. Catharines, Ontario – ruining lives and leading to suicides. Despite being out of print for years, *To Sir with Hate* was recently nominated for the Polaris Music Prize's 'Heritage Prize,' recognizing influential Canadian albums from decades past.

Like their friends in Change of Heart, Fifth Column operated as a self-contained DIY unit, recording and touring on a shoestring budget. It would take five long years until their next full-length, *All-Time Queen of the World*, was released, again on their own label, Hide Records, in 1990.

In the interim, the band went through some major membership changes, notably the 1987 addition of bassist Beverly Breckenridge. Her playing smoothed out the band's sound, her Joy Division–influenced basslines driving gripping, psych-punk epics like 'Like This.'

Another lineup shuffle not long after the album's release resulted in a major shift in the Fifth Column sound. G.B. Jones moved from drums to guitar, and the kit position was filled by a series of male drummers, including Don Pyle of Shadowy Men. Michelle Breslin, later of It's Patrick and sad-oceanspacebear, joined to double up the guitar attack. Fifth Column was suddenly a turbo-charged rock band.

After seeing a schlocky 1977 Canadian horror film called *Cathy's Curse*, Jones decided she wanted to write a song with Azar named after a line from the movie: 'All Women Are Bitches – Repeat!' That was the closest Fifth Column came to writing an anthem. No longer just a piece of kitschy Canucksploitation, the phrase became a condemnation of systemic, learned misogyny.

'All Women Are Bitches' came out on a seven-inch single in 1992, by which point Nirvana had transformed the music industry and focused worldwide attention on indie music coming out of the Pacific Northwest. For the first time in almost a decade, Fifth Column had an outside label backing them up, and what a label: K Records, run by Calvin Johnson of the Beat Happening was crucial to the corduroy-clad revolution. Its hometown of Olympia, Washington, was ground zero for Riot Grrrl, spawning Bikini Kill, Bratmobile, Heavens to Betsy, Excuse 17, and others. Things really detonated when Everett True – the British music critic who discovered Nirvana – featured the record as 'Single of the Week' in UK music mag *Melody Maker*, then the cooler competitor to the NME.

On the home front, Fifth Column were invited to play the side stage of Lollapalooza at Molson Park in summer 1993. The following September, almost fourteen years after they formed, they were on the cover of *Now*. That 'making-it-in-Toronto' milestone coincided with their appearance at the Kumbaya festival at the doomed Ontario Place Forum, an event that was going live-to-air on MuchMusic. The TV people asked them not to play 'All Women Are Bitches,' so of course they played it. The band claimed that Much never aired their videos again.

Performing for ecstatic American audiences on tour, the band found a joy in playing live they had rarely felt until then.

CA: I loved the American shows. I loved Bikini Kill. Playing with Bikini Kill, that was the experience I was looking for since 1981, and all it took was a thirteen-year wait.

Kathleen Hanna (Bikini Kill, Le Tigre): We didn't see Fifth Column until pretty late, '94 or '95, and it was this legendary group of women. We'd seen the movies, read the zines, totally obsessed. They came to town and they were absolutely lovely. I just remember thinking, 'Why are we the ones who get all the attention? They're such a better band than we are.' (to Kevin Hegge, *She Said Boom*, 2012)

CA: I remember we did this one show in New York with Huggy Bear. It was such a rambunctious show, I could've sworn we were a dance band. Things got so wild, the stage broke.

Sadly, the band never felt they received the same rapturous response when they played in their hometown.

CA: There was a guy who worked for [a label] who saw us at the Rivoli, and he came up to me and said, 'We need to have a meeting.' So I went to his office. And he said, 'You need to break up. This is just the most horrible music.' We would get endless feedback that if we wanted to get a larger audience, we needed to change our sound. And we just never listened to them. But I think because of K Records, and having more clout through the US and UK press, the Torontonians went, 'Oh! Wait a minute.' People started to look at us differently. Which implies a great deal of shallowness. I always marvel when that happens, because I think, 'Don't you know what you like?'

It was getting increasingly challenging to manage the various demands and requests for their time, especially for G.B. Jones, who had become something of a countercultural, multimedia superstar.

GBJ: I had a gallery in New York, and was showing work there, doing work for various other galleries and magazines, making films and acting in films. I was working literally around the clock. If I wasn't doing a drawing, doing a movie, or practising with the band, I was writing letters. I would be getting a hundred letters a week that I'd go through and answer by hand. Thank God there was no email then, that's all I can say. I used to go around every day drinking so much coffee, smoking a billion cigarettes, and telling everybody, 'I'm on the verge of a nervous breakdown.' I don't think all that helped keep the band together. Naturally, everyone else wanted to do more – they wanted to tour, and I was just exhausted, and going, 'No, I don't want to do it, I don't want to do it.' It was just like *Beyond the Valley of the Dolls*.

The disappointment of turning down a UK tour offer was the final straw for a frustrated Caroline Azar, who by then had become the band's driving force.

CA: I walked. I did, I walked. I wanted to get to England and that wasn't the consensus. All signs were telling me that I had to walk away.

Fifth Column played their last gig in early 1995 in Ottawa. In 2007, Scott Kerr, by then part of queer electro-punk crew Kids on TV, began a series of Fifth Column tribute nights at Sneaky Dee's.

CA: My favourite thing post-breakup was those tribute nights; it was [the next] great generation of bands, like the Hidden Cameras. I loved every single interpretation of the songs. I had a job in New York, so I had to wear a pin-striped suit. And I came right from the airport to Sneaky Dee's, and a little girl came up to me and said, 'Is one of your kids in the band?' Every time some of these kids played, they'd come right over to us and they'd say, 'Did you like what we did?' And we'd say yes and we'd kiss and hug them – it was like we were their parents!

Azar and Jones continued careers in the arts. Returning to her love of theatre, Azar has directed over twenty plays, as well as music videos for Sylvia Tyson and Bob Wiseman. Jones makes art in mixed media, including film, and began collaborating with the Hidden Cameras in 2003.

THE CLUB BOOM
1984-87

The booming economy of the eighties brings live music
and DJs to new, unexplored parts of town, including the
Annex and the Waterfront – but Queen West still dominates.

Hundreds of gig-goers were out and about the night of June 12, 1985, bouncing from club to club, up and down Queen. The Club Crawl for Freedom of Choice brought together the four main live venues on the strip for a one-night mini-festival. Ten dollars granted admission to the BamBoo, the Rivoli, the Horseshoe, and the Cameron for the night, with all proceeds going to support the Morgentaler Defense Fund. Anti-abortion terrorists had firebombed Dr. Henry Morgentaler's clinic, destroying the Toronto Women's Bookstore in the process. The Fund was established to help improve access to abortion in Canada.

The Club Crawl lineup was a snapshot of Queen West's diversity: soca-popsters Compass, swing-jazzers Canadian Aces, and a reunion of reggae-rockers V at the 'Boo; dancey post-punks Vital Sines and queer new-wave popsters Bratty & the Babysitters at the Riv; former Yorkville psych denizen Luke Gibson and soft-rockers the Jitters at the 'Shoe; country and jazz singers Handsome Ned and Molly Johnson at the Cameron. The format was later adopted by CKLN-FM for its annual Street Crawls.

The club scene was booming in the mid-eighties in Toronto. The economy had mostly bounced back from the recession, and 1984 saw the emergence into popular culture of the 'yuppie.' Socially liberal and libertine but fiscally conservative, the stereotypical Young Urban Professional was a twenty- or thirty-something who had decided to put off putting down roots in favour of a decadent, materialistic, extended adolescence. And the city was growing: the Toronto metropolitan area had almost doubled in size since the early sixties.

New, larger clubs opened in parts of town previously unexplored or thought forgotten. Two combination live/dance club venues opening in summer '84 served the new, moneyed demographic: the Diamond (now the Phoenix) at Sherbourne and Carlton, and the Copa, in Yorkville.

Denise Benson (DJ, writer): *There was such a division between people who went out to live shows and people who went to dance clubs. And yet there was so much more of a merger inside the clubs than is necessarily remembered. There'd be* DJ *nights, or nights where there were* DJs *leading into live shows, going back into* DJs *...*

Jane Siberry, backstage at the Diamond, 1984.

Locals that played the Diamond included Jane Siberry. One could categorize her music as 'art-pop,' as her '84 album *No Borders Here* (on indie Duke Street Records) mixed influences ranging from folk and jazz to ambient and electronic. 'Mimi on the Beach' made for a very odd pop hit, but it gained respectable airplay on Canada's new video channel, MuchMusic. A sign of things to come, Siberry was the first of several eccentric, atmospheric Toronto artists who earned a large following. After the release of 1985's *The Speckless Sky*, she could fill Massey Hall.

In the fall of '85, RPM opened on the deserted waterfront at Queens Quay and Jarvis – a good location for evading residential noise complaints, but not for transit or other amenities; the club ran a shuttle bus from Union Station. RPM became a go-to spot for Garys shows for out-of-town bands as well as regular DJ nights with a more underground/alternative flavour, most notably CFNY DJ Chris Sheppard's Sunday night blend of rock and electronic music. In 1995, RPM became the Guvernment and the Warehouse under the ownership of legendary owner Charles Khabouth.

Benson: *It was so empty at night. I remember leaving RPM so many times and you'd just wander along the bottom of the city and barely pass anybody.*

The fall of '85 also marked a challenge to Queen West's live-music dominance. Close to the University of Toronto's downtown campus and along a subway line, the Annex is a neighbourhood of cute Victorian houses populated by profs and students. Its commercial strip along Bloor Street was replete with European-style cafés.

Albert's Hall, across the street from the Future and upstairs from the Brunswick House pub, had booked vintage New Orleans jazz since the early seventies. In 1981, Derek Andrews, formerly of the Edge, took over as booker and made it *the* place to hear Chicago blues. Veteran club booker Yvonne Matsell also got her start there, and in 1994, soulful singer/songwriter Jeff Buckley would play two storied nights at the venue.

A block or two west was Lee's Palace, which had been a movie theatre from 1919 to '57, then a burlesque cabaret called the Blue Orchid, then the Oriental Palace. In the punk days, the second floor had been a venue called The Rock Palace. Local businessman Chong Su Lee capitalized on the growing popularity of the Queen West scene by opening a larger concert venue to serve the student and hipster crowds. With its sixteen-foot ceilings, raised stage, and five-hundred-plus capacity, Lee's became the 'step up' venue for bands who had outgrown the Cameron/Horseshoe/Rivoli/BamBoo.

Lee hired artist Alex 'Runt' Currie to create a colourful, intricate mural that made Lee's an Annex landmark. The second floor opened in 1986 as alternative DJ club the Dance Cave, with indoor murals by graphic artist Fiona Smyth. Swaying drunkenly at 'the Cave' after downing cheap tequila shots became a rite of passage for black-clad U of T students.

A block down Bloor, a Hungarian dining lounge named Ildiko's, which went through a few other names, including the Starwood and the Bridge, booked hardcore punk shows during the roughly two years it lasted – much to the displeasure of neighbouring Annex homeowners. Otherwise, hardcore never had much of a stable home. Crazy Steve from the Bunchofuckingoofs tried running a club, DMZ, which bounced around locations, leaving behind a trail of trashed toilets and fuming owners.

Kensington Market wasn't yet a hotbed for venues. The Goofs' (and their many menacing attack dogs') domination of the Market may have scared off outsiders, or the conflict with the area's day uses may have prevented the development of much nightlife. A few spots came and went, though. Punk and hardcore bands like Madhouse and Living Proof played Quoc-Té, a dark Vietnamese basement bar in that billed itself as 'Toronto's ultimate psychedelic underground.' This is likely the same address that later, as Club 56, hosted legendary early-2000s DJ nights Evil Genius, Peroxide, and Expensive Shit.

Dancey post-punks Vital Sines marked the end of an era at the Beverley Tavern.

Meanwhile, back on Queen West, it was the end of an era. Right before Christmas '85, Beverley Tavern management made the sudden decision to stop booking live bands, ending a decade-long run as a spawning ground for the new wave in Toronto, starting with the Dishes and Martha and the Muffins. The original Queen Street dive couldn't keep up with the new door/bar split system made the standard by the Horseshoe.

There was no Last Booze-Up at the Bev. In avoiding the destruction that would have come with a last hurrah, the management also robbed the community of a chance to give the seminal space a proper farewell.

Ian Blurton (Change of Heart): *I still have the sign. There was a sign that said, 'This way to the attic,' the upstairs room. I broke it off the wall the night it closed, when they stopped having live bands. I was like, 'Fuck this.'*

The Bev returned to its roots as a watering hole for Queen West workers, though now they were more likely to be stockbrokers than slaughterhouse workers. oca students repopulated the bar, downing cheap pitchers of draft after class. The Beverley finally shut its doors for good in 2003. It is now a falafel joint, with no heritage plaque yet.

More worrisome than the loss of long-time venues was the economic boom's impact on the artists who had made the area what it was. The Victorian and Edwardian warehouses and industrial buildings surrounding the Queen West strip fell to the wrecking ball or were converted into pricy lofts. As the city cracked down on illegal live/work spaces, displaced artists moved further west to the post-industrial spaces around Parkdale.

Despite the expansion of the live music circuit, its creative centre of gravity remained the Queen West strip. On July 19, 1986, at the Horseshoe Tavern, a release party was held for one of the essential Canadian reggae records. *Revolutionary Tea Party* by Lillian Allen was steeped in deep dub reggae rhythms but had a dark, menacing atmosphere akin to the heavier sounds coming out of Queen West.

Allen's lyrics and vocal approach especially set the record apart: coming from the tradition of dub poetry, she spoke out against injustice and oppression in Canada – especially toward immigrants and racial minorities – with a rage and candour mostly unheard by the mainstream until then. Released on her own Verse to Vinyl label, *Revolutionary Tea Party* was produced by the Parachute Club's Billy Bryans; the backing musicians included members of both the P. Club and Truths and Rights – in a way, the music on *RTP* is as close as we'll get to hearing the cross-genre collaboration of V on record.

The album leads off with 'I Fight Back,' describing the struggles of domestic workers and people whose very existence in settler countries is questioned. 'They label me immigrant, law-breaker, illegal,' Allen seethes over wiry post-punk guitars and dub beats, foreseeing the sound of Massive Attack's *Mezzanine* a decade later. Elsewhere, 'Rub A Dub Style Inna Regent Park' boldly named a Toronto neighbourhood associated with the Black and Caribbean diaspora. Though the album was recognized with the 1986 Juno Award for Best Reggae/Calypso Recording – the categorically lazily shoving together two very different musical genres – reggae and dub poetry were still marginalized. Regent Park was not a place you were going to hear about on pop radio.

QUEEN STREET JAZZ

Queen West in the mid-eighties witnessed an insurgent new jazz scene that stole the music away from the concert halls and back to the clubs. Groups like Whitenoise and Gotham City blew a surprisingly danceable racket through the Cabana Room, the Rivoli, the BamBoo, and other clubs on the strip. The 'Queen Street Jazz' groups were strongly influenced by American saxophonist Ornette Coleman and his own developed theory of 'harmolodics,' with which he created a driving 'free funk' hybrid.

Glenn Milchem (Whitenoise): *Today people only dance to stuff that's familiar, like 'I know this song, it's on the* Guardians of the Galaxy *soundtrack!' But in those days, people would dance to an Ornette Coleman cover. We'd play the BamBoo club and there'd be 250 people dancing to some weird song in 9/8 that the sax player wrote. It was kind of amazing.*

Much like the conservative rock scene, Canadian jazz was (and is) a tough place for innovators, with record labels only supporting bebop-and-big-band traditionalists. Like hardcore bands, the QSJ groups put out their own albums on cassette.

Whitenoise, led by saxophonist/vocalist/composer Bill Grove, were a relentless party band. Gotham City may not have swung as hard, but they were badass in a low-key way. Led by another saxophonist/composer, Nic Gotham, the trio played film-noir spy music, perfect for lurking in the shadowy confines of the Rivoli. Gotham later formed the jazz /new music orchestra Hemispheres and relocated to Riga, Latvia, in 1998, where he became a national music icon before cancer took his life in 2013.

SHADOWY MEN ON A SHADOWY PLANET
Having an Average Weekend
1984-94

January 26, 1985 – The Rivoli was getting a facelift. Business was booming for Queen West's quirkiest club. A front bar and restaurant were getting added to the main floor, giving the clientele of artists, filmmakers, and other creative types a daytime place to hang and eat. Canada had lifted itself out of the early-eighties recession, and on a Saturday afternoon, even in January, there was plenty of foot traffic moving past.

'Look! Look!' exclaimed the handmade signs. Those not staring down at the sidewalk as they shuffled past were drawn over to the storefront of 332 Queen West. The windows were papered over for the reno, but someone had cut holes in the paper, creating a window through the window. Inside, a band played. They had no singer. Without the need for a PA to amplify vocals, the trio could just set up and play all afternoon, which they did, in a 'Shopper's Preview' for a gig a few weeks later in the club's back room. It was one of the band's very first shows, and they were already a sensation. They were unlike any other band, and had a name unlike any other: Shadowy Men on a Shadowy Planet.

Don Pyle (drums): We picked the name because we thought, this is a ridiculously long name. We liked that it sounded like a movie rather than a band.

Besides, we were only planning to play once, so it didn't matter what we were called.

Forming in the spring of 1984, Shadowy Men on a Shadowy Planet hadn't even considered playing live until their pals in Sturm Group offered them an opening slot at a Rivoli gig. Once in a while a new band comes along with instantly mythical status, the mix of pedigree and personal popularity resulting in everyone else in the scene knowing they're going to be great – and hoping for it, hungering for something awesome and new.

Shadowy Men were certainly new – and definitely novel. They were instrumental, at a time when it was unheard-of for a rock band to forgo a singer. Their sound shimmered with bright, reverb-laden guitar influenced by the surf-rock sound of sixties artists like Dick Dale and the Ventures. Many years later, they would record 'We're Not a Fucking Surf Band,' but it was hard to not hear that gnarly California twang in their sound. In their hands, though, it had a curiously naive, optimistic Ontario air about it. They weren't the first surf-inspired band in town – that honour is claimed by Mark Malibu & the Wasagas – but Shadowy Men predated the full-on surf revival sparked by the *Pulp Fiction* soundtrack a full decade later.

But the biggest thing that set them apart? Shadowy Men were *fun*.

DP: On the Toronto music scene at the time, things had gotten super dark. The most popular bands were Breeding Ground, Vital Sines, Sturm Group … it was super goth-y. A lot of people using drugs. We were definitely lighter and brighter.

Nervous about how they would be received without a singer to focus the audience's attention, Shadowy Men got a female friend to rollerskate through the crowd, holding up signs announcing the song titles. Arts and crafts – camp consumer kitsch and thrift-shop fashion – would play a huge role in the band's aesthetic; one of their seven-inch singles came in a Jiffy-Pop stove-top popcorn package, all five hundred copies stuffed by hand by the band members themselves.

As fun as their stage shows and art concepts were, Shadowy Men could have gotten away with simply being an awesome band: their musicianship was exceptional. Guitarist Brian Connelly was a savant-like virtuoso, while bassist Reid Diamond's melodic basslines anchored the songs in that meaty post-punk way. Amazingly, super-solid beat king Don Pyle had only just learned to play the drums five months before that first show.

Such DIY gusto is unsurprising given that a few years earlier, all three had been members of the punk band Crash Kills Five, which during its brief 1980–81 lifespan issued a couple of great singles. Pyle, a Toronto native and Crash Kills Five's singer, documented and eyewitnessed the first wave of punk rock, attending shows as a young teenager and taking crucial photographs later collected in his 2011 book *Trouble in the Camera Club*. Diamond and Connelly, meanwhile, were transplanted Calgarians who had moved to Toronto in '79 after the breakup of their band Buick McKane, one of the earliest Alberta punk groups.

Shadowy Men were soon joined on stage at their Rivoli gigs by a high school friend of Diamond and Connelly's from Calgary, a comedian named Bruce McCulloch, who told jokes between sets. McCulloch had a brand-new sketch troupe that soon began booking their own gigs at the club. Shadowy Men's instrumental sound – alternately cheery and creepy – worked great for interstitials, and they began accompanying the five-man troupe, who called themselves the Kids in the Hall. Thus began a decade-long partnership that would ultimately bring Shadowy Men their greatest notoriety: in 1989 their signature song 'Having An Average Weekend' began a second life as the theme song to the Kids in the Hall's legendary comedy TV series.

For people of my generation, there is no more iconic a representation of Toronto than the early *Kids in the Hall* opening sequence, a loving series of portraits of the city's neighbourhoods and denizens. If Toronto ever had a national anthem, it would start with Reid Diamond's unmistakable three-note bass riff.

DP: I was twenty-three when I started playing drums, and at that time I thought, 'I'm too old to start learning an instrument!' Anybody I knew in bands had been playing for a long time. But within a year we recorded the first single, which had 'Having an Average Weekend' on it. It's been the one thing that I've earned the most money out of. We had that song within six months of me starting to play drums, so you never know what's going to happen.

Shadowy Men on a Shadowy Planet set out on a successful touring and recording career of their own, one that increasingly saw them looking beyond the Rivoli and Toronto to reach an audience. By the early nineties, they

found themselves out of step – or rather, uncomfortably in step – with the wacky-band craze of Barenaked Ladies and Moxy Früvous.

DP: I understand why a lot of people thought we were just kind of like a stupid novelty band. I can't deny it because we did some silly things – we did fucking 'Batman,' we packaged the record in popcorn ... There was a lot of humour in what we did, and there were certain things that happened in Toronto with other bands that were doing things humorously that really made us back off from that very quickly.

Shadowy Men began to quietly drop the elaborate sets and rollerskating sideshows to focus on being a band. At the height of their instrumental powers, the trio benefited from a groundswell of support from influential members of the burgeoning American indie underground.

Their debut album, *Savvy Show Stoppers* – a collection of their early singles and EPS – was released by UK label Glass Records in '88, but the label immediately went bankrupt. The album was re-released by Montreal indie label Cargo Records in 1990. Shadowy Men cheekily embraced civic pride by putting Viljo Revell's New City Hall on the album cover – in the form of a kitschy tourist postcard overlain with their cardboard-cutout namesakes.

Cargo went on to release Shadowy Men's two fantastically named, proper full-lengths, 1991's *Dim The Lights, Chill the Ham*, and 1993's *Sport Fishin': The Lure of the Bait, the Luck of the Hook*. The latter was recorded in Chicago with Steve Albini, one of the most notoriously outspoken and respected/feared figures in American indie-rock. Albini had become a fan of the band, and engineered the album at a cut rate.

The trio's other cheerleaders around the globe included legendary BCC DJ John Peel, Everett True, the UK *Melody Maker* writer who discovered Nirvana, and Calvin Johnson of K Records and lo-fi pioneers Beat Happening. Shadowy Men toured North America twice with Beat Happening, appearing at Johnson's famous International Pop Underground Convention festival in

Olympia, Washington, alongside Fugazi, Bikini Kill, and L7, in 1991 – the idealistic height of 'The Year Punk Broke.'

On September 4, 1994, Shadowy Men played a one-off festival at the Ontario Place Forum – the last rock concert at the venue before its ignominious demolition. The day was entitled 'Kumbaya,' organized by jazz singer Molly Johnson as an AIDS hospice fundraiser, the rest of the lineup featuring fellow Queen Street stawarts Fifth Column and Mary Margaret O'Hara alongside more mainstream acts like Tom Cochrane and 54-40. Following the gig, the band announced a long-planned sabbatical, from which they would not return.

DP: I feel like we ended at the proper time. As far as our popularity in Toronto, we could feel that we'd been rising, rising, rising, rising … and then we had just plateaued.

Connelly's musical vision had been increasingly at odds with Diamond and Pyle's, who were keen to record an album with American outsider musician Jad Fair. The rhythm section teamed up with the Sadies' Dallas Good to record with Fair, backing him up and also playing on their own as Phono-Comb, with Fifth Column's Beverly Breckenridge joining on bass.

Connelly formed the more surf-rock-aligned Heatseekers and later Atomic 7. Pyle joined electro-dub rockers King Cobb Steelie and expressed his gay identity on the dance music project Greek Buck and later Black Heel Marks. After starting the multi-media project Danny & Reid's Motion Machine, Reid Diamond passed away after a six-year battle with cancer on February 17, 2001.

Their legend only growing over the years, Shadowy Men on a Shadowy Planet reunited in 2012 for Calgary's Sled Island festival, with Dallas Good filling Diamond's snazzy shoes on bass. With their original albums all since reissued – the band admitting *Oh, I Guess We Were a Fucking Surf Band After All* in the title of a 2016 box set – Toronto's ambassadors of thrift-store cool still tour and perform on the regular.

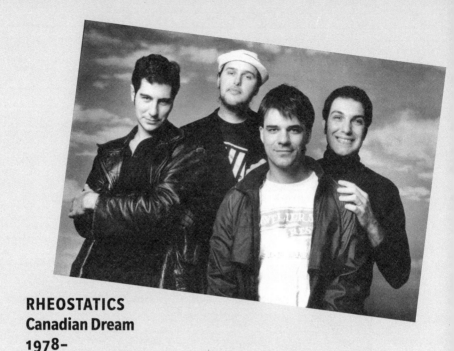

RHEOSTATICS
Canadian Dream
1978–

Dave Bidini (guitar/vocals): I was in the band room at the Edge, and it was fucking gross but it was so glorious. The romance of playing that role, that character, being a musician – it was enthralling. The band we were opening for, Popular Spies, had a flute player, and he was sitting up in the dressing room, smoking. I remember I said to him, 'Do you have any advice for a young band, mister?' And he took a drag on a cigarette and said, 'Yeah, don't ever break up.'

I think everyone who's been playing in bands for a while asks themselves, what if your high school band never broke up? The Rheostatics are one of the few that can answer that question. In a way, Toronto's most beloved yet uncategorizable band has been all about giggling at the mirror of their own self-identity. Born on the cusp between the Boomers and Gen-X, they grew up with arena-rock culture and were therefore able to laugh at/with the awesome silliness of 'being in a band!' Self-reflective yet never narcissistic, Rheostatics were the perfect group to boldly explore the inscrutable Canadian identity.

Forming in Etobicoke in 1978 while in the early years of high school, the Rheostatics recently celebrated their fortieth anniversary. Though the band did break up in 2007, its semi-regular reformations make it feel like they've never really gone away. The band seemed strangely destined for greatness since their teenaged inception, but they were also wisely unhurried, taking their time to grow into the artists they thought they could be but didn't quite believe they would be.

That first Rheos gig at the Edge in October 1980 is the stuff of local legend, and it's almost as if the band knew that going into it. Or perhaps they've been good at cultivating their own mythology all along. Then-frontman Dave Bidini, at sixteen, was already an accomplished journalist with self-confidence beyond his years.

DB: We recorded a demo, and I gave one cassette copy to the guys who ran Ready Records and another copy to Gary Topp, but I never heard anything from him. Then one afternoon, I was covering the Festival of Festivals [now TIFF] for *Sunshine News*, a really poorly named national high school newspaper. I was in the lobby just having a coffee, and a guy comes up to me and says, 'Are you Dave Bidini?' And I was sixteen! I said, ' … yes?' And he said, 'I'm Gary Topp, I just talked to your mother.' I was like, 'What?' He said, 'I just phoned your mom and she told me you were covering the film festival. I listened to your cassette tape and I think it's really good and I want to book you guys at the Edge.' I was so happy, I called the guys, we were so excited. It was packed for the gig and all our friends were there from Kipling Collegiate and my parents were there, their friends were there. But the gig itself was like running from a wild animal. We just played on terror basically, just fucking terror. And then we were done and everybody left, because it was a Tuesday night. The headlining band said, 'Where are your friends going?' We said, 'They've gotta go home, man, they've got to catch the subway!'

The Rheostatics were a different-sounding band in those early years, playing an awkward, goofy new-wave funk. With the rhythm section consisting of rocksteady bassist Tim Vesely and zany, jazz-schooled drummer Dave Clark, the band later filled out their sound with a horn section. The early Rheos played around the post-punk Queen West circuit, mostly at the Beverley or the Cabana Room, simultaneously impressed by, and terrified of, older peers like Fifth Column, Rent Boys Inc., and the Dave Howard Singers. They did their first out-of-town show in Kitchener, Ontario, in 1981, opening for their heroes in L'Étranger, and that proved to be an eye-opening experience about the dedication required to be in a band.

DB: We drove up in Tim's parents' Volvo and played our show. L'Étranger weren't around, they were opening for Dead Kennedys that night in Toronto and were driving up to play the show right after. We finished our set and immediately went to our dressing room, the hash pipe came out, and we were just having the giggliest, funnest time. All of a sudden, the fucking door opens and these troglodytes in leather jackets and ripped jeans show up, and they're *quivering*. It's L'Étranger, and they had just come from the show, where they were drenched in spit and blood from the Dead Kennedys crowd, and booed off the stage. They were still, after that van ride, still so fucking freaked out by it. But it made me think, that's what it is to be in a band, to have that shared experience, traumatic or joyful, but you're in it together. Then they went out to play and they were amazing. And it just made me realize that we were just kids having a giggle but they were a *rock band*. That's what it takes. You've got to fight a war to get where you want to be.

It took the Rheostatics seven years to go from playing their first gig in 1980 to releasing their first album, *Greatest Hits*, in 1987. Why the wait? For one thing, the guys were in no rush to commit to the lifestyle of their post-punk peers – which involved living downtown, amidst the glamorous squalour of bohemia, cutting the umbilical of parental support. The Rheos took pride in their dual identity: coming downtown to play dirty rock shows and then retreating to the comfortable bubble of suburbia.

DB: We'd all been told, our entire lives, that this kind of life was not a real life. Go to school, get an education, get a job. That was the prevailing senti-ment – why would you want to be an artist, why do you want to be in a band? There's no future. So it took us a long time before we committed. And I also do think, on a level, just doing a couple of shows a month, that's kind of great. That was enough in a way. We liked hanging out in the suburbs. We liked playing hockey and baseball. It's a strong flavour, that band life. And for us it might have been just a little bit too strong. I don't know if we were ready to bite in just yet.

Another factor was a lineup addition in 1984 that changed the direction of the band's sound – and their future. Martin Tielli was a few years younger than the founding members, but Bidini admits he was a more talented guitarist and vocalist. Tielli was also more rooted in the austere folk music scene. His inclusion smoothed out the Rheos' sound – pulling it toward more atmospheric art-folk – while his reedy, soaring voice became one of their sonic hallmarks. This 'classic' quartet lineup made them into a Canadian indie Beatles: Tielli the sensitive Harrison, Bidini the punk visionary Lennon, Vesely the accessible McCartney, and Clark the zany Ringo.

The more serious sonic direction wasn't at the expense of humour, and their newer songs like 'The Ballad of Wendel Clark,' an ode to the rugged Maple Leafs forward, embraced their love of hockey and Canadiana. In the summer of '87, they set out on a cross-Canada tour to promote their first album, on tiny X Records, and perform in Vancouver at the short-lived Canadian Independent Music Festival. What it became was a life-changing national odyssey that solidified what the band was all about once and for all. The big, empty, mysterious, and charming country that lay beyond Toronto city limits was their source of inspiration. They became obsessed with Canadian culture and music, covering Gordon Lightfoot's 'The Wreck of the Edmund Fitzgerald' while Bidini almost single-handedly brought Stompin' Tom Connors out of retirement.

DB: Who fucking takes two and a half months to tour Canada? You can do it in twelve days if you wanted to, but we had no idea what we were doing. We spent ten to twelve days in every city. It was terrible routing, and our car broke down, and 13 Engines had to drive us back across Canada. But that's when we became a band, really, and that's when we found our sound. I'd seen the world a little bit, but Clarky and Martin had never really been anywhere – it was the first time for them beyond the suburbs. So for them, going to Regina was like going to Paris. Like, 'Wow, I'm in *Regina*! I've read about this place in geography class!' We started writing all these Canadian songs. Everybody said, 'You've got to drop the Canadian shit, you're not going to get signed, you're not going to sell any records.' And we were like, 'What are you talking about? We just had the most profound experiences of our lives. You're telling us that they're not valid?' It made us dig in a little bit harder.

You can hear the change when comparing '87's *Greatest Hits*, recorded prior to the tour, with their live recording for CBC Radio's *Brave New Waves* six months later in February 1988, the band playing with more intensity and gravitas. But later that summer, they made the ill-advised decision to tour Ireland, based on dubious contacts from one of Bidini's old school friends. The disastrous tour – complete with intra-band strangulations and members disappearing for days on end – caused the band to split.

Their separation lasted over a year, until they made amends and re-formed in fall 1989, with the intention of finishing the album that first Canadian tour had set in motion, which ended up becoming their career-defining statement. Though they were still a relatively small band at this point, playing for seventy-five people at the Rivoli, they had grand artistic aspirations.

DB: As a musician, you're really only required to work for two hours out of the day, and the rest of the time is just sitting around. We would just all get together, and if we were at the Royal Albert Hotel in Winnipeg, we would all get together in someone's room and would just jam. And we wrote dozens and dozens of songs. We wanted to reflect that experience on record. So we went to Reaction Studios on Stafford Street. It was the greatest recording experience of my life, because it was a sound we wanted to cultivate that we could hear coming alive. We dreamed this epic record that would tell the story of our country through our experiences.

Melville – released in spring 1991 by upstart indie Intrepid Records, run by Graham Stairs, formerly of Popular Spies, the band they opened for at that first gig at the Edge – showed the band at their most emotionally affecting, a true love letter to the expanse of the great Dominion. The videos for its lead tracks 'Record Body Count' and 'Aliens (Christmas 1988)' received substantial MuchMusic play, raising their profile nationally. *Melville*'s success coincided with a pre-Nirvana upswing of mainstream interest in independent music, driven by the runaway popularity of their friends in Barenaked Ladies.

Melville also marked the start of a long-lasting creative partnership with Michael Phillip Wojewoda, who went on to produce 1992's follow-up, *Whale*

Music, and later drummed for the band. *Whale Music* also saw the Rheos sign with US label Sire. The album's title was inspired by the 1989 Paul Quarrington novel, and the Rheostatics scored the 1994 screen adaptation. Though Canadian film is usually a graveyard for audiences, the soundtrack yielded the band's only top forty hit, Tim Vesely's catchy 'Claire,' which also appeared on their '94 album *Introducing Happiness*.

Despite this commercial breakthrough, and their status as one of Canada's most critically acclaimed groups of the decade, Sire dropped the group after that. Their fourth album was also drummer Dave Clark's last – he effectively switched stools with Don Kerr of the Dinner Is Ruined, joining that band while starting up an improvised orchestra, the Woodchoppers' Association, fully embracing his passion for jazzier free-form experimentation.

The Rheos went on to tackle loftier high-art projects such as *Music Inspired by the Group of Seven*, commissioned by the National Gallery of Canada in 1995, and continued to connect with mainstream audiences by touring with the Tragically Hip's Another Roadside Attraction festival. They became treasured institutions in Toronto with their annual club residency Green Sprouts Music Week, launched at the Ultrasound in the nineties.

It was at Massey Hall that the Rheostatics played their 'farewell show' on March 30, 2007. But they couldn't stay away, and the group has reunited semi-regularly since 2015. Despite their 'national institution' status, some of these gigs have been at venues as small as the Dakota Tavern. With Bidini launching the neighbourhood newspaper the *West End Phoenix* in 2017 and the band releasing a new album, *Here Come the Wolves*, in 2019, the Rheostatics are more a part of Toronto's local community than ever.

THE EXPORT BOOM
1987-91

While Canadian hip-hop is born at the Concert Hall,
roots-rock takes over Queen West and 'adult alternative'
acts make surprise breakthroughs. But louder, weirder
bands are pushed underground.

With Toronto's club circuit for original music solidified by the late eighties, the local music scene was finally poised to start exporting talent beyond the city limits at levels not seen before – this time without anyone needing to relocate to another country.

It was a weird time for pop music. The Can-rock spin cycle was moving so fast that acts like Toronto's ex-new-wavers Platinum Blonde could go quadruple platinum and then get dropped one album later. Worldwide, hair-metal rockers like Bon Jovi and saccharine teen idols like Rick Astley were ruling the pop charts, their Canadian equivalents Bryan Adams (Vancouver), Corey Hart (Montreal), and Glass Tiger (Toronto) a strange mix of both. Pre-grunge 'alternative music' – featuring cleaner guitars and more atmospheric textures and electronic beats than post-punk – was starting to edge into the mainstream via bands like the Cure and Depeche Mode, well supported in Toronto by CFNY.

Meanwhile, hip-hop and rap music was bubbling up from south of the border. Ron Nelson's hip-hop parties made the Concert Hall (a.k.a. the Masonic Temple on Yonge Street) the hip-hop embassy in Canada, with legendary battles between New York and Toronto crews, including one in March 1987 featuring Scarborough's Rumble and Strong vs. DJ Scott La Rock of BDP, just a few months before he was shot to death. The architects of Toronto hip-hop's first wave, notably Maestro, Michie Mee, and Dream Warriors, got their start on Nelson's stage.

Christopher 'Thrust' France (rapper): *The Concert Hall was like the Apollo of Toronto. That stage made every prominent artist in our scene. If you couldn't perform at Concert Hall, then you couldn't get the stamp of approval from the city.* (to Kevin Ritchie, *Now Magazine*, June 7, 2017)

Though the Concert Hall was its central meeting spot, Toronto's hip-hop community was a Metro-wide phenomenon. Parties in basements, high schools, and community centres, with sound systems like the Sunshine Sound Crew and Kilowatt, had been happening since the late seventies in suburban neighbourhoods like Rexdale, Jane and Finch, throughout Scarborough, and in downtown communities with large Black populations, such as St. Jamestown and Eglinton West, a.k.a. Little Jamaica.

Queen Street was tuned to a different frequency. During the late eighties, roots-rock was the sound most often heard drifting out of QSW's live music clubs. Later rebranded alt-country, roots-rock was the sound of former new wavers discovering the joys of folk, country, bluegrass, and the blues. Earnest and striving for authenticity, the sound struck a nerve in the plastic eighties.

Toronto roots-rock was best exemplified by Blue Rodeo. Fronted by Jim Cuddy and Greg Keelor – alternately Lightfoot-smooth and Costello-snarling – along with a wild-card improvising keyboardist, Bob Wiseman, the quintet played their first show in February 1985 at the Rivoli, quickly building up a following and headlining the Diamond within a year, though the Horseshoe, with its perfect mix of honky-tonk and Queen West cool, was the club they became most associated with.

Toronto roots-rock forefather Handsome Ned was probably smiling down on them when Blue Rodeo had an unexpected hit in 'Try,' the second single from their '87 debut, *Outskirts*. Nine months earlier, Ned had died tragically of a heroin overdose; his funeral became a mass wake at the Cameron House and down Queen West.

Though Blue Rodeo never had their hoped-for US breakthrough, they became one of Canada's biggest bands, a domestic treasure, still going strong fifteen albums later. Their success opened doors for other roots-rockers. The Tragically Hip were also a rootsy quintet, though they hailed from Kingston, Ontario, two hours east, and leaned more on the blues-rock gas pedal. Frontman Gord Downie was more of a possessed performance poet than a lead singer, the locus of their furious live shows. The Hip also had a long relationship with the Horseshoe, playing their first T.O. gig there in '86, and winning over A&R reps at the bar during the frenzied bidding war that led to their '89 breakthrough album, *Up to Here*.

Even more than Blue Rodeo, the Hip would – sometimes uncomfortably – wear the mantle of 'Canada's band,' superstars at home but cult artists in the rest of the world. Downie's 2016 brain cancer diagnosis was a national tragedy, the band's farewell tour a collective nationwide grieving. Passing away in October 2017, Downie will be missed like few others.

Glenn Milchem (Blue Rodeo): *When Blue Rodeo got popular, that changed the Toronto scene entirely. Suddenly there was an explosion of roots bands. If you were going to play in Toronto, you were going to play in a roots band. Once Rodeo hit, there were plaid shirts and cowboy shirts everywhere.*

The downside of this trend is that it ended up wiping away most of what was left of the arty post-punk scene that Rodeo drummer Milchem's earlier band Vital Sines came up in. The loss of the Beverley left a void that the Cabana Room happily filled once again. With his folky post-punk trio L'Étranger winding down, in 1987 singer/song-writer Andrew Cash unplugged his electric guitar and started a Monday night residency at the Cabana. This led to a surprise deal with Island Records. Numerous other Toronto roots-rock groups ended up with videos on Much-Music: Crash Vegas, Skydiggers, the Leslie Spit Treeo.

Ian Blurton (right) and Rob Taylor co-led alternative scene stalwarts Change of Heart.

The roots movement also impacted the more underground, *post*-post-punk bands in the late eighties. (The term 'alternative' was only just coming into use.) Cabana Room regulars the Lawn, evolving out of Woods Are Full of Cuckoos, incorporated lap steel slide guitar into their jangly college-rock sound, best heard on their lost '86 masterpiece *Peace in the Valley*. Pigfarm played a hectic brand of country-punk that made them a local answer to Arizona's Meat Puppets. Change of Heart's psych-pop-flavoured indie-rock took on a rootsy flavour by their third album, 1989's *Soapbox*. And you could argue that the whole trend toward jangly college-rock, popularized in the US by REM and Violent Femmes, and locally by Plasterscene Replicas and Chalk Circle, had a bit of roots-rock seasoning.

Most of these bands had either been putting out their own records or signing to small homegrown labels like Fringe Product or X Records. This group of bands also received regular coverage in *Nerve* magazine – the scrappy, oft-hilarious alt-culture started out of Ryerson by Nancy Lanthier and retired zinester Dave MacIntosh, which ran from 1984 to '88 – as well as the more mass-market *Graffiti*.

Nancy Lanthier (co-editor, *Nerve* magazine): *No publication was as loyal to the local music scene as* Nerve. *Before Nirvana, all these bands and indie labels received no radio play and were initially supported by quite small audiences. This was our scene and we worked hard every month to pull together enough advertising to pay for production and rent.* Nerve *was powered by volunteers. Our writers wrote about what they loved.*

One group from this scene decided to skip over Canada – at least when it came to record labels. Starting out as Ikons, the band debuted as 13 Engines in April '87 at the Cabana Room. Quickly, the quartet signed to a US indie label out of Detroit, Nocturnal Records, and even briefly relocated to Michigan.

Tapping into the droning, heavily amplified folk-rock sound of Neil Young & Crazy Horse, 13 Engines allied themselves with the burgeoning, laconic, 'slacker' American indie-rock style of Dinosaur Jr. and the Replacements. This approach took them further than their Toronto peers – they ended up signing a major worldwide deal with SBK Records (also home of Vanilla Ice) in 1991, on the cusp of the grunge revolution.

International buzz was something that had mostly eluded Toronto bands since Martha and the Muffins. That changed in November 1988, when two major-label releases by Toronto artists received a boatload of critical acclaim, especially in the fickle British press: mercurial singer/songwriter Mary Margaret O'Hara's uncategorizable ambient-pop masterpiece *Miss America*, and Cowboy Junkies' *The Trinity Session*, famously recorded live in one day, with one microphone, inside Toronto's Church of the Holy Trinity.

Margo Timmins of Cowboy Junkies, who brought a kind of hush to Toronto's roots-rock movement.

Slow, quiet, dark, smoky, heartfelt, and atmospheric, Cowboy Junkies' sound explored the depths of American blues and country ballads, combining it with the introspective side of the Velvet Underground. Lou Reed famously said their cover of 'Sweet Jane' was his favourite. They brought the same hushed quiet to their live shows, silencing a sold-out Diamond Club when promoting the buzzy record in February '89.

While Mary Margaret O'Hara vanished into near-myth (as a recording artist at least), the Junkies became one of North America's hardest-working bands, touring incessantly and releasing fifteen albums. As their sound moved away from the dreamy 'slowcore' of *The Trinity Session* toward more straightforward country-rock, the Junkies helped define the new sound of 'adult alternative.'

By the late eighties, being 'independent' or 'unsigned' was looking like a good career move. A third album gained international buzz in late '88, one with a less grown-up sound: *Love Junk* by the Pursuit of Happiness. TPOH plied the sound of power-pop, that late-seventies bastard child of new wave and hard rock exemplified by Cheap Trick, the Cars, and Toronto's the Kings. They rose to fame with their indie video for the self-deprecating 'I'm An Adult Now,' which featured the band playing in front of an empty parking lot next to the BamBoo.

Another indie music video from this era became a permanent part of the city's psyche. The Shuffle Demons were a beret-and-kaftan-clad crew of neo-beatnik bebop jazz players as likely to be heard busking on the corner of Yonge and Dundas as onstage at the Horseshoe, bringing a fun, populist appeal to the genre. With 'Spadina Bus,' they were likely the first band to romanticize the people's transit, the under-loved TTC. Their album *Streetniks!* went on to sell 15,000 copies, making it the best-selling Canadian independent album of all time up to then.

There is a fine line between 'goofy' and 'wacky.' Starting with the Shuffle Demons, Toronto bands started to cross it. Another band of the same ilk, the parodic funk band the Look People, a sort of Day-Glo Talking Heads obsessed with camp Canadiana, could veer into smug showboating. You couldn't fault either band for their musicianship, though: bandleader Richard Underhill and his fellow Demons were serious jazz players, and the Look People were a fantastic live band.

The Bourbon Tabernacle Choir were also top-notch musicians, whose ability to make Toronto crowds loosen up and dance made them one of the biggest-drawing locals of the era. Swelling to a nine-piece soul/funk orchestra, the BTC brought back the organic sounds of Motown and Stevie Wonder during a synthetic age — though to modern listeners they might sound a bit corny.

As fun as all this showmanship was, it opened the door to one of the most embarrassing eras in Toronto music history: *Wacky Bands.*

Before the horrors of Moxy Früvous, it was still safe for underground bands to goof off. The popularity of earnest roots-rock pushed a lot of weirder music to the late-eighties margins, but a new crop of DIY bands were more about cranking it up and having fun. Sixties garage-rock saw a big revival, with Cabana Room dwellers like the Dundrells, UIC, and the Ten Commandments going back to the original punk rock. Across North America, countless young bands resurrected this sludgy, primitive sound, as well as the fashion that went with it: moptops, turtlenecks, polka-dot shirts – though the Dundrells, for their part, preferred hockey jerseys. UIC produced the most definitive album of this era – 1986's ecstatically furious *Our Garage.*

The Cabana Room wasn't the only place for underground bands to play in the late eighties. Between July '87 and May '88, the Silver Dollar Room, at Spadina and College, was taken over for an amazing run by indie promoter

Dundrells cranked it up at the Cabana Room in the mid-eighties.

Elliott Lefko, not only hosting noisy US imports like the Flaming Lips and Pixies but also becoming the new location of Elvis Mondays. This freak scene included cEvin Key of Vancouver industrial rockers Skinny Puppy (then decamped in Toronto) and CFNY DJ Chris Sheppard doing a bizarre multi-media night called SNUB Tuesdays – the acronym meaning 'Slimy New Underground Bubbles.' Putting passion before profit, Lefko had been bounced from club to club for losing them money, and the same thing happened again at the Dollar. But Lefko had the last laugh – he went on to be one of the city's top promoters at MCA Concerts, eventually relocating to L.A., where he became a bigwig at Goldenvoice, one of the world's largest concert companies.

Elliott Lefko: *The Silver Dollar was special. It was my first club. It was owned by my friend's father, who was known as the Slum Landlord. His apartments were horrible and he treated people terribly. But he gave me a shot. He gave me the keys and let me book whatever I wanted. Of course, it all came crashing down eventually and I was fired.*

Around the time of his booking regime at the Silver Dollar, Lefko also tried his hand at running a record label. Under the Right Side Records imprint, he reissued *New Heroin*, the debut album by A Neon Rome, which had first come out on French indie label New Rose. The band had built up a substantial

Psych-punk band A Neon Rome turned heads with publicity stunts and onstage antics.

local following thanks to the notoriety of the posters they put around town that said 'Free Erotic Films – Attention Heroin Addicts.' The Elvis Mondays alumni were the apex of Queen West's neo-psychedelic movement, but drew upon the deep well of proto-punk bands like the Patti Smith Group. The unpredictability of their music was matched only by possessed vocalist Neal Arbic's onstage antics, which involved plenty of blood and smashed glass.

In spite of their cult following, A Neon Rome had more success creating mythology than music, their second album left unreleased. Most infamously, Arbic became a Buddhist, shaved his head, and took a vow of silence. The band was supposed to star in a Canadian indie film, but they broke up before shooting began. Director Bruce McDonald instead fictionalized the band, renaming them 'The Children of Paradise.' The resulting 1989 film, *Roadkill*, was the ultimate rock'n'roll road film. The fictional singer, who also shaved his head and took a vow of silence, was played by real-life vocalist Shaun Bowring of Toronto electro-rockers Teknicolor Raincoats, now owner of the Dundas West venue the Garrison.

Following the end of the brief noise-rock era of the Silver Dollar, left-field bands moved down the street to the short-lived Siboney, above a furniture store on Augusta Avenue. Notable bookings during the Kensington Market club's '88/'89 lifespan included the Canadian debuts of My Bloody Valentine and the Sugarcubes, both gigs presented by the Garys.

There was also the Slither Club, in the dingy basement of the Paddock, a grimy dive bar at the 'wild west' corner of Queen and Bathurst. It's best remembered for its smell, after an ill-timed sewage leak. Opening in the fall of '87, the Slither became the new home of Elvis Mondays post–Silver Dollar. At some point in 1989, it changed its name to the Soup Club, but it was toast within a year.

Ian Blurton (Change of Heart): *I remember we played the Slither on New Year's Eve [1988/89] and literally everyone was on acid. Like everyone, the audience and all the bands, except for us. It was a weird vibe, so bizarre. I think somebody had gotten some incredible acid and it was just like, 'Well, anyone who buys a ticket ...'*

Further west, the Apocalypse Club, in Little Italy, took up the reins for underground rock, with Elliott Lefko taking over booking and 13 Engines christening the room in March '89. Lefko handed the keys to an ambitious young booker from Ottawa, Jeff Cohen, the following spring, who brought in more hardcore, metal, ska, and reggae. But the doorstep of Ossington was just a bit too far west back then, and the Apocalypse ended with a whimper in fall '91. The spot is now the famed Latin drag club El Convento Rico.

Other new venues cropped up on College – and stayed there. Sneaky Dee's, a Tex-Mex restaurant that served a mean platter of nachos, opened its doors at its original Annex location on Bloor in '87 and booked jazz on Monday nights. Folk, punk, and indie bands soon followed, and in spring 1990, the club moved to its now-iconic current location at College and Bathurst. Previously, the spot had been a dance club called the Caribou, where DJ Denise Benson started her beloved Dyke Nite. In 1989, Sneaky Dee's even opened a short-lived *uptown* location at Yonge and Davisville. But College Street would remain on the music scene's margins for another solid decade.

As the eighties ticked over into the nineties, Queen West held strong as the epicentre of the club circuit, despite the encroaching threat of commercial gentrification. Some old-timers say the strip began to change when City-TV and MuchMusic took over the historic warehouse building at Queen and John in '87, while others blame the incursion of clothing chain stores Le Chateau and Club Monaco.

At the start of the nineties, Queen West's eastern end was anchored by a new small live venue, the Ultrasound Showbar, opening in April 1990 on the same block as City-TV/Much. Booked by Yvonne Matsell, a British expat who had come from booking Albert's Hall on Bloor, the 150-capacity Ultrasound was a small room with big presence – there was a red velvet curtain behind the stage, the furniture was new, and the sound system was top-notch. It was a step up from the Cabana Room for bands starting out.

Yvonne Matsell (booker, Ultrasound Showbar): *They wanted a blues-themed club. I booked a bunch of local acts, including Big Sugar. A lot of young indie bands started coming to me, asking for shows, so I started to realize that I didn't need to stick to one genre, I could mix it up. I started to book these young bands, and suddenly, the Toronto music scene started to explode. We became the showcase venue of choice. Record labels wanted to do all their new releases there. We were also practically next door to MuchMusic, which during that time was the most fun, off-the-hook music station and we started doing their 'out of the studio' interviews with their VJs.*

The group that would galvanize the indie-music revolution in Canada – as an economic model if not an aesthetic one – got one of their many storied starts on Matsell's stage. When Barenaked Ladies was formed by Ed Robertson and Steven Page at Woburn Collegiate Institute in Scarborough, they played light, acoustic folk-pop that was sweetly humourous, if not plain wacky.

The duo built up a local cult following after they debuted their first 'video,' for 'Be My Yoko Ono,' self-recorded live on City-TV's public video booth Speaker's Corner. BNL gigged endlessly at all the small clubs, rapidly rising from weeknights at the Ultrasound to selling out the prestigious Bathurst Street Theatre.

BNL made headlines when their '91/'92 New Year's Eve show at Nathan Phillips Square was cancelled, after a City Hall staffer said their name objectified women. Local papers made hay of the 'political-correctness-run-amok' story, conservative mayor June Rowlands took the heat for looking clueless, and the free publicity fuelled sales of their homemade indie cassette ('The Yellow Tape'), which eventually sold 100,000 copies – a platinum certification. This began the boom of local bands stocking their self-releases in the consignment section of chain stores like HMV.

By 1992, Barenaked Ladies had proven there was a serious market for indie music. *The Yellow Tape* broke the record broken the previous year by the Lowest of the Low's *Shakespeare My Butt* – self-released on CD, then still an expensive proposition for indie bands – who had built up a rabid, devoted following for their punkier, moshpit-friendly take on folk-pop. LOTL's philosophical lyrics spoke to the world-weary U of T undergrads of the Annex, who helped sell out multi-night stands for the band at Lee's Palace.

I wasn't the biggest fan of Barenaked Ladies, and LOTL weren't exactly to my taste either. But I have to give both bands props for their DIY hustle, and the doors they opened for others. With everyone still retching from the memory of the plastic eighties, the public was ready for something more genuine and relatable — as others have pointed out, the rest of the world had the distorted angst of Nirvana; Canada had the acoustic cheeriness of BNL.

But the Export Boom wasn't limited to Toronto's rock bands or singer/songwriters. Nor was its impact confined to the downtown core. By covering Public Enemy's 'Fight the Power,' however goofily, on *The Yellow Tape*, Barenaked Ladies became big champions of hip-hop – the music that eventually would give Toronto its biggest global megaphone.

TORONTO HIP-HOP'S FIRST WAVE
1989-91

Homegrown hip-hop hits the mainstream via four breakout
recording artists and the support of community radio stations.

On February 3, 1990, six thousand screaming teenage fans mobbed the
HMV at Square One mall in Mississauga for the official album release
party for *Symphony in Effect*, the debut album by Maestro Fresh Wes. The
lead single, 'Let Your Backbone Slide,' had already challenged New Kids on
the Block for the top chart spot on the city's lead pop radio station. Homegrown hip-hop had arrived.

Wes's album promotion dates included gigs at huge suburban nightclubs
like Super Stars, where he opened for Young MC, and headlining the Marquee,
a massive club in the sleepy deep east end. Six months earlier, he was playing
the annual CKLN benefit at the tiny Rivoli.

Born to Guyanese-Canadian parents in 1968, raised in North York and
then Scarborough, Wes Williams was turned on to hip-hop by DJ Ron Nelson's
Fantastic Voyage on CKLN. In 1982, Nelson featured him as a guest on the
show, where he rhymed over roller-disco classic 'Bounce, Rock, Skate, Roll.'
In 1983, under the moniker Melody MC, Wes formed the Vision Crew at
L'Amoreaux Collegiate at Warden and Finch. Five years later, he walked past
a Tuxedo Royale store, which inspired him to wear a tux to match his new
moniker as Maestro. Demos produced with DJ LTD led to an indie video,
'I'm Showing You,' airing on MuchMusic. Manager Farley Flex landed Wes
a breakout appearance on City-TV's *Electric Circus*, where the rapper
premiered 'Let Your Backbone Slide.'

Maestro: *'This is a throwdown.' The reason why I wanted to start a cappella is
because I'm a huge fan of Public Enemy. When you look at Chuck D, every song
is like a punch in the face with the first line. That was just me saying, 'I'm here.'*

So yeah, I did it, I went out and I performed the song for the very first time. Stevie B from LMR *Records just so happened to be performing that day.* (to CBC Radio, July 23, 2019)

Noted Miami freestyle artist Stevie B hooked Wes up with his New York label, distributed and marketed by Attic Records north of the border.

Most Toronto Gen-Xers can recite 'Backbone''s unmistakable lyrics by heart. With a deep voice and flow reminiscent of Big Daddy Kane, Wes rapped over a catchy, dance-floor-friendly beat, reeling in house music fans as well as pop kids. Though its US chart impact was modest, domestically it became the first Canadian top forty rap record.

Symphony in Effect was an uneven debut album, however, and in my humble opinion, his sophomore album, 1991's *The Black Tie Affair*, is superior. The cheery single 'Conductin' Thangs' saw Maestro amping up his local Scarborough namechecks over a speedy sixties ska beat. But it was 'Nothin' at All' that really saw Wes boldly sidestep mainstream concerns, as he embraced Afrocentric consciousness on a searing track that celebrated the accomplishments of prominent African-Canadians.

Though he was the first to release an album, Maestro Fresh Wes wasn't the first Canadian hip-hop artist signed to a US record deal. That honour goes to Michie Mee. Born in Kingston, Jamaica, in 1970, Michelle McCullock emigrated to Canada when she was a child. Inspired by a Lillian Allen performance at her school, she started rapping after seeing the 1984 film *Beat Street*, and entered one of Ron Nelson's rap battles at the Concert Hall, famously destroying New York MC Sugar Love. What set Michie Mee apart was her seamless integration of Jamaican patois into her rhymes.

Michie Mee: *I add a lot of reggae to my sound. It comes natural to me, so when I combine them all, it's like, 'Oh my God, she's from Canada, she's rapping, which is American, yet she has the influence of the Jamaican in it.'* (to CBC Television, 1988)

Forming a duo with DJ L.A. Luv (a.k.a. Philip Gayle), Michie Mee set about a recording career. While visiting her aunt in the Bronx, Michie made friends with Scott La Rock and KRS-One of Boogie Down Productions. The pair produced the 1987 single 'Elements of Style,' with KRS-One giving the seventeen-year-old emcee a warm introduction on the track. The buzz led to a deal with Brooklyn label First Priority Music. She appeared on a track with

MC Lyte that expressed female solidarity: 'We are women. Hear us roar!' The duo were invited to open for Sinéad O'Connor at her Toronto debut at the Diamond in 1988.

Michie Mee and L.A. Luv's debut album, *Jamaican Funk – Canadian Style*, wouldn't see its release until 1991, but the record and its title track were proud expressions of the emcee's Jamaican-Canadian identity, and instant Toronto hip-hop classics.

Another major Toronto hip-hop export was Dream Warriors, proudly from Jane and Finch, a neighbourhood tarnished with a reputation for youth crime and gang violence. The duo consisted of King Lou (Louis Robinson) and Capital Q (Frank Allert), who were born in 1970 in Jamaica and Trinidad, respectively, and became friends in junior high. Lou was Michie Mee's neighbour and collaborated with her as a songwriter and backup dancer.

Jane and Finch duo Dream Warriors brought a whimsical sense of humour to Toronto hip-hop.

King Lou (Dream Warriors): *When we first came out, we were hard and negative. It was speakers and sneakers, and we were rapping for our Jane and Finch neighbourhood. We found out that when we were talking loud, no one was listening, so we decided to talk softly and carry a big stick. … Everybody in that neighbourhood had their own hardcore things going on. Some people think that only Black people live there, but that's not true – there's just a lower standard of living. You had some Bob Marley blasting from across the street and next door they might be pumping out [Motorhead's] 'Ace of Spades' on one side and hardcore hip-hop on the other.* (to Tim Perlich, *Now Magazine*, April 4, 1991)

Dream Warriors formed in 1988; their lo-fi sound incorporated jazz, reggae, ska, and other quirky sampladelic elements. But labels were indifferent – A&R probably thought songs like 'Roll of the 12-Side Dice' were way too weird – until the Warriors' demo landed on the desk of Island Records UK publicist Nick White, a.k.a. ex-Rent Boy/zinester Nick Smash, who had become a hip-hop journalist since moving to London.

Nick Smash: *I actually interviewed Scott La Rock on the phone. And this was just a couple of weeks before he was killed. He was telling me that they were working with some Toronto DJs and emcees. I thought, really? How cool, I'm from Toronto. So I got in touch with their manager. He told me there was a really good scene in Toronto because Ron Nelson was doing his regular DJ clubs. Obviously it was a really cool underground that was really thriving.*

Dream Warriors were suddenly the unknown Canadian group with an overnight UK buzz. Their first single, 1990's 'Wash Your Face in My Sink,' received critical praise in the British press and radio play across Europe. Canadians paid attention when their second single, 'My Definition of a Boombastic Jazz Style,' sampled Quincy Jones's 'Soul Bossa Nova,' which had also been used as the theme song for the cheesy Canadian game show *Definition*.

The resulting album, *And Now the Legacy Begins*, was an instant smash critically and performed respectably on the charts. The week of its April 1991 release, Dream Warriors were on the cover of *Now Magazine* and head-lined the Concert Hall. *Legacy* made numerous critics' best-of lists worldwide at the end of the year. So did another now-essential Toronto hip-hop album, *Breaking Atoms* by Main Source.

Main Source were based out of Queens and fronted by an American, the bespectacled Large Professor, but the other two-thirds of the group were brothers from Toronto, K-Cut and Sir Scratch. Though their family relocated to NYC when they were little kids, they spent their summers back in Canada, and thanks to their Guyanese and Jamaican heritage, they heard plenty of soca and reggae growing up.

K-Cut: *Breaking Atoms was a collective [effort]. Large Pro would bring the ideas – he would have something already put together, but then we would go in the studio, and then we would add all the other elements. He came with the* *bones but we all collectively put the icing on the cake.* (to 'Views Before the 6' podcast, 2017)

Breaking Atoms, co-produced by influential beat-maker Pete Rock, wove together samples from vintage soul, jazz, and reggae numbers like Sister Nancy's 'Bam Bam,' and helped shape the dreamy, hazy sound of Golden Age hip-hop. Yet it may best be remembered for marking the recorded debut of rap legend Nas, who appeared as a featured artist on 'Live at the Barbeque,' at age seventeen.

K-Cut also produced half of Maestro's jazzier *Black Tie Affair*, which alongside *Breaking Atoms*, *And Now the Legacy Begins*, and *Jamaican Funk – Canadian Style*, made up the 'big four' albums of 1991: the Year Toronto Hip-Hop Broke. These early-nineties architects are now recognized as making up 416 hip-hop's first wave.

But they were still operating in a relative vacuum of support, especially when it came to radio. Toronto did not have a single radio station dedicated to Black music – and would not until FLOW 93.5 went on air in 2001 – a shameful state of affairs that the hip-hop community protested with a collective track entitled 'Can't Repress the Cause,' a cheeky acronym for 'CRTC' (Canadian Radio-television Telecommunications Commission).

Organized by rapper Devon Martin, the track was released under the name Dance Appeal with a party in September 1990 at the Spectrum on Danforth, its star-studded cast including Maestro, Michie Mee, Dream Warriors, and rapper HDV, alongside reggae ambassadors Lillian Allen, Carla Marshall, Messenjah, and Leroy Sibbles. The video definitely got the message out, though, through hip-hop's most consistent mass-media champions, MuchMusic and its *RapCity* show.

Toronto hip-hop's largest hub of support, arguably, came from community radio. Shows attracted not only loyal listeners but also in-studio guests, MCs, and DJs, making them a real scene in themselves. One could argue that community radio shows are for underground hip-hop what dive-bar venues are for punk and indie-rock.

Ron Nelson's groundbreaking *Fantastic Voyage* ran from 1982 to '89 on CKLN, every Saturday from one to four, after which he passed the time slot to DJX, who hosted the *Power Move Show* from then until 2000.

Nic Murray (Da Grassroots, LAL): *Saturday one-to-four was kind of a religious thing for me for a very long time. Saturday still feels kind of weird to me, actually, between one and four. It feels like I should be doing something else, you know?*

Another program started up in '89, airing later on Saturdays and a quick flip to the right on the dial: *The Masterplan*, hosted by MC Motion and John-Bronski with DJs Power and DTS. The University of Toronto's campus radio station, CIUT 89.5, first started broadcasting on the FM dial in early '87, and eventually installed a fifteen-thousand-watt transmitter, allowing its signal to be heard as far away as Buffalo.

Six months earlier, in June '86, York University's CHRY hit the airwaves. Its weak fifty-watt signal couldn't be heard downtown, or really anywhere that far from York's suburban campus. Writer Del Cowie was lucky to grow up within CHRY's frequency range and he says the station's programming was a huge influence on him, pointing out, in Northside Hip Hop's *For the Record* book, that CHRY played hip-hop, R&B, and reggae daily, making it effectively a Black radio station. The station also hosted infamous DJ battles, the Metro Mix-offs.

Within CHRY, CIUT, and CKLN all on the air, the late eighties marked the start of a Golden Age for community radio in Toronto – coinciding with the Golden Age for hip-hop. This continued for a good two decades until CKLN controversially had its licence revoked in 2011. In 2015, CHRY was rebranded as mainstream urban-format VIBE-FM, leaving CIUT as the only FM campus station in the city. *The Masterplan* is still on the air.

Overlooked by the Canadian industry and mainstream media, the hip-hop scene would go underground at the start of its more DIY second wave (Ghetto Concept, Da Grassroots, k-os, Thrust, Dan-e-o) in the mid-nineties. It would bounce back into the mainstream at the turn of the millennium with emcees like Choclair and Kardinal Offishall, who helped popularize the city's identity as the 'T-Dot.' Toronto hip-hop's latest wave would take over the world, and give the city another nickname.

PHLEG CAMP
In the Rocket's Red Glare
1989-93

There are moments in your life when you don't realize until much later that you're witnessing something incredible – something you would have missed if you hadn't been in the right place at the right time. I feel blessed to have been able to witness firsthand the unique evolution and trajectory of Phleg Camp, a post-hardcore trio with a stunning grasp of dynamics, their songs growing from folky quiet to full-on lockgroove noise assault. As sludgy guitar bands came into fashion in the early nineties, the band's instrumental prowess and imaginative song structures set them apart from their peers.

Phleg Camp were mythologized heavily during their short existence. Their beautifully packaged vinyl singles gave them a gravitas other locals, who had only put out tapes or maybe a CD, often lacked. They went to Chicago to record with Steve Albini, racking up then-substantial 'indie cred.' Their songs had strange and impenetrable titles to match the music. And the three members were also unapproachably distant and aloof, adding to their allure. There were rumours that they were drug addicts who all lived together communally. But Phleg Camp remain mostly forgotten now, left out of the historical record, their albums out of print.

The three members of Phleg Camp met at Thornlea Secondary School in Markham, Ontario, a sprawling suburb directly north of the city. An alternative high school with a strong music program, Thornlea featured a talented cohort of musicians in the late eighties. One of the numerous bands in the school scene was Entangled, which included Hayden Desser (nineties indie-folk superstar Hayden), Noah Mintz (later of hHead), and a Grade 9 prodigy, Gavin Brown, on drums. This future-past supergroup is said to have sounded like 'U2 meets Supertramp.'

Gavin Brown (drums): We played a lunch hour concert. The student council was very into music events and there was always a band playing. And then these guys came up to me and said, 'Hey, we're in a band, and we want to do a different band.'

The other band, which briefly included Jose Contreras, later of By Divine Right, was called Feet Like Fins – their name borrowed from a song by UK alt-pop band Cocteau Twins. Guitarist Eric Chenaux was three years older than Brown, and bassist Sean Dean was two years older than Chenaux – at twenty, he was already a musical encyclopedia, turning his bandmates on to the legendary CBC late-night radio show *Brave New Waves* and seminal bands like Gang of Four.

Sean Dean (bass): I was a new-wave artsy-type kid. Eric was a guitar player, interested in rock'n'roll, country, blues and old-time American musicology. He was a smart kid who was interested in philosophy, and questioning the blandness of acceptable behaviour that regular high school kids went along with. We hit it off, even though we were very different.

Eric Chenaux (guitar): Sean was more musically adventurous than most people I knew and was an incredible guitar player. Maybe because he had a bass or because he's just generous, he switched to bass and I played guitar, which made no sense. And then we heard Gavin Brown. And he was just insane. So we stole him!

SD: We all had very different musical tastes, but we instantly came together, jamming and writing songs. Eventually we got into the punk/all-ages/hard-core scene and our music started to reflect that. We all knew we wanted to commit our lives to music, in whatever capacity we could.

The late eighties were the halcyon days of Dischord Records – the influential Washington, D.C., record label founded by Ian MacKaye of Minor Threat. In 1988, MacKaye's new band, Fugazi, were at the vanguard of the post-hardcore sound with their socially conscious, dub- and funk-influenced buzzsaw attack. Fugazi and another Dischord band, Soulside, would heavily shape Phleg Camp's early sound.

GB: I think part of our ideology was to be as shocking as possible – through whatever we thought that was musically. The idea was to be weird and fuck people up.

At some point in '89 – they aren't sure exactly when – they headed downtown to make their club debut. They gigged at the Slither Club, underneath dive bar the Paddock, at the corner of Queen and Bathurst. With roots-rock the dominant sound of Queen West clubs, heavier bands were pushed to the margins.

But Phleg Camp were on their own path. Though they took some inspiration from elders like Change of Heart, Nomind, and Rocktopus, the young Markham trio also made an immediate impression on their more established peers. They found early champions in the likes of Jeff Beardall, of noiserockers Guilt Parade, who helped them record their first demo tape. And John Yates, a San Francisco graphic designer who ran a small label called Allied Recordings, who released a series of seven-inch singles for the band. Phleg Camp suddenly had international distribution.

EC: That opened up the world outside of Markham. We started trying to think about touring in whatever way we could. Sean was the main motivator for most of that. He just knew how to do it. He was a pretty good organizer. Phleg Camp wouldn't have happened without him.

In those days, it was fairly easy to sneak across the border and avoid the punishing cost of visas. But not many Canadian bands did it. America was (and is) big, bad, and scary. Phleg Camp set out where most other Toronto bands feared to tread – and without tour support from a big label. But what a smart move that was.

The US had a large network of DIY venues in community centres, church basements, punk houses, and progressive clubs. The 'Get in the Van' network (as dubbed by Henry Rollins) had also been established for a decade by then. Phleg Camp quickly found themselves welcomed into this nationwide community.

Not just sticking to nearby towns like New York or Chicago, the band also toured out to the West Coast and through the Deep South, where they found new fans in surprising places. In Florida, a singer in a band they met had been playing their music non-stop at a bar he worked at.

GB: It was the very first time that I ever remember, other than in Toronto and the surrounding area, going somewhere where there was a pre-knowledge of our material. It was very shocking to us, actually. We were always calling people and begging for a hundred bucks and a place to sleep. And then we showed up in Pensacola and there were five hundred people there. They were dancing and singing along. It was very weird!

Touring the back roads of America had a huge influence on these three young men, their music, and their lives, which quickly became deeply inter-twined.

EC: It was obviously exciting. You have an experience of growing up in high school and you have a feeling that there's something happening elsewhere. And that was a big elsewhere. There is something amazing about that – never mind meeting people and playing concerts, but just being in a van with people and sharing an experience that is rich and scary and mildly dangerous, sometimes precarious. All of those things are not descriptors of a suburban lifestyle.

Thanks to their adventures south of the border, Phleg Camp loomed large when they returned to Toronto for hometown gigs. This mystique was reinforced by their lack of interest in the usual rock-star posturing. Their 'image' was defiantly anti-image – very nineties. But the band had a clear visual aesthetic, combining the *Thrasher*-mag-style, black-and-white, fish-eye-lens skate photography of their friend Rob Ben, a.k.a. Robzine, with Dean's hand-drawn lettering and artwork. The effect was enigmatically beautiful.

This inscrutability extended to the band's lyrics and song titles. 'The Head Is No Pillow.' 'I Am A Cerebral Ball of Wax.' 'Cut the Robe Shit.' Chenaux's lyrics were mostly phonetic and lacking in much literal meaning. But the titles often came out of the band's shared language, which became weirder as they became more insular. And their hermetic aloofness was rooted in a very real shutting-out of the outside world.

GB: We weren't very sociable humans. We just kind of stuck to ourselves. We spent a lot of time together, we were in the van all the time. [We developed] that remoteness and that insular lexicon, these weird things that only meant things to us. And that leaked into the music, that became the 'brand.'

Though they came across as intense, serious young men, Phleg Camp were not without a sense of humour – it was just very, very dark and bizarre. When they appeared in *Now*'s local band 'Spotlight' in 1992, they described their sound as 'music for Miss Lala and her wonderful two-headed girl.' Their answer to the weekly stock question 'Weirdest moment on the job?' was: 'Recently we played a basement in Toronto full of people and we were all tripped out and felt alienated, fearful, lonely, ashamed, and realized our lives were in a shambles.'

Maybe they weren't joking.

At some point in '91/'92, Phleg Camp's music changed. Growling, Jesus Lizard guitar riffs now tangled with thunderous basslines and hypnotic, almost hip-hop drum beats – a near-transformation from their earlier Dischord-inspired days. Song structures  became sprawling and unpredictable, with long instrumental codas. Minimalism and repetition were key. This was a stoner's dream, perfect for transfixed head-nodding enabled by the super-strong hydroponic weed then making the rounds. The band members enjoyed lighting up, but their new music was inspired by even stronger substances.

EC: We were experimenting with psychedelics quite a bit. There was some incredibly good LSD around at the time. It had a huge impact on just the way you listened to music. We started listening to more psychedelic music of all kinds, whether it be the Grateful Dead, Indian classical music, or funk music from the seventies.

Warped country and bluegrass licks also started edging in, inspired by another huge cultural input: America. Their tour-van playlists included plenty of Neil Young alongside jazz and dancehall reggae, and the band began playing a crushing cover of Young's 'Powderfinger.'

In early '92, they drove to Montreal to record this new set of material for a live session for *Brave New Waves*. They were pursued by Montreal-based Cargo Records, also home of Change of Heart and Shadowy Men on a Shadowy Planet, but were indifferent to the quest for a wider audience.

GB: I remember playing a New Year's Eve show with Change of Heart and some guy from Cargo Records being there, but we were all so fucked up, I don't even remember talking to the guy. And all of a sudden we have a record deal. And I don't remember reading a contract. I don't remember if there *was* a contract.

Through their friends in Shadowy Men, Phleg Camp connected with über-indie engineer Steve Albini. They headed down to his studio in Chicago in the fall of '92, a few months before he tracked *In Utero* for Nirvana. The trio re-recorded much of the *Brave New Waves* material along with newer songs like 'Rockets Red Glare' and 'Hi-Hat' – which has a hot lead-off beat that's begging to become a hip-hop sample (if it hasn't already) – for what was intended to be their debut album.

SD: It was an amazing experience for us. Musically, and intellectually. Steve is an amazing, intelligent, and honest music legend, able to teach us so much about the industry we were set on joining. The album was recorded and mixed in about a week. It inspired us so much, but at the same time we also became aware of our idiosyncrasies and limitations. After recording in Chicago, we planned to go on tour for three months. At the time, we thought that was manageable. But in reality, it was crazy. This went on for a couple of months, but in Colorado we started to get worn down. The travel, and being away from home, was making us crazy, so we decided to bail on the rest of our tour dates.

Released in spring 1993 on Cargo, Phleg Camp's debut album, with the suitably strange title *Ya'red Fair Scratch* – was raw and redlined in trademark Albini fashion. Though the oversaturated audio almost undermines the album at times, it still captures the band's unhinged power and fury. The band wasn't in love with the final product, though, and Albini was uncredited on the sleeve.

EC: The CBC recording is far superior to the Steve Albini sessions. I think the world of Steve Albini, but it wasn't good timing. And we had already recorded the songs weirder and better.

I personally don't agree with Chenaux's assessment. *Ya'red Fair Scratch* is fantastic, upping the band's intensity and weirdness factor – the result being one of the top ten Toronto albums of all time. For a while, it was my go-to album to play for visitors who wanted to learn more about the local scene. There's a good reason the band members may have less fond memories of the record, though: by the time of its release, the band was falling apart (again). The almost cult-like intensity of their work ethic, combined with their drug use, had begun to take its toll.

GB: That shroud of Phleg Camp became who we were. Because the band was a lifestyle, there was no life outside of the band. We lived together, we ate together, we smoked together, we spoke this language of our own. It was a living art project. A reactive, artistic, living, breathing organism. And I think like every organism, they die. It runs out of fuel.

EC: There's an intensity to that age. And it's not always an intensity that can be carried on into your mid- to late twenties. People change.

Today's newfound awareness of mental health issues in the music industry is welcome and overdue, but there doesn't seem to be much discussion around how the idea of the band – or arts institution – can become a devouring entity, one that demands constant sacrifice of the energy, resources, and well-being of its participants. Feeding the ravenous beast appeared to be most draining on the band's youngest member, Gavin Brown, who was barely out of his teens as it came to an end over the summer of '93.

GB: It became very unhealthy. I couldn't continue playing in Phleg Camp. I would be dead.

SD: We had healed up mentally, so we went back on the road to promote the record with another multiple-month tour of North America. We lasted about a month. Things began to feel strained and we were seeing distance between us. Eric and Gavin were feeling bored with the band set-up, tonality, and genre. We played that tour through to Churchill's Bar in Miami, Florida. We were staying out at my parents' winter home when we decided to break up the band.

I remember feeling the wave of sadness ripple through the Toronto music community as the news spread of the band's demise – mostly by word of mouth. Phleg Camp were our underground heroes. It was sobering to think we'd hear no more from them.

In the year following the breakup, Brown and Chenaux played together as the much more subdued duo Life Like Weeds. Brown moved out from behind the drum kit to duet with Chenaux on acoustic guitar and voice. Their shows were reverential affairs, with silent audiences sitting on the floor. Sean Dean started a new power trio in 1994 called the Sadies. They picked up the cow-punk end of Phleg Camp, but after Dean traded his electric bass for a stand-up, they dove fully into psychedelic Americana. Still a regular touring act twenty-five years later, the Sadies are one of North America's foremost exponents of alt-country.

Phleg Camp was a supergroup before its time. I can't think of another seminal band with members that are not only still involved in music, they are all successful figures in their other chosen fields. While Dean still lives the van-bound life of a touring rock musician, Eric Chenaux delved fully into the avant-garde, finding his true calling amongst Toronto's burgeoning free-improv community. Since 2006, he's been a critically acclaimed solo recording artist for Montreal's Constellation Records, and has called France home for the last decade. As for teenage drumming prodigy Gavin Brown, he is now one of Canada's most successful record producers. His journey out of the narrow confines of hardcore punk began with him supplying his kit prowess to hard rock bands like Big Sugar and Danko Jones in the later nineties. His extensive producing credits include gold- and platinum-selling albums by Billy Talent, Metric, Three Days Grace, and the Tragically Hip.

GB: It's a good life. All the evil notions of major labels, I've never experienced that. The only people who have ripped me off are independent record labels. When I deliver a record to RCA, they go 'great,' and they put it on the radio and they pay us. Hardcore didn't have very much patience for things other than it. Because any outside forces would change the brand, you know. For trying to be open-minded and liberal, the scene was really closed-minded and dogmatic.

Few bands busted beyond genre walls like Phleg Camp, who truly embodied the forward-thinking spirit of post-hardcore. Though it was an experience they needed to spend a couple of decades distancing themselves from, it's one they are starting to look back on fondly.

EC: I loved playing guitar with Gavin and Sean playing the drums and bass, they were just … what a force.

GO WEST: THE DRAKE
BEFORE THE DRAKE (AND DRAKE)
1991-93

The grunge era revives noisy guitar rock in the wilds of Parkdale, while the rave scene emerges from empty, darkened downtown warehouses.

Brendan Canning (hHead, Broken Social Scene, etc.): *All I remember is that it was further, further west. And that was where you could still get Chinese food for four bucks next door. It wasn't developed. There were no fucking art galleries from Ossington to Dovercourt.*

Parkdale was a virtual no-man's land in the early nineties, crime-ridden by safe Canadian standards, and in those days its psychological borders spilled east past the Dufferin Street train bridge into West Queen West. Pre-millennium, the stretch of WQW between Trinity Bellwoods Park and Dufferin was deserted.

Around Queen and Dovercourt, there wasn't much to check out beyond the sporadically booked Great Hall – where I saw an incredible show by New York noise-rockers Sonic Youth in 1990. Promoter Elliott Lefko oversold the venue, leaving hundreds of ticket-holders stuck outside. A 'riot' ensued, according to SY's Thurston Moore, before the venue's power blew, and Moore led the crowd in a 'rousing singalong' of 'Search and Destroy' by Iggy and the Stooges. Despite the impression that show made on my ears, they weren't yet adventurous enough to check out shows downstairs in the Music Gallery, then located on the Great Hall's lower level.

What drew me to the west end as a teen was a small music venue – the new home of Elvis Mondays. In 1991, the Drake Hotel was a rooming house with a dingy basement bar, full of tables with overflowing ashtrays. It had a tiny stage and an even tinier backstage, basically a walk-in closet. This is the very same Drake reopened as a boutique hotel by tech millionaire and art lover Jeff Stober in 2004, the same basement venue now called the Drake Underground.

The stage at 1150 Queen Street West awaiting the next hopeful at an Elvis Monday.

Everyone involved in music scenes has a formative venue that shaped everything they love about seeing live music: mine was 1150 Queen Street West, aka the 1150. I saw some mind-blowing shows there, but more importantly, it was where I first discovered the value of community, where I first made friends from the music scene.

Geoff Marshall (Antimatter): *It was scuzzy. It was ours.*

The first person I met there was Brendan Canning, then the affable bassist of hHead, a loud grunge-rock trio who were seemingly on every cool show bill.

Brendan Canning: *Noah [Mintz] and I met at Brock University. We did a bunch of covers and played a couple of gigs in St. Catharines. Then we went backpacking in Europe and came back and started the band in the spring of '91. On that backpacking trip we saw Jane's Addiction, Sonic Youth, and Babes in Toyland. Noah and I were an acoustic duo at that point. And after that we were like, 'No way, we're gonna start a rock band, this acoustic guitar shit is fucking lame!'*

I first saw hHead at the 1150, opening for Love Battery, a band from Seattle on Sub Pop Records. Though Sub Pop had had an underground buzz growing since the mid-eighties for disseminating the sound of grunge, it had since supernova'd to global prominence as the label that discovered Nirvana. *Nevermind* was released in September '91 and instantly changed the music world, making alt-rock commercially viable.

The grunge years were heady days. There was an exciting sense that the doors were opening to previously marginalized music. William New, godfather of Elvis Mondays and Groovy Religion, took over booking the 1150 in November 1991, overseeing a groundswell of younger, hungrier, artier guitar bands – while creating a refuge for eighties vets of the Beverley and Cabana days. At the 1150, I discovered not only hHead but also the Dinner Is Ruined, Grasshopper, the Lawn, the Leather Uppers, and many others. But I saw hHead more times than I can count: they were the 1150's unofficial house band, and New even let them rehearse there for free during the day.

Grasshopper: *Best stage I've ever played on in my life. 1150 was the best, man. That's when it was a fuckin' crackhead hotel upstairs. Like evil, like you* didn't *go upstairs.*

I first saw Fifth Column at the 1150, opening for indie-pop icons the Beat Happening. I caught the Dave Howard Singers after their decade away in the UK, unaware I was witnessing a domestic pioneer. And in August '92 I saw the first Toronto gig by influential San Diego math-rockers Drive Like Jehu, who were one of the tightest bands on the planet at that point.

Jehu had built up local buzz through incessant play at new Queen West indie record store Rotate This and coverage in the new free music monthly *Exclaim!*, which had begun publishing that May. Some of the magazine's contributors performed at the 1150, and William New was an *Exclaim!* co-founder.

As the first local music paper to launch since the demise of *Nerve, Exclaim!* filled a void, but it was not alone – six months earlier, in October '91, *Eye Weekly* began publishing as the first serious competitor to *Now*. The new alt-weekly's copious music coverage leaned more on the edgy sounds of hip-hop, electronica, and noisy indie rock – plus its writers were much funnier. And CHRY expanded its presence with shows featuring reggae, rap, punk, and indie.

Bill Reynolds (former editor-in-chief, *Eye Weekly*): *There was a general feeling that, although Now's editorial stance was more or less right, it was boring and doctrinaire and humourless and cookie cutter. The thought was,* *hey, why don't we put out an entertaining alternative weekly? Why does it have to be boring and preachy?*

Ian Danzig (publisher, *Exclaim!*): *There were definitely a lot of positive things happening with music at the time, but everyone involved with the publication felt an overall frustration with the lack of coverage for local artists.* Exclaim! *was just an extension of the* DIY *culture that dated back to the punk and post-punk era of the seventies and eighties. We were all pretty naive in the best way.*

Matt Galloway (CHRY, *Now*, CBC Radio): *It felt like everything was really happening at the same time. Rotate This was a huge part of that – you'd go and buy records, but also talk about the records that you didn't know about. Same with Play De Record and Vortex. There were a lot of people writing about local music at* Now *and* Eye, *playing the music at* CKLN, CIUT, *and* CHRY – *and the Edge [*CFNY*], when Kim Hughes was hosting* Live in Toronto. *It felt like people were really invested in supporting their own.*

The 1150 also had its own unofficial in-house zine, *Corpus*, published by show-goers 'Deb and Brooke,' with contributions from various band members. *Corpus* might be the all-time-perfect local scene zine, informative and hilarious, with cheeky takedowns of Torontonian pretentiousness and Anglophilia. Deb and Brooke were given an advice column in *Exclaim!* in recognition of their contributions to humour and sludge-rock.

Other important moments at the 1150 included the first Toronto show by Halifax indie-popsters Sloan and the release party for *Smile*, the critically acclaimed fourth album and magnum opus by Change of Heart. Later moving to Toronto one by one, the Nova Scotians gave their props to Upper Canada when Sloan guitarist Patrick Pentland wore a Change of Heart T-shirt in the video for their breakthrough hit, 'Underwhelmed.'

A collective of musicians from the 1150 scene, led by Antimatter's Geoff Marshall, came together on Easter '92 to stage an ambitious indie rendition of rock opera *Jesus Christ Superstar* at the club.

Marshall: *A bunch of us were sitting around the backyard and we started a drinking game where we would cast ourselves in different ensemble pieces. I think we went through* The Brady Bunch *and* Gilligan's Island *till we got to* Jesus Christ Superstar. *It went quiet for a second and then we realized it might actually work. I somehow got twenty-six Toronto artists and musicians to work* *on this crazy project. I thought no one would show up to see it on a long Easter weekend. There was a lineup of four hundred people down the block and up a side street waiting to get in the two hundred-capacity 'theatre.'*

The 1150 *Jesus Christ Superstar* was such a hit that they remounted it that summer on the side stage at Lollapalooza at Molson Park in Barrie, Ontario. The troupe played later in the day than Pearl Jam, who were only the second band of seven on the main stage.

Marshall: *Elliott Lefko provided a school bus and a case of beer or two. Two weeks before Lollapalooza, I had gotten a call from Andrew Lloyd Webber's lawyer. After a very entertaining conversation, he allowed us to play as long as we promised to 'never do this again.'*

They kept their promise.

Though the 1150-era Drake is not as mythologized as Crash 'n' Burn, the Garys-era Horseshoe, or the Edge, it deserves an equally vaunted place in Toronto music history. It was similarly short-lived – lasting just fourteen months, it closed its doors suddenly in January '93 after a change in ownership. I was gutted.

Dale Morningstar (the Dinner Is Ruined): *That place filled a void for sure. Not the cachet of the Rivoli or Horseshoe, but it served up the rock'n'roll*

The 1150 made a new home for Cabana Room vets like gnarled-roots rockers the Lawn.

in a big old basement like it was meant to. We played there once and the power died mid-set – a storm outside and pitch black inside. We carried on acoustically, sitting on the edge of the stage – people lit candles and gathered round. It was sublime.

William New moved his booking operations to the main floor bar (and later the basement) of the Edgewater Hotel, on Roncesvalles Avenue. If the 1150 was considered far west, Queen and Roncesvalles felt like the edge of the world. It was where Queen Street ended, and the streetcars went to sleep at night at the Sunnyside Loop, with the expanse of suburban Etobicoke beyond. William knew the Edgewater's remoteness was a tough sell, and his booking tenure lasted only seven months.

Elliott Lefko, then working for MCA Concerts, brought in some stellar out-of-town bands to play the Edgewater's tiny stage that spring and summer, some for no-cover Elvis Monday nights. I caught mind-melting shows by Michigan's His Name Is Alive, New Zealand's Bailter Space, Memphis oddballs the Grifters, Providence freaks Six Finger Satellite, and Washington, D.C.'s Hoover and Pitchblende. There was many a long, stunned streetcar ride home.

★

Noise-drenched grunge-rock trio Grasshopper played 1150 Queen Street West almost every week.

William New jumped from the Edgewater in October '93, taking an offer to become full-time booker of the El Mocambo, heading right back into the heart of the city's live scene. New made the old stomping grounds of dinosaur rock a home to more adventurous sounds.

The El Mo and Sneaky Dee's, a short hop down College at the corner of Bathurst, were the go-to spots for Toronto indie-rock in the mid-nineties. But Sneaky Dee's' initial run as a live venue was cut short in the spring of 1995, when the bar's management decided to kill off live bands upstairs and replace them with more lucrative DJs, cashing in on the popularity of alterna-dance nights among the U of T crowd. They ruined one of the city's best small stages by filling it with seating booths and erecting a railing across its front. I was *pissed*.

The Music Gallery made a similar geographic move in the fall of 1993. After nine years at the corner of Queen and Dovercourt, the long-running CCMC clubhouse moved back into the heart of the city, to a gorgeous, architect-designed marvel on Richmond Street West. Leased from cultural developers Artscape, Toronto's premier new-music concert hall featured a glass foyer in the front and a spacious black box theatre in the back. At the time, I was barely aware of its existence.

The 1150 and the Edgewater weren't the only small clubs opening doors to new corners of the west end. Circa '91–'93, Melanie Kaye, the original singer of all-woman punk band Chicken Milk and later Smear, booked border-smashing post-hardcore shows in the back of the tiny Niagara Café, on Queen West opposite Trinity Bellwoods Park in Little Portugal.

Melanie Kaye: *The Niagara was primarily a bar for older Portuguese men in the front room and the back room had a stage and a small PA that was left unused for the most part. The owner and I had a good rapport, although I knew from the get-go this was going to have an expiration date as the punk bands I was going to book and his regular clientele would not exactly jibe. Being inclusive was important to me, so I would offer younger people that were starting to book bands a night where we would co-present shows.*

In parallel with noisy guitars suddenly dive-bombing suburban stereos, electronic beats burbled up between cracks in Toronto's asphalt in the early nineties. Or were they air-dropped from a transatlantic flight? Though the music originated in Chicago and Detroit, the world's first raves were held in the UK, coinciding with the acid house movement and the 'Second Summer of Love' in 1988. DJ Mark Oliver may have been one of the first Toronto people to spin the new, minimal four-on-the-floor sounds at the Tasmanian Ballroom, an unassuming club at Jarvis and Adelaide.

The long-celebrated Twilight Zone started Toronto's warehouse scene in the eighties, with semi-illicit dance parties starting to take over vacant spaces through the Garment District south of Queen Street, often on the one-way thoroughfares of Richmond and Adelaide.

Denise Benson: *I think back to this time period and it's hazy. I didn't even drink or do drugs at the time, but it's still hazy because it was late nights. I remember going to parties where the promoter was talking to a real estate agent, and got keys to this old church that's for sale. And bam, there's a party there.*

After the Twilight Zone closed in 1989, more above-ground, licenced clubs began to appear in this area, such as Go-Go, where Mark Oliver and James St. Bass spun house and other dance music genres, soon becoming Toronto's most popular and ubiquitous DJs. This clustering of nightclubs marked the beginnings of what would become Clubland, or the 'Entertainment District.'

In the summer of 1990, a group of nightlife denizens took over an empty warehouse at 318 Richmond West and named it 23 Hop. At first a rental hall that hosted various late-night parties and boozecans, 23 Hop became ground zero for Toronto's rave scene. On August 31, 1991, Exodus Productions threw a party featuring the Booming System crew: English and Scottish expats Malik X, Mark Oliver, Dr. No and Sean L, who wanted to bring the exciting sounds then taking over the UK to a city that, to their ears, was pretty dead. Another British emigré, Alx of London, threw what's considered to be Toronto's first rave, 'Chemistry,' on December 13, 1991, in an east-end ware-house at Queen and River. Flyers for the party were rolled up and handed out in test tubes.

Toronto soon developed one of North America's biggest rave scenes, but in its early years, the community was small, with a lot of the same DJs playing the circuit of clubs and parties. Malik X had a radio show on CKLN and DJed the beloved Acid Jazz Wednesdays at the Cameron House.

Exodus continued developing the rave scene at 23 Hop, filling the raw space with fog, lasers, and massive amounts of bass. The communal spirit of the dance floor was enabled by the introduction of a new party drug, ecstasy. Techno was so new that people still called it 'industrial dance.' Rave music encompassed many subgenres that were beginning to fragment and emerge in their own right – breakbeat later became drum'n'bass, a genre for which Toronto became one of the world capitals outside the UK.

In '93, Nitrous came in with even bigger parties, usually in abandoned warehouses. Among their organizers was Don Berns, a.k.a. Dr. Trance, an American radio DJ who had come to Toronto to work as program director for CFNY and got swept up in the city's emerging rave scene. At least twenty years older than most of his friends on the dance floor, Berns showed that in the electronic music community, 'all ages' worked in both directions.

All the familiar elements were there – glowsticks, chillout rooms, smart-drink bars. But though rave was growing, it was still mostly secret, illicit, and underground, with venue locations communicated via telephone hotlines. In deserted corners of the city, kids congregated after midnight and danced until dawn, or beyond.

Overground, the Canadian music industry was waking up with an eighties hair-metal hangover, flailing around to sign anything Nirvana-ish. A 1992 album release with major label backing, *Fully Completely*, by the Tragically Hip, was intended to fulfill the band's long-awaited commercial breakthrough in the States. That this didn't happen cemented the Hip's status as Canadian rock heroes misunderstood by the rest of the world.

I don't think any of the industry brass expected that the world's biggest hit of fall '92 would be sung by a white Toronto dancehall reggae singer. 'Informer,' by Snow, a tale of the artist's charges of attempted murder, spent seven weeks at number one on Billboard. While 'Informer' blasted out of car radios across the GTA, the Toronto Blue Jays won the World Series. Torontonians felt an unfamiliar stirring – civic pride. Maybe things were changing?

KING COBB STEELIE
When Will This Struggle End?
1991–2014

Grunge was the worst and best thing to happen to independent music in Toronto (and the world). It spawned a lot of garbage, but music industry doors were suddenly open – briefly – to smaller, scruffier entities previously left waiting outside. And the reaction against the revolution's new orthodoxy created some truly interesting music.

King Cobb Steelie are one of our gifts from the bounty left by the success of Nirvana. Singer/guitarist Kevan Byrne's previous band, Heimlich Maneuver, actually opened for the Aberdeen, Washington, trio at their first Toronto gig, on April 12, 1990, at Lee's Palace. But that brush with near-future fame only pushed young Byrne away from distortion-drenched rock primitivism toward the enlightenment of the dance floor.

Pulling in elements of dub, funk, electronica, and hip-hop, King Cobb Steelie were the rhythm-oriented outliers on countless flannel-heavy show lineups. Though their sound was, at first, jagged and anthemic enough to pass as grunge, they aspired to greater sonic sophistication and delved further into dubwise space with each successive release.

Yet they remain something of an enigma. Reflecting the youthful idealism of the decade, the band was defiantly anti-commerce – in 1992, they put out their first seven-inch for free, pressing three hundred copies that they gave away to everyone who paid the five-dollar cover at their gigs. Yet they also signed to EMI and did many of the other weird promotional things Canadian bands had to do.

Putting out vinyl was merely a dream to Byrne's earlier band, who only mustered a cassette release during their four years together. Growing up in Vancouver and Montreal, before settling in Oakville as a teen – where he played in early hardcore band Section 8 – Byrne formed the initially goofy, garage-rocky Heimlich Maneuver while attending McMaster University in Hamilton in 1986. They broke into the Toronto scene via the Cabana Room, winning over Rivoli booker Carson Foster and becoming the go-to local opener for many of the noisier US bands Elliott Lefko was bringing across the border. Toward the end, the trio's sound aspired toward the poppy, heartfelt guitar rock of bands like Soul Asylum.

Kevan Byrne (guitar/vocals): Our music was pretty derivative. I was becoming really interested in hip-hop and electronic music and I tried to introduce those elements into Heimlich, which was ridiculous. The other two really weren't having it.

Byrne quit the band almost immediately after the Nirvana gig. A year later, in 1991, he went back to school in Guelph, an hour and a quarter west of Toronto. A walkable, historic college town, Guelph had its own vibrant music scene, including a well-attended summer folk festival, Hillside. Byrne joined a reggae band called Special Mission, which included two members of Messenjah. The project was short-lived, but he found his musical soulmate: bassist Kevin Lynn.

KB: When we started talking about music, it was incredible because we almost had the same sets of influences. His interest in music felt as broad as mine, but he was even broader. He was interested in all of this improvisational music; he introduced me to Derek Bailey and all this crazy stuff that I had no context for. He was so weird as a player, it was so visceral and idiosyncratic, it could not come out of anybody else.

The pair had first met at the University of Guelph's campus station, CFRU, when Lynn had interviewed Heimlich Maneuver for his radio show. Lynn was an Alberta transplant whose bruising yet mesmerizing bass style became the backbone of the King Cobb Steelie sound. The two Kevs quickly recruited a second guitarist, Al Okada, and Byrne's old Section 8 bandmate Gary

Dutch, and they began playing around Guelph's tiny downtown, at clubs like the Albion Hotel and Jimmy Jazz.

With chicken-scratch guitar and funk beats, KCS harkened back to the dancey post-punk sound of Talking Heads and *Sandinista*-era Clash, yet even then, they were experimenting with primitive samples and looping. Taking their name from a marble, King Cobb Steelie balanced a childlike sense of humour – they had a song called 'Talking GI Joe with Lifelike Beard and Hair and Kung-fu Grip' – with lyrics filled with self-loathing over participating in a capitalist system. They became Guelph's most popular band, their rep spreading fast thanks to their infamous free seven-inch, the decision to give it away both a political statement and a canny marketing move.

Kevin Lynn (bass): People started coming to the shows and were super appreciative, so we had an idea to make a record that would be a thank-you for the people who had been supporting us by coming to see us play.

Their breakout Toronto gig came in May '92 at basement clubhouse 1150 Queen Street West, when they opened the CD release party for Change of Heart's *Smile*. After that, things started happening for the now-six-piece band, whose rhythmic aptitude was expanded by COH percussionist Mike Armstrong and sample-scientist Steve Clarkson. They met music-biz upstart Amy Hersenhoren, who was working for Raw Energy Records, a local indie label with distribution from A&M, and assembling a CD compilation surveying the lo-fi Canadian music underground. *On the Road*, released in March '93, turned out to be a seminal document, also spotlighting the likes of Eric's Trip, the Dinner Is Ruined, hHead, and the Wooden Stars. Hersenhoren became KCS's manager.

That spring, Raw Energy unleashed the band's debut self-titled full-length, recorded at Toronto's Reaction Studios and produced by their friend Don Pyle of Shadowy Men on a Shadowy Planet – though the term 'producer' was loose, as Pyle was really just there to lend a hand, in the band's spirit of collectivism.

KB: With all things KCS, they just kind of happened. It was like, 'You're a producer, you're a manager, you're in the band now.' We very much operated that way, it was based more on relationships. If we got along with somebody or they were helping us in any way, we tended to suck them in and make them part of our little culture.

King Cobb Steelie featured rock anthems like 'Duotang,' but the debut album's most interesting moments come toward the end, when dub influences take over in a spacey suite of instrumentals. The album immediately went into heavy rotation on Canadian campus radio and CBC's *Brave New Waves*. By mid-'93, the band had enough pull to pack the Rivoli or the Horseshoe.

KB: We went on tour not long after that. And we quickly found out that the only place where anybody was going to show up was Toronto or Guelph. You'd go out to Saskatoon and there's literally four or five people there – four or five *very* rabid fans.

Later in the year, through Pyle, the band connected with Steve Albini with the aim of recording an EP, but the band wasn't happy with the results and shelved the recordings. Around the same time, Hersenhoren was in discussion with the Canadian office of EMI Records about an idea that she credits to Sloan manager Chip Sutherland: the major label would subsidize the creation of a new 'indie' label, Lunamoth Records, whose roster King Cobb Steelie would curate – thus capitalizing on their buzz but retaining their street cred.

KCS had signed a publishing deal with Warner Chappell, giving them the financial freedom to produce their second album on their own terms – and own the masters. They got their first pick of producer: Bill Laswell, whose extensive credits included Brian Eno and Herbie Hancock's 'Rockit.' Much like their debut, *Project Twinkle*'s strongest moments were instrumental dub excursions like 'Italian Ufology Today,' where Laswell gets to sprinkle his magic pixie mixing dust.

The album's September 1994 release coincided with the emergence of the post-rock subgenre. Just a few months earlier, Tortoise released their self-titled debut, while journalist Simon Reynolds coined 'post-rock' in the pages of *The Wire*. The lone Canadian outlier in this nascent global movement, King Cobb Steelie identified with it from afar but weren't recognized as part of the trend.

Project Twinkle was lauded at home, receiving a five-star review from Tim Perlich in *Now* (rare praise for a local act) and a nomination for the Best Alternative Album Juno. But it sold poorly. KCS parted ways with Hersenhoren and their label; she went on to run Lunamoth solo, where she released records for Hayden, Wooden Stars, and Ui before the plug was pulled in '96.

Amy Hersenhoren: It was a deal that I did to try and benefit my bands and not for any sort of ego-driven reason. It was a terrible, terrible idea. It caused a lot of tension amongst people and it ended up not being a great ending.

KB: That was a fairly acrimonious departure by both parties. But we've remained friends, we still email back and forth and see each other at shows.

The band went through some lineup changes post-*Twinkle*, with Don Pyle replacing Clarkson on sampler and Sam Cino taking over from Dutch on drums. Their new material smoothed out their sound and slowed down the tempos, with Kevan Byrne's vocals taking on a deeper, more chilled-out flavour. This coincided with the global success of UK trip-hop acts, and EMI recognized the group's renewed commercial potential, signing them directly.

For their third album, they looked across the pond, recruiting London-based Guy Fixsen, a member of early post-rock band Laika and producer of dreamy indie records by My Bloody Valentine, Slowdive, and Stereolab. *Junior Relaxer* came out in April 1997. Its local release party was a sort of generational torch-passing held at Lee's Palace; the opening act was Do Make Say Think.

Junior Relaxer yielded the closest thing KCS got to a hit, with 'Rational' receiving decent rotation on MuchMusic's alternative video show *The Wedge*. The sombre song name-checked Mexico's Zapatista freedom fighters and wrongly executed Nigerian environmental activist Ken Saro-Wiwa, for whom the band played a memorial benefit in Toronto later in '97.

KB: Those lyrics were an expression of trying to reconcile my own personal alienation with the larger struggles of people like Saro-Wiwa, who are systemically oppressed, and whose oppression benefits many of us in wealthy countries. I just wanted to connect the personal and the political, because at the time I remember feeling so powerless and depressed about events happening in other parts of the world.

The combination of a more accessible sound and thoughtful, socially conscious lyrics brought the band to a wider audience; they played European dates alongside the likes of Cornershop and Spearhead. But despite a respectable 10,000 units sold domestically, the label seemed unsatisfied.

KL: We started writing songs and recording demos for the follow-up. EMI were really not into them and wouldn't commit to anything. So after they hemmed and hawed for a long time, we just asked to be let go, and that was it.

In 1999, relocated to Toronto, they began performing around town under the name Junior Relaxer to explore their more instrumental, improvisational side – including a free weekly residency at Rancho Relaxo.

For their fourth album, 2000's *Mayday*, King Cobb Steelie had slimmed down to just three members. Byrne, Lynn, and Armstrong recorded the album at home. Despite the support of a new label, US indie Rykodisc, and a more streamlined pop sound with hip-hop beats and scratches from DJ Serious and the vocal talents of Michelle McAdorey (ex–Crash Vegas), *Mayday* didn't break through, either. The band only had one album left in them, 2004's *Destroy All Codes* (Outside Music), by which point the members were absorbed with the responsibilities of fatherhood and careers.

But King Cobb Steelie quietly continued for another decade, releasing a final EP, *Goodbye Arcadia*, in 2014. They celebrated the 2012 re-release of *Project* by performing the album front to back at the Horseshoe Tavern – an indication their music had finally, fairly, been canonized.

GUH + SLOW LORIS
The Twenty-Eight-Year Gig
1991–

S ome bands run their course, break up, fade away ... the members pack away their instruments and move on to more stable and lucrative callings in life. Others continue, the years ticking over without notice. The members of GUH fully gave themselves over to their muse, closing in on three decades ago. Beatific laughter has been their medicine for the craziness and the broke-ness of the musical lifestyle. Playing live is where these musicians feel most alive, and they are always playing. In some ways, the history of GUH is one long twenty-eight-year gig.

GUH aren't an easy band to describe. Are they jazz? Classical? They have bagpipes, but they sure aren't Celtic rock. They get incorrectly tagged as 'improv' even though they clearly read off music stands. The last time I saw them, in 2019 at their latest home base, the Monarch Tavern, they were an instrumental dance band with dub and Ethio-funk basslines. For an 'avant-garde' group, they sure know how to start a party.

GUH were also a quintessential product of Toronto in the nineties: a band that could only come out of (then-) cheap rent; cheap (usually free) beer; abundant, play-when-you-want rehearsal spaces; supportive institutions both grassroots and academic; countless small venues to perform in; and an endless supply of talented musicians to pull into their orbit. Sound a bit like

Broken Social Scene? GUH's Brian Cram was something of a guru to Kevin Drew, and part of the very first BSS gig.

It can be difficult to pinpoint a leadership or identify core members of GUH, given how many people have come and gone through the years. But the origins of GUH can be traced back to the late eighties / early nineties in Belleville, Ontario. Henry Muth (bagpipes), Andrew Henry (drums), Julian Brown (original bassist) and Craig Barnes (longtime manager and current bassist) knew each other from high school and jazz camp. In 1991, Henry, Muth, and Brown moved to Toronto, taking over a dilapidated student house on Lappin Avenue – what was then the far west end.

Two other old friends, drummer Blake Howard and guitarist Ruben Huizenga, from small towns northwest of the city, also moved into the same house. Howard and Huizenga had been playing together in rock bands since high school, their most recent incarnation a prog/funk-metal band named Glueleg. While keeping that band going, Huizenga got absorbed into the 'house' band. Andrew Henry came up with the name, inspired by the sound Ruben's guitar made while he played Slayer riffs: 'Guh guh guh guh.' Their surreal sense of humour was there from the start.

Blake Howard: They played a show at Nag's Head North or something, then the next show was at the Niagara Café. And I heard GUH and I was like, 'I gotta be in this band. Let me in there!' So they let me in and I played a weird percussion setup for the longest time.

Putting together a stand-up drum kit from unwanted cymbals, roto-toms, and a fire bell, Blake Howard added a double-drum element that has been key to the band's sonic impact ever since. GUH was a very different band in 1992: darker, heavier, industrial-strength rock, in the vein of Soundgarden or Swans. Vocals were more prominent in their sound, with Brown and Muth harmonizing on a cover of Leonard Cohen's 'Who By Fire,' heard on their first cassette, 1993's *Fanky Baby Madstar* EP.

GUH played around the emerging rock club circuit: the Cameron House, Lee's, Ultrasound, as did Glueleg; but as Huizenga's band took off in popularity, he split with GUH, and Howard split with Glueleg. A few years later, Glueleg graduated to the Edgefest circuit alongside I Mother Earth and Our Lady Peace. GUH's new guitarist, Jason Clarke, from Dundas, Ontario, met the Lappin crew through a 'musicians wanted' ad he'd placed in the back of *Now Magazine*.

Jason Clarke (guitar): I went up to the house and the whole of GUH was living there. I just kept coming around and hanging around, and then I went and saw them play at Sneaky Dee's. I never heard any band play that stuff before.

In early 1993, GUH moved out of Lappin and into a warehouse space on Mowat Avenue that included a large jam room and a few adjoining bedrooms where some of the members lived, including Andrew Henry, who worked around the corner at Upper Canada Brewing. It became very convenient to roll over some kegs and help pay the rent by throwing a party.

A community of bands and musicians who jammed or crashed there developed around them – including heavy indie rockers Venus Cures All and garage punks Adventure Playground, among others. But the band's sound began to evolve away from rock, and from playing 'songs,' after Julian Brown's departure, not long after the addition of a new member he had met in the U of T Jazz program, trumpeter Brian Cram. His playing was as intriguingly enigmatic as his backstory.

BH: When we first met Brian, he was pretty hilariously mysterious. He was maybe twelve years older than me, because he's also a rat, in Chinese astrology. He looked like he had been through a lot, he was smoking a lot of marijuana, and then you'd get the sense that he was also somehow very rich. But don't talk about it! And he was playing jazz trumpet, though he didn't really even know how to play jazz trumpet.

The elder Cram inspired the rest of the band to fully indulge their muse, with a unique personal philosophy that was part Buddhist, part Nietzsche.

Craig Barnes (bass/manager): You live your life happy and free. You create things and you're thankful for what you have, and you keep giving to what you have to make it grow. Brian brought a lot of that energy to us and we all have it in us. But he allowed us to focus and grow in that way because he was a bit older and definitely very comfortable with his lifestyle. And we were young and impressionable.

Around the same time, a GUH splinter group formed. Clarke, Cram, and Howard were recruited for a new musical project started by Daryl Smith, guitarist from neo-psych band Yeti, co-founder of brunch haunt La Hacienda, and co-owner of Chemical Sound, a new recording studio on Portland Street south of King. With bassist David Walsh, who had played with eighties hard-core punk trailblazers Nomind and Afhakken, completing the lineup, the new group jammed during downtime at the studio and Smith rolled tape. True to their name, Slow Loris played long, unhurried, cinematic, instru-mental jams – with found sounds and overhead voices – that could suddenly turn dramatically heavy. With Change of Heart's Ian Blurton adding a third guitar to some tracks, it could get crushing.

BH: We would run into each other while walking around Queen Street. Jay was like, 'You want to play the drums with this thing too?' And then Jay had the idea of going around with a tape recorder and recording weird incidental sounds and putting them on, like part of the subway.

JC: We didn't have vocals, so we thought we'd just put atmospherics in it. We'd walk around Union Station and the arcade underneath it.

Slow Loris were very ahead of their time – in 1993, the only thing they could be compared to was 'slowcore' US bands like Slint or Codeine, but their self-titled CD anticipated the sound of Godspeed You! Black Emperor and other groups of the first post-rock wave. It still holds up, twenty-five years later.

Upon its release, the EP caused an immediate buzz in the Toronto under-ground music community, eventually selling out its run of one thousand copies. They began to perform live, including a legendary set at a boozecan in Sorauren Park in the west end. In January '94, they were booked for a show at the Rivoli, opening for a new band on Sub Pop called Red Red Meat.

Amy Hersenhoren (concert promoter): It was my first show as a promoter, when I worked for Sub Pop. No one would book Red Red Meat, so I did it. We sold out the Rivoli with Slow Loris as the supporting act. Slow Loris sold *all the tickets* – but no one knew that. I looked like a superstar. Slow Loris were amazing. People freaked out over that first record.

Slow Loris were then booked for a much higher-profile indie-rock show, opening for Pavement and Codeine on March 25, 1994, at the Palladium. They followed this up with a seven-inch single on Derivative Records. But that marked the end of their sudden rise to indie stardom, as the band lost interest in playing live.

Slow Loris only released one more album, 1996's fantastically titled *The Ten Commandments and Two Territories According to Slow Loris*. In spite of the support of a bigger label, US/UK indie Southern Records, the subtler, jazzier, studio-only venture didn't make the same impact as the debut. Some things have a moment, and then it passes.

★

As for GUH, the summer of 1994 was a transformative one for the group. While Andrew Henry played pummelling rock drums for Venus Cures All, the rest of the core band spent the summer busking across Europe. Bohemian madness ensued, including losing Cram for a whole week.

BH: We had to hitchhike around everywhere. We'd divide ourselves into groups of two and try to get to the next city.

GUH returned from Europe as stronger performers, able to handle anything, and especially adept at commanding stages beyond rock clubs. The band's sound was more refined and orchestrated – though still strange. They had also amassed a significant amount of original material. The band spent most of 1995 recording, doing four sessions at different studios.

In March of '96, GUH celebrated the release of their debut album. It wasn't your average CD release party – they set up and played in the back of Kos, the all-day-breakfast diner. And it wasn't your average CD. GUH gave music journalists their ledes by making their debut a triple CD.

CB: We had to clear the palate to make room for the future. There had been so much recorded at that point.

'Triple CD' garnered enough coverage in *Now*, *Eye*, and *Exclaim!* to help the band build a substantial following, and it marked a brief period when avant-garde music was hip in Toronto.

The Rivoli became GUH's home base, though they'd make occasional forays into more institutional settings, performing at the Music Gallery and the Art Gallery of Ontario. But Toronto's mainstream jazz community never really embraced them. They didn't play the Rex Hotel until 1997, and as of 2019, they have still never played the Toronto Jazz Festival.

GUH followed up the sprawling triple with a more focused statement for their second album, 1997's *Flog* – also their strongest album. Producer

Brenndan McGuire overcame some of their previous studio challenges by recording them in natural stereo, like the big bands of the olden days.

CB: Recording the band is a challenge because it's a live band. We're a street band. We're a club band, a festival band. Getting the sound of a live band onto a compact disc was challenging because the band's big. Through the U of T Jazz program, we had access to tons of musicians, really hot players who could come and read a chart or play a solo.

While *Flog* was a deep listen, their third album, *We Are Sunburning*, was a breezier, almost summery record, showcasing them at their dance-band best. By its 1999 release, GUH were stretching out their performance horizons even further, playing alongside Super-8 films at Toronto's Splice This! film festival and connecting with the city's bike community by performing at the 'free pancake breakfast' as part of Bike Week. They were also the first band to play the *Exclaim!* Hockey Cup. And they claim to have played every craft brewery in town.

Continuing to buck convention, rather than driving to the big cities to promote their most accessible album, they embarked on a tour of B.C.'s Gulf Islands, playing houses and churches.

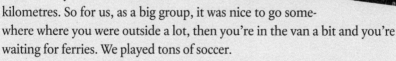

CB: We were on the road for a month and we only drove a thousand kilometres. So for us, as a big group, it was nice to go some- where where you were outside a lot, then you're in the van a bit and you're waiting for ferries. We played tons of soccer.

GUH opened for Do Make Say Think at their first CD release party in December 1997 at Club Shanghai, beginning a relationship that would alter both groups' paths. Cram and other GUH members lent their horns to the instrumental post-rock collective, and Cram joined them on their European tour later that year. He later recruited members of Do Make Say Think for his existential-art-metal project Gesundheit, taking them on numerous gruelling tours through the squats of Eastern Europe.

But as the careers of the groups that they and Slow Loris influenced and inspired took off, GUH began to slow down, with members starting families, some moving out of the city. In 2001, they recorded what was supposed to be their fourth album – at the Gas Station, after its move to Toronto Island – but it wasn't released until 2009, under the apropos title *Unearthed*.

James Keast (music journalist): As they get older, GUH is completing their transformation from an eccentric oddity into a national institution that will eventually take its place amongst the Kronos Quartet or the Art Ensemble of Chicago as great innovators misunderstood in their own time. (*Exclaim!*, October 1999)

Time has not yet done GUH's legacy justice. Partly because the band would likely laugh at such canonical notions. But also because Toronto is pretty bad at celebrating our 'great innovators' in music, especially if they fall outside the singer/songwriter tradition.

GUH continues to play. Though they haven't made a new album in almost two decades, they gig at least a few times a year. For them, it's a family thing, a dedication to the music and its social dimension.

JC: Everybody in GUH still plays. They've always played. I can't think of anybody that stopped playing, so that's why it's easy for us to just keep going.

CB: For me I see it as the expectation of playing music. When we get together, we're playing – and when we're not together, we're playing.

BH: We always just thought we're gonna play this until we're dead, because that was the only way to get through this world or something. In your naive but also wise mind, you're going, 'This is the only way through here.' Oh, we're just going to be playing GUH until the end.

ALL AGES, ALL HOURS
1993-96

While grunge-pop goes big-time, a more politicized
underground scene emerges, with all-ages music happening
at all hours in DIY venues, warehouses, and boozecans.

In the wake of the Halifax Pop Explosion – which began with Sloan, followed by Moncton, New Brunswick, foursome Eric's Trip, the first Canadian band scooped up by Sub Pop – Toronto was ready to anoint its own home-grown grunge heroes. The 1150's former house band, hHead, had been building buzz since appearing on the '92 CFNY New Music Search CD and opening for everyone from My Bloody Valentine to Stone Temple Pilots. In the fall of '93, hHead were the surprise winners of CFNY's Discovery to Disc prize – a princely $100,000 sum. Less than a year later, the trio signed to an American label, IRS Records, the original home of REM. Mostly, though, the alt-rock bands getting signed in Canada were the slick ones – I Mother Earth, Moist, Our Lady Peace. Canadian indie music mostly remained 'indie.'

In 1993, some of the most exciting 'Toronto' music was happening elsewhere in Ontario: Guelph had dub-funk collective King Cobb Steelie, Ottawa had wonderful art-rockers the Wooden Stars, London had lo-fi tunesmiths Spool. But while those bands were somewhat sophisticated and 'adult,' a slew of poppier groups were capturing the attention of the burgeoning teen scene.

No one embodied this all-ages moment better than Sonic Unyon Records, the Hamilton-based indie label started by the members of noise-pop band Tristan Psionic. They grew into an indie-music distribution empire, built hand-to-hand by its founders' relationships with record retailers across the country – killing two birds, they used their band tours as store-servicing routes.

Grunge-popsters Treble Charger achieved liftoff at many mid-nineties all-ages shows.

Mark Milne: *We're not exceptional brains or anything. Ask yourself logical questions. If you want to start your own independent record label and sell seven-inch singles, well, ask yourself, 'Where can I sell seven-inch singles?' If you ask enough people, you'll find out.* (to Mike White, *Exclaim!*, May 1995)

The Unyon went on to release a slew of CDs from Ontario bands, ranging from Hamilton grungers Shallow North Dakota and shoegazers Sianspheric to Toronto's sensitive folkie Hayden and indie popsters Treble Charger. Treble Charger (formerly NC-17) were likely best the exemplars of teenage post-grunge indie music in Toronto, even though the members were all over thirty. Their tuneful, twin-guitar jangle-core on tunes like 'Tenth Grade Love' seemed purpose-built to make a sea of Converse-and-flannel-clad kids jump up in unison, while 'Red' represented the Platonic ideal of the indie-rock power ballad.

The Sonic Unyon crew brought a welcome lack of pretension to the indie scene. Treble Charger celebrated their signing to the label with two boxes of doughnuts outside of Honest Ed's. In their own backyard, the Sonic Unyon crew threw massive multi-band festivals like WoolSock – named after Psionic's gonzo bassist, Wool – as well as countless all-ages shows. Their acts regularly sold out the Opera House, an 950-person venue in the east end, at Queen and Broadview, housed in a turn-of-the-century vaudeville theatre, complete with a gorgeous arched stage and adjoining Juliet balconies.

The east end had never been a hotspot for music venues, except for a few larger halls on Danforth Avenue, like the Music Hall (now the Danforth, one of our few tolerable thousand-plus-capacity clubs), the Palladium, and the Spectrum. More traditionally residential than the west end, Queen East never achieved the density of clubs, restaurants, and galleries of its western twin. But to kids coming in on the TTC from the suburbs, that didn't matter.

The Opera House and the Palladium catered to the underage crowd with stacked multi-band mini-fests like 'The Grunge That Stole Christmas,' featuring most of the Sonic Unyon roster along with Ottawa funk-metallers Furnaceface, Hamilton indie-popster Killjoys, and Toronto heavy grunge-rockers Rusty, another crew of thirty-somethings who would have a main-stream breakthrough with their '95 single 'Wake Me.' Ecstatic teens with long dyed-green hair and plaid shirts tied around their waists jockeyed in the epoch-defining mosh pits, immediately a punchline on *The Simpsons*.

The mid-nineties all-ages era at the Opera House supported more diverse sounds. Blue Dog Pict, an arty prog-rock band fronted by Keram Malicki-Sánchez – who by day was the star of YTV youth drama *Catwalk* – built up a devoted following of free-thinking high-school freaks, sold a respectable number of their self-released CDs via the indie racks at HMV, and staged some pretty elaborate shows.

Keram Malicki-Sánchez (Blue Dog Pict): *We loved the Opera House because it was so epic and made us feel like bona fide rock stars. The entire basement was the green room. It is also where we shot the pilot for* Catwalk, *which was like going full circle. One time we did a show called* Dead Dog Saloon. *We brought ten bales of real hay and placed them strategically around the stage, and sourced some round saloon tables and gingham table covers. Then our friends loaded up some puppets, we dressed up like cowboys and played the whole show like it was a sketch on* The Muppet Show.

Promoter Jonathan Ramos, still one of Toronto's longest-running hip-hop promoters, got his start there. The first show he put on was the Pharcyde, on June 21, 1993, at the Opera House. The opening acts were rising Toronto funk/soul band Bass Is Base and stand-up comedian Russell Peters. There weren't many other venues that supported live hip-hop or R&B at the time.

Jonathan Ramos (promoter): *There weren't consistent shows coming to Toronto, and half of the ones that did come had issues: bad production, short sets, violence, artist no-shows, lack of proper security, late starts, bad promoters. None of the 'concert venues' were supportive. They wouldn't book hip-hop on weekends and charged exorbitant rent on the days they did allow you in. There was a stigma of violence and (even worse) lack of bar sales attached to the genre.*

Hip-hop culture inspired Grasshopper, the stoner-grunge trio and 1150 regulars who had become local heroes by the time they released their '94 CD *Stereovision*. If you were a teen in Toronto in the mid-nineties, you probably attended a few big multi-band bills at the Opera House with Grasshopper at the top. Riffing on the juvenile nostalgia that was coming to define Gen-X, Grasshopper's well-worn T-shirts lifted the *Sesame Street* and Spider-Man logos, beginning a trend of bands incorporating breakfast cereal and other nostalgic childhood pop-culture iconography into their merch designs. It was cute and fun, but it didn't help with elders' perception that our generation was apathetic, immature, and apolitical.

★

In some respects, the all-ages show movement became the music scene's *cause célèbre*. It was an easy thing to get behind: making the music accessible to everyone, especially 'the kids' shut out of licenced bars, bored and hungry for something to do. There was also the exclusion of families and older people unable to attend shows that often didn't get going until eleven p.m. The Toronto music scene had always taken place in licenced bars and clubs, at least at the emerging-band level. But playing shows in bars was getting fucking *boring*. As fun as it was to play the El Mocambo, where the Stones played and all, it could feel like dinner theatre, with the audience seated at tables, sipping bottled beer, clapping politely between songs.

The old cliché about Toronto crowds not dancing was true, though not necessarily because we were uptight or reserved; most small venues weren't laid out to encourage standing at the front without it being awkward. The first people to go up to the front of the stage would have to be very brave, or drunk, to not feel completely self-conscious. This created what one friend called the 'zone of death' – an empty space in front of the band where no one dared tread. And that created a sense of remove, a mental moat, between band and audience. As a performer, it was easy to start to resent listeners who weren't listening.

At an all-ages show, it could be completely different: the kids were *into* it. Playing out-of-town became something to work toward. With less going on, small-town crowds were way less jaded. For them, it was new and fresh and exciting. In theory, at least. At plenty of all-ages hardcore shows, kids sat cross-legged on the floor.

Idealistic scenesters wished to bring some of that energy to downtown Toronto – to create new spaces for people to play, where the focus was on the music rather than binge drinking, where there wasn't a club booker breathing down your neck about bar sales. This opened up previously neglected, overlooked parts of the city, which was exciting and occasionally terrifying. You felt like an urban explorer. In twenty-first-century hindsight, this has the whiff of colonialism – and unwittingly, it trod a path that led to Toronto's out-of-control gentrification. But artists, like all marginalized people, must go where space is affordable and plentiful.

The hardcore punk scene saw a resurgence in the mid-nineties, with a new crop of bands like the Blundermen, Hockey Teeth, and BlowHard playing shows at Classic Studios, a low-ceilinged basement space located on Ossington, just north of Queen. The hardcore scene became more politicized, aligned with activist groups like Anti-Racist Action, and there was more effort made to put on all-ages shows and provide sober spaces, as many embraced a straight-edge lifestyle. The community became more organized, as well: you could call the Hardcore Hotline to stay up to date on all the latest shows.

In addition to punk, Classic Studios also hosted metal, indie, hip-hop, house, and techno. The venue was booked by Project 9, a berserk, brass-driven avant-funk collective led by three Salvadoran brothers of the Bahá'í faith: Alvaro, Boris, and Ulysses Castellanos. They drew big all-ages crowds at their own gigs, regularly throwing benefit concerts for charities such as the Redwood Women's Shelter.

Vibrant all-ages hardcore, punk, and underground rock scenes developed in smaller towns and suburbs across Ontario, especially in the 905 suburbs. One of these was in Durham Region – and Project 9 had a hand in booking its most storied venue, a pizza place in Ajax called Pizza Pino's. They convinced the owner that kids would come order pizza if they could book bands. But the underagers were happier to buy beer, and most shows ended in brawls, like something out of *Repo Man*. It all sounded insane, and I'm still not totally convinced this place even existed, but to quote another nineties icon, *I want to believe.*

Ulysses Castellanos (Project 9): *Pizza Pino's ended with a bang. I was playing in a band called Bobdogdog, and we played mostly noise. We concocted the most fucked-up stage show. I was going to come out wearing a Brian Mulroney mask, and brandishing a Stihl chainsaw, and I was going to saw through a bunch of stuff we threw on the floor. Pizza Pino's didn't have a stage, so we were literally playing in an eight-foot-square area. I dressed in a suit covered in Christmas lights which short-circuited when my lips touched the mic. The jolt* *was so huge that it sent the mic flying and hit someone in the face. Then I blew up a bunch of firecrackers off my chest.*

The all-ages era was supported by a renaissance in self-published zines. Even though there was more indie-friendly print media than ever, titles like *Circle, Ductape, Girltalk, Paint the Houses, Pumpkin Seed, Rivet, Saucy,* and *Superkeen* were still some of the only ways small bands could get coverage. And in a marked contrast with a decade earlier, the majority of these Ontario zines were made by young women, living beyond city limits.

Zine culture itself became magnified in the nineties, with the magazine *Broken Pencil,* which catalogued and reviewed zines, starting up in Toronto in '95, alongside annual events including the Cut & Paste Zine Fair and BP's own Canzine. In those idealistic, anti-authoritarian years, zines were an attempt to take back the media from the hands of corporations, and to stick it to the Man by using his photocopier.

Anarchism was fairly *au courant* in the nineties. In 1991, American writer Hakim Bey (a.k.a. Peter Lamborn Wilson) introduced the idea of the TAZ, or 'temporary autonomous zone' – the idea of creating a space beyond establishment modes of control. Inherent in the definition of a TAZ was its sense of impermanence. In Toronto in 1993, an idealistic collective of performance artists came together with the idea of creating their own temporary autonomous zone.

Symptom Hall was anomalous among Toronto 'music venues.' Firstly, it wasn't really conceived as a music space at all. It drew on the deep well of the artist-run centre tradition that animated Toronto's arts community in other disciplines: theatre, dance, film, video, and beyond. Secondly, it was located on Claremont, a residential side street, south of Dundas West, in a beautiful, spacious old community centre in which they saw limitless possibility. Experimental theatre shows and performance art spectacles took over the building, including mock funerals for dead pets. People lived there too, and theatre-goers might stumble upon someone's stag party – which consisted of watching art films on Super 8.

Matias Rozenberg (musician, Symptom Hall volunteer): *In 1996, I came across a group of ridiculous weirdos at an art/music event at a warehouse* *studio. They were running a workshop which combined formal clowning techniques with bizarre psycho-spiritual rituals. Each person was unique, hilarious, and inspiring. Right away, I was hypnotized by them (not literally) and jumped in their van to follow them blindly to wherever the fuck they were going. We ended up at their home base, Symptom Hall, a place I didn't even know existed! After that, I was hooked and hung out there constantly.*

As might be expected, the stress and cost of operating a volunteer-run performance space stretched the collective thin, and numerous fundraising parties turned Symptom Hall into more of a music space. These boozecans would often run all night, and the neighbours on Claremont were surprisingly co-operative (or possibly afraid).

Later on, Symptom Hall became a more regular venue, hosting shows by GUH, Smallmouth, and acid-jazzers Jukejoint. But it's probably best remembered in the music community for hosting the first Toronto show by Montreal post-rock collective Godspeed You! Black Emperor, in 1997. A year later, the landlord sold the building and it fell to the wrecking ball, 160 Claremont is now occupied by some bland townhouses.

★

Who's Emma? That was the question, and the question mark was part of the name. In 1996, Dr. Alan O'Connor, a cultural studies professor at Trent University in Peterborough, Ontario, began his sabbatical year by putting the theoretical into practice. A gay rights activist who was deeply involved in the hardcore punk scene, O'Connor wanted to see if it was possible to create a temporary autonomous zone in Toronto.

Like 5 Arlington in Ottawa, Who's Emma? opened in Kensington Market as a combination punk record shop, anarchist-book-and-zine seller, vegan café, and workshop space – providing 'informal education' on everything from bike repair to doing live sound. It was also an explicitly queer-positive, feminist, women-friendly space, and Mondays were run by women volunteers only. The name was inspired by Russian-born anarchist activist and writer Emma Goldman, who had lived (and died) in Toronto in the Depression Era.

The original Who's Emma? space was truly tiny – the café had room for one table. The opening party in October '96 took place outside on the sidewalk; the bands that played were horror punks the Sinisters, old-school hardcore crew Politikill Incorect, and electro-shock rocker Corpusse. Over the course of the school year, O'Connor increasingly empowered the volunteer collective that ran Who's Emma? to come up with a consensus-based decision-making framework; by the end of it, he stepped aside and handed it off to them.

The following spring, in April '97, Who's Emma? moved directly across the street to a larger storefront space with a basement where shows could happen, and it became a more regular venue for live bands. One of its first bookers was Will Munro, artist and later founder of beloved queer DJ night Vazaleen.

Though it was located in the 'drunk punk' Market, home turf of the Bunchofuckingoofs, Who's Emma? increasingly booked more straight-edge hardcore bands on tour from the US. One of the band bookers was teenaged punk Mike Haliechuk, who a few years later co-founded Fucked Up, one of Toronto's best-loved hardcore exports of the twenty-first century.

Mike Haliechuk (Fucked Up): *I started doing a weekly shift at Who's Emma? and wanted to contribute more, so I ended up doing most of the LP ordering for a while, and then also started booking the basement. The first show I ever did was the Dillinger Escape Plan. I made them all pasta that I brought downtown from my parents' house.*

In the summer of 2000, Who's Emma? suffered two back-to-back robberies. Unable to absorb these blows, the space closed its doors permanently that September.

Jim Munroe (author, video-game maker, Who's Emma? volunteer): *To me it was a miracle it existed in the first place, given that it was an anticapitalist store and political community space run by volunteers. It was a beautiful and brave experiment, a temporary autonomous zone that burned brightly.*

The building became home to vintage instrument shop Paul's Boutique; next door is popular dive bar Ronnie's Local 069 – both businesses have employed countless local musicians. With I Deal Coffee's patio across the street, and numerous scruffy, bohemian neighbours sitting daily in their front yards, this stretch of Nassau Street still feels like a TAZ. Kensington Market is one of the last downtown 'hoods that resists gentrification.

Massive warehouses like 9 Hanna provided affordable rehearsal spaces for bands in the mid-nineties.

In the summer of 1994, a new band I was jamming with borrowed rehearsal space from friends in noisy indie-pop band Neck. All I knew is that it was in a warehouse around King and Dufferin, a mostly derelict area of old warehouses. I remember making my way to a massively long building that looked like a Star Destroyer had crashed next to the train tracks. The parking lot was dirt, and there was a car parked every hundred feet or so. I was told most of them contained sex workers and their johns.

Up a dark flight of stairs, we came out onto a seemingly infinite hallway. Neck's unit had high ceilings, huge windows overlooking the highway and railway lands, a little loft bedroom, and a hangout area decorated with Christmas lights. We cranked our amps and improvised late into the night; the music became repetitive, hypnotic, a product of the unbounded freedom of the creative space we found ourselves in. It had been a munitions factory in World War II, and was almost certainly toxic. There was a massive open space down the other end, and we'd ride around it on old bicycles and skateboards. At night, we'd get onto the roof and climb up onto the billboards overlooking the highway.

The name and address of this place was 9 Hanna, one of a handful of old buildings that made up what we called the 'warehouse district.' Five years later, it would get rebranded – and redeveloped – as Liberty Village. The area had a long and checkered history. In the nineteenth century it was home to two different prisons. Upon release, ex-cons would walk out onto Liberty Street; hence the name.

For a hundred years, the area was home to industrial factories where carpets, appliances, and tractors were manufactured and easily shipped onto the railroad. In the late seventies and early eighties, industry started moving out and the artists started moving in. Rent was dirt cheap, but since the units weren't zoned for residential, you usually had to install your own kitchens and bathrooms – and keep your sleeping arrangements on the DL. But you could make noise at all hours.

Alastair MacLeod (Neck): *When the studio at 9 Hanna became available, I jumped at the chance to move in there. One night, an old friend from Winnipeg had come to town and I (drunkenly) thought I'd locked myself out. I asked my neighbour, Gary Taxali, if I could climb through his window to get in my studio. When I crawled in my window, it shut on my leg and I still have a scar.*

MacLeod's next-door neighbour Taxali became a world-renowned, award-winning illustrator. He was never bothered by our noise – in fact, he said he *enjoyed* drawing and painting while listening to us. Others weren't so patient: the story goes that a one-time major-label artist who was laying tracks at a studio down the hall tried unsuccessfully to bribe Neck with beer to stop practising.

For a few short years in the nineties, the warehouse district was a creative utopia for Toronto musicians – *Paradise by the Highway*, as memorialized in the title of the lone album by Venus Cures All, one of many bands that lived and rehearsed and occasionally performed there. They released a double seven-inch single in 1995 on local labels Whiskey Sour and Aural Borealis, and their growing local buzz was only amplified when they got to tour the States alongside American indie-rock heroes Seam and Versus, as part of the *Ear of the Dragon* tour, promoting a compilation of indie musicians of Asian descent: bassist Sally Lee is Korean-Canadian.

The CD release party for *Paradise by the Highway* took place January '96 inside the Gas Station, the studio where it was recorded. Run by Dale Morningstar and Don Kerr of the Dinner Is Ruined, the Gas Station was the hotspot for indie bands to record in, located in a gorgeous red brick building on Fraser Avenue in the warehouse district.

Indie sludge-rock foursome Venus Cures All on the Toronto stop of the Ear of the Dragon Tour, El Mocambo, 1995.

Venus Cures All rehearsed a block away from the Gas Station, in a low-slung former commercial space at 37 Mowat Avenue. Drummer Andrew Henry lived there along with members of his other band, GUH. There were several units in the building, including a notorious boozecan called 'the Bunker,' run by the building's 'rental supervisor,' a biker named Dee Troyit. Other bands that lived or rehearsed there included the Rheostatics, By Divine Right, and Satan's Archenemy G.O.D.

Craig Daniels (The Leather Uppers, the Stinkies): *There were several spaces off a loading dock where all the people knew each other, and each place had several band members living in each space. People would literally go from one jam to another, as they would be in multiple bands jamming in those spaces. It was fun to hang out in the chairs right on the loading dock and drink and chat about whatever. It was basically a stoner, indie rock'n'roll Brill Building.*

Jay Clarke (GUH): *There would be a lot of impromptu playing, because there was always somebody to play drums or bass at any given time. And I think that really made everyone better players, because they were just playing a lot.*

Dallas Good and Sean Dean from the recently formed insurgent country band the Sadies took over a unit that had previously been a sign manufacturer called Lucky Signs.

Dallas Good (The Sadies): *My brother had moved into 37 Mowat in the late eighties. The unit next to mine. It was amazing. He put on speakeasies a whole*

Dream-rockers It's Patrick! were among the family of bands that jammed in the warehouse district.

lot and would use my dad's PA and light system. He had great local bands playing there a lot. By the time I moved in, it was getting shittier for bands because all the loft spaces were being used illegally for residential spaces. Even though it was zoned for making a racket, we slowly had to turn down – and ultimately get the fuck out quickly to make room for the wealthy.

Though Dallas and his brother Travis were the sons of Bruce Good, of seventies country/bluegrass icons the Good Brothers, they came up in the eighties punk scene. Prior to moving to Mowat, Dallas lived on Dovercourt, in a building south of Queen where the denizens regularly threw boozecans to make the rent – bands like Phleg Camp, Guilt Parade, and Dallas's pre-Sadies group the Satanatras played. With last call at one a.m. and less happening overall in the city, there was a hunger to keep the party going.

Late-night speakeasies happened all over the city, a tradition going back decades. In 1994, the Matador Club celebrated its thirtieth anniversary. The heavily mythologized country and western dancehall on Dovercourt wasn't a boozecan per se – they didn't sell alcohol, but they *did* sell plastic cups of pop and you *could* find the woman with the hockey bag that *might* sell you a mickey of hooch – but with opening hours posted from one to four a.m., it was easily the most visible beacon of Toronto's after-hours nightlife.

North of Parkdale, in the Sorauren Avenue area, was a lovely loft space called Lump of Squid, where you might see King Cobb Steelie or the

Rheostatics playing for a packed dance floor of fashionable people you wouldn't usually see at indie shows. The vibe was fun and artsy and carefree – not the sketchy after-hours you might get dragged to today.

Then there was 50 Wabash, an abandoned building *inside* Sorauren Park, where I saw eerie, cinematic instrumentalists Slow Loris blow minds in 1994 at a party thrown by artist/entrepreneur Joy Gough. Given that boozecans were illegal – serving alcohol after hours, without a licence, in potentially condemned buildings – you'd think there would have been plenty of busts. Not so much, according to Gough.

Joy Gough: *We didn't [have any issues] other than noise complaints. I had the cops come to one of the last ones I ran, they said 'turn it down' and left us to go on. Door staff didn't let people leave with drinks and told them to keep it down. I eventually sold only canned beer to stop smashed bottles on the street. We did a clean-up before sunrise. I regularly cleared my cash, hiding it in another studio, and didn't have all my alcohol in the space. I was aware if I was busted I'd lose it all. I also did crazy soundproofing for every party. No tales of woe, and nobody that I knew had any arrests either.*

★

To a certain degree, the underground Toronto music scene in the nineties was split up into cliques, without a lot of crossover. You'd see the same three bands play the same show bill together, over and over. As unhealthy as that could be for the wider music community, it was important for developing a sense of camaraderie and helping us all develop our own voices.

The scene I was part of coalesced around the summer '94 release of the *Leisure Terrorists* CD compilation, released by co-op artist-run label Theta State Recordings. *Leisure Terrorists* was in some ways an indie-pop statement: there were ragged lo-fi bands like Kat Rocket and MAdE; smoother, more Anglophilic-sounding bands like 122 Greige and the Orange Near; and noisier yet still tuneful post-punk bands like Neck and Parts Unknown. (Most of the same circle co-founded Wavelength five years later.)

My band from university days, noise-pop quintet A Tuesday Weld, called it quits only a few months after the comp was released, and my next group, Secret Agent, was louder, angrier, and more experimental – the sounds I'd absorbed at the 1150 had sunk into my bones. We still played shows and shared space with our popwise friends – other bands that rehearsed at 9 Hanna included a new dream-pop band, Mean Red Spiders, and mood-rockers It's Patrick!, led by Fifth Column guitarist Michelle Breslin. (Their name came from an unintentionally hilarious life-insurance TV commercial.) But we also befriended other bands more stylistically in line with us.

One was Venus Cures All; another was Smallmouth, which had ties to GUH. With Slow Loris come and gone by summer '94, Smallmouth took up the duties for representing slowcore and math-rock, bringing much-needed intensity to Queen West stages like the Ultrasound and the 360.

Smallmouth's sister band, Pecola, were a revelation. They were insanely tight, eye-poppingly intense, and didn't really sound like anyone else; their herky-jerky rhythms and turn-on-a-dime dynamics always smashed expectations. They even wrote a pop song now and then – but it was weird and fucked-up.

Jamie Fleming of noise-rockers Pecola: master of eyeball-popping intensity.

Craig Thompson (Pecola): *From my perspective, it was key to challenge audiences. We used to play hardcore shows and we were pretty far from hardcore, so that was challenging (maybe?) to the people watching us. We played an all-ages show once and all the kids were sitting on the floor, and I remember Jamie [Fleming] walking through them playing guitar and vocalizing – that was pretty amazing. I've also always been drawn to that aesthetic – anything outside of the typical 4/4, two-guitar attack. Alt-rock and grunge were big back then so anything that did not sound like that was heavenly for me.*

Smallmouth and Pecola both self-released cassettes in '95. It was hard for them to find much of an audience until they were discovered by a music lover and cartoonist named Phil Klygo, who had started writing for *Exclaim!* and publishing his own fanzine, *Skull Geek Bible.*

Phil Klygo: *I started visiting the* Exclaim! *offices in 1994. It was always a treat to go through their drawers of artist/band/label submissions. I started picking* *out small label and* DIY *releases, stuff that had been sitting there for months, things that looked cool, and a lot of it local. One of the gems that I found in the vaults was the first Pecola tape. I was obsessed with their sound immediately, so powerfully raw and tight.*

Klygo had some money saved up and decided to turn Skull Geek into a record label as well as a zine. This filled a gaping void, as there were precious few indie labels supporting the local scene, besides Sonic Unyon, Squirtgun, or Rusty's Handsome Boy Records. In 1996, Klygo released Pecola's first seven-inch EP – which included a comic by Tony 'Ratboy' Walsh, as well as a Smallmouth CD and a Secret Agent single. A fourth band joined the Skull Geek fold – Slowgun, a fuzzy indie-pop band. All four bands played together at numerous showcases, usually held downstairs at the El Mocambo.

Prior to Skull Geek coming along, my friends and I felt pretty alienated from the music business. In June 1995, a collective I was part of called Re:define, along with friends from Kat Rocket and Parts Unknown, organized a two-night music festival called 'No Labels' – a middle finger to both major labels and reductive journalistic pigeonholing – at the Freak Show, an all-ages club on Richmond Street. The point was to present what *we* thought was the best stuff happening in the Toronto underground scene. It was mildly disastrous financially – I don't even remember if anyone paid to get in; it may have been the bands all playing to each other – and it was the only event that ever happened under the Re:define banner. But at least we have the memory of the bass amp catching fire and belching thick black smoke.

The Freak Show occupied the former address of Toronto's original rave club, 23 Hop, which started booking an all-ages alterna-dance night called 'the Freak Show' on Wednesdays in the fall of '93 that eventually took over the space's identity. By early '95, they had begun booking live bands, including Radioblaster, Grasshopper, Project 9, rap crew Yet Another Posse, hardcore punks Hockey Teeth, and swamp-rockers Suckerpunch. This incarnation of the Freak Show didn't last long, however, and by the end of the year, the place had become cheesy mega-club the Joker.

In the mid-nineties, I dreamed of seeing audiences respond to Toronto bands with the same fervour as they did to out-of-town heroes like Fugazi. I wonder why this couldn't have happened through more crossover between the indie-rock and the rave scenes. But the answer is still there when I go to shows now: the social tension between wanting to dance and wanting to *watch a band.* I still crave the same ecstatic, communal effervescence from a crowd at a live show that comes so easily to a dance floor empowered by a DJ. Those moments it *does* happen are rare and precious. And what we were doing wasn't really what 'the kids' wanted to hear. The few people coming to see the Skull Geek bands were dwarfed by the popularity of the rave scene.

In the mid-nineties, Toronto raves began to explode in size and ambition. Promoters were getting increasingly adventurous, wandering beyond secretive warehouse spaces to take over larger and higher-profile buildings. In 1993, Atlantis Productions (formerly Nitrous) held the first rave at the Ontario Science Centre, the public science museum up in Don Mills. A poured-concrete marvel, designed by architect Raymond Moriyama, that flowed down the side of the Don Valley ravine, the OSC perfectly matched rave music's sense of retro-futurism. Despite increasing concern from authority figures, occasional raves were held at the Science Centre over the next six years.

Electronic music events spread to other public spaces that twinged nerdy nostalgia among 'eighties kids.' In July 1994, the ambient duo Deepspace – producer/guitarist Jeff McMurrich and keyboardist Dave Lovell, a.k.a. DJ Davy Love, later of Blow Up fame – performed their 'placid house' at the McLaughlin Planetarium, as part of an event called 'From Here to Tranquility,' to celebrate the twenty-fifth anniversary of the moon landing. The planetarium being famous for its 'Laser Floyd' shows, it was easy for Lovell and McMurrich to work with the in-house laser artist to craft visuals, while DJs played before and between sets.

The following spring, a collective of fresh, idealistic, and socially conscious promoters – who came together under the name Transcendance – also put on a live show at the planetarium, featuring British ambient artist Scanner. Sadly, the McLaughlin closed its doors permanently later that same year. Turned off by the increasing commercialism of the rave scene, Transcendance created thoughtful, meditative events that were more like art installations.

Stephanie Seifert (Transcendance): *The electronic scene in T.O. was male-run, with mostly a very different vibe. We created a new niche, run on the principles of equality, art, and community. [This proceeded] to piss off the small group of male rave producers.*

In March of '96, Transcendance put on their best-known event, a near-mythical warehouse party in the Junction, with the UK's Autechre alongside Windsor, Ontario, minimal-techno pioneer Richie Hawtin and Toronto ambient duo Legion of Green Men. The collective parted ways after a suspicious house fire at their shared apartment. Co-founders Beverly May and Ian Guthrie continued to promote events, the latter with Building Blocks and Fukhouse.

Drum'n'bass and jungle – the furious fusion of reggae and techno that had blasted out of London at breakbeat speed – also began to get a foothold in Toronto, a moment marked with the Syrous party 'Judgment Day,' complete with *Terminator 2*–themed flyer. Local DJs like Marcus Visionary were among the first to popularize the frenetic sounds over here, making Toronto a world jungle hotspot.

The evictions from the warehouse district began in '95/'96: the City and property owners had big plans to redevelop the area. One by one, musicians reluctantly moved out and started finding other homes and jam spaces. 9 Hanna was demolished. On December 1, 1996, the province changed the liquor laws, allowing bars and restaurants to serve until two a.m., which spelled doom for the boozecan scene. All-ages shows became more infrequent as licenced venues returned to their reliance on bar sales to stay afloat. The all-ages, all-hours music scene was on life support.

Blake Howard (GUH): *Everybody at the warehouse was pissed off, of course. And we got a lawyer and the lawyer was straight-up with us. She said, 'This is great that you're really upset and it's great that you called me, but you're never going to win. You have no chance against these people. They are just going to come in and take it.'*

KAT ROCKET
The Art of Never Winning
1992–99

Toronto produces a lot of talented artists with plenty of artistic integrity – idealistic, uncompromising, 'difficult' to the point of self-sabotage. Toronto is also the headquarters of the Canadian music industry, where A&Rs vulture around fresh-faced buzz bands, their 'interest' rarely landing anything more than the *rumour* of interest, creating a potentially toxic brew of disappointment and dashed hopes. No one represented this conundrum in the nineties more than Kat Rocket.

Kat Rocket stood out amongst Toronto's noise-rock scene of the early '90s due to their embrace of melody. Still a puzzle box of a band – sonically rooted in the lo-fi American indie-rock of Pavement, Sebadoh, and Guided by Voices, the UK shoegaze/dream-pop of My Bloody Valentine and Ride, and a range of classic rock, psychedelic, country, and trip-hop influences — Kat Rocket deserve a bigger place in Toronto's musical memory. They left behind a handful of great songs, brought to life by Stella Panacci's disaffectedly impassioned voice.

What became Kat Rocket started in 1991 at Earl Haig, a high school with a renowned arts program in the Willowdale neighbourhood of North York. It began with skate-punk band Stew, who wrote songs about their local doughnut shop, Petit Place. Through classmate Sean Waisglass, of Fugazi-inspired Mudfish, they discovered the 1150/Drake scene. And through another classmate, they became connected to an all-ages scene just east of the city.

Stella Panacci (vocals, drums): I auditioned for the arts program at Earl Haig, and I got in as a double major for music and dance. I took the bus every day from Pickering.

Pickering is a suburban town far enough from downtown Toronto to have developed its own local music scene. Panacci got Stew a gig at a hall there, and they contributed a track to the CD comp *Stereophonicus Disruptus*. But by the time of its release, Stew was already no more.

Darren Donaghey (guitar/bass): I remember feeling stifled by our hardcore band, and then I met Mikko and Dave. They had this Ween kind of sound, writing really weird songs, and I was transfixed and wanted to play with these guys.

Kat Rocket's original lineup featured a different frontman, singer/guitarist Mikko Mallinick, while Donaghey played bass and Panacci played drums and sang backup. Guitarist 'Little Dave' Solursh, a tiny, manic, dreadlocked hippie, filled out the band's sound with psychedelic textures. Originally called God's Kid Brother, they played their first show at an Earl Haig talent show in September 1992, covering songs by Ride and the Jesus and Mary Chain alongside a handful of originals. Their first gig as Kat Rocket – or rather, Catrocket (as they originally styled it) – was a few weeks later at an Elvis Monday at the 1150.

SP: We spent a whole afternoon going through the dictionary in the food court at Mel Lastman Square. That's how we came up with the name Catrocket. We just put two things together!

'I Hate Myself and I Want to Die' was what Kurt Cobain had threatened to title the third Nirvana album, and Catrocket beat him to the punch, cheekily pinching it for the title of their four-song demo tape, released in summer '93, months before the release of *In Utero*. (A year later, the title wouldn't be so funny.) The demo contained one fantastic song – 'Lost,' a soaring dream-pop anthem with heartbreaking lead vocals and lyrics by Stella Panacci. That was the band's 'lightbulb' moment: Stella was their greatest asset.

DD: We wanted Mikko out of the band. We came up with a story: let's break up the band, and re-form the band. And that's what we did.

Returning as Kat Rocket, the band solidified Stella and Darren as the song-writing core. A series of Stew / Earl Haig alumni filled out the constantly rotating lineup. In the spring of '94, they made their new identity official, self-releasing a two-song seven-inch on their own label, Hoodwink Records. 'Lost' was the A-side. As if to throw the A&R guys off the scent, they titled the single *Coffee Shop Philosophers*. Kat Rocket were clearly sending the message 'this band doesn't come with a business plan.'

SP: My friend Sandy went to Dunbarton high school [in Pickering] and there's a Tim Hortons near the school. One day the principal came up to them and said, 'You're all just a bunch of coffee shop philosophers!'

Double-doubles and danishes, crullers and chain-smoking: the doughnut shop is where Canadian adolescent dreams are hatched. In summer 1994, the band met up at their North York local, Petit Place, with the heads of a record label to discuss plans to release an EP. But these weren't major-label staffers with expense accounts to cover the chocolate glazeds. Theta State Recordings was an artist co-op, run by members of local indie-pop bands. It had just put out its first release, a compilation CD, *Leisure Terrorists*, that its founders hoped would put Toronto on the global indie-music map.

Kat Rocket's contribution, 'Slacker Boy Blue,' was a bona fide indie-pop anti-anthem. The song referenced *NewMusic* journalist Daniel Richler's sole novel, *Kicking Tomorrow*, but Panacci's lyrics were really a sisterly kick at bandmate Donaghey's sad-sack ways. But as a fan of the '91 Linklater film, 'slacker' was a badge he wore with pride.

DD: The song came from Stella always calling me that – because I *was* a slacker! 'Get off your ass, you're in your basement all the time!' I remember us writing it together: I wrote the chords, she wrote the words, but I didn't know that she was actually making fun of me as we were writing the song.

Kat Rocket began to receive substantial coverage in *Now* and *Eye*, as well as the local Oshawa paper, which was noticed by a forty-something communications specialist named Mario Panacci, who read the story and thought the drummer/singer in the band photo resembled his long-lost niece.

SP: But we never used our last names. I went by Stella Marie, he was Darren Danish! I didn't know my Italian side until I was nineteen years old. And he thought, 'This could be my niece Stella.' And then I got a phone call at York

University one day, and he said, 'Are you Stella Panacci? I think I'm your Uncle Mario.'

Donaghey remembers the story differently, recalling that Uncle Mario came to see them at an Opera House all-ages gig, opening for then-massive Grasshopper, and approached them afterwards. Either way, Uncle Mario immediately saw their potential.

SP: He thought we were the best thing since sliced bread, man. He invested his whole life and a lot of money into us.

DD: He was looking for something. He didn't want to do his job anymore, and when he found Stella and the band, he was very excited. He was super supportive right from the start.

SP: He tried to encourage us, and we were so rude. We were so laissez-faire and uninterested.

DD: Well, *you* told him that you weren't interested, but I said that we were! Even though he was your uncle, I said, 'Yes, we do need help.'

With Uncle Mario's aid, in May 1995 the band released their debut EP, *Town Disguised as a City* – the title a gentle slap at Toronto's parochial streak. Theta State Recordings had since folded, but the connection led them to Chemical Sound, where they spent most of '94 labouring in the studio, gigging occasionally at the Cabana Room or Sneaky Dee's.

DD: The CD release at the Rivoli was hilarious. The manufacturing plant didn't get the CDs done on time and we were yelling at them, and they said, 'We'll get you some cassettes first.' Danko Jones was the emcee, as 'The Great Entertainer.' And Stella cut Little Dave's dreadlocks off onstage!

SP: And then I whipped them into the crowd. People were going to grab them like they were a wedding bouquet. His Mom still has one in a Ziploc.

Town Disguised as a City garnered plenty of campus radio play across the country, and in August '95, Kat Rocket went on tour to Halifax – alongside my own band, Secret Agent. (I had happened to see their very first show, and soon after we became friends and collaborators.) We played some great shows, but the audiences were just as apathetic as back home. But making it all the way out to the coast in our early twenties, in the faces of near-constant vehicular mishaps, felt like a huge accomplishment.

Kat Rocket's lineup had been bolstered by a new, dead-cool bassist, John Calabrese, who Stella had met at York U, while Secret Agent had recruited an incredible new drummer, seventeen-year-old Justin Peroff. By the end of the tour, both had quit each band, clearly frustrated with the disorganization and calamities. Ironically, Peroff ended up joining Kat Rocket after their drummer quit. Five years later, he'd co-found Broken Social Scene. As for Calabrese, he put his business and bass skills together to co-found Danko Jones with the eponymous frontman.

Peroff didn't last long in Kat Rocket. Despite the revitalization of a solid new bassist – Paul Pfisterer, who became a key anchor for the remainder of the band's existence – Peroff left partway through the recording of their first full-length album. The band doesn't blame either of them now, seeing the follies of their youthful quest for artistic purity.

SP: We were too cool. We just wanted to be so artsy and true – not 'fake,' not 'contrived.' But it's like everything's fucking contrived, right?

Justin Peroff (drums, Broken Social Scene): Kat Rocket had this hip-hop cool about them. They were this unique funk indie thing with this really cool Italian skater girl. Stella was like Gwen Stefani before Gwen Stefani.

In mid-1996, Kat Rocket finally unveiled their first full-length, *Captured by the Dream Company*. The album title coyly referred to the band's tentative courtship by the industry – they were in talks with Sony and Warner.

DD: As everyone was being signed at the time, we purposely made a difficult record to prevent us from being 'captured.'

A blend of studio and home recordings, the album is disjointed and disorienting – though not always in a bad way. Donaghey and Panacci partly attribute this to everyone else being perma-stoned and playing everything much slower than intended. The album's bright spots come when the band puts down the bong and amps things up, as on lead track 'Art of Never Winning' – the only track that Peroff ended up playing on. The album made the *Toronto Star*'s list of the best local indie CDs of '96, Lenny Stoute calling it 'bold pop psychedelia with clever twists.'

Though the band promoted the disc with shows in Ottawa and Montreal, they were again stuck in the same old Toronto indie band trap of nowhere-to-go-from-here. At this point, they considered whether the escape route might be a major label, after all. Their friends in MAdE – also a Pavement-influenced indie-pop band with a woman on drums – had signed to Universal, releasing *Bedazzler* in 1997 and receiving some mainstream airplay.

Kat Rocket were picked up by MAdE's producers, Alfio Annibalini and Daryn Berry, and received a FACTOR grant to make their next record. This album would have a big budget: the production duo had big plans to shop it to labels. But the band found the process torturous – tracking each instrument individually, playing to click tracks, not even seeing each other for weeks – which began to create a rift between co-founders Donaghey and Panacci.

DD: It was great and terrible at the same time. It was an incredible learning experience, but we pretty much broke up right after that. I felt like I was losing control of 'my' band. The producers had an idea of what they wanted to do and it was different.

SP: We broke up musically. I think that's what we did, we divorced musically. We both fell out of love with the whole concept, at that point. We were like, 'Fuck this! It's getting real – we don't want real, we want fantasy!'

Finally released in May 1999 at Ted's Wrecking Yard – once again on their own Hoodwink Records – *Colours on the Inside* was the last chapter of Kat Rocket's fantasy story. Panacci started a solo career, under the name Stella Luna, while Donaghey and Pfisterer started a music production company.

Toronto in the nineties didn't know how to make space for creative, ambitious yet unfocused youth like Kat Rocket to find their voice. Indie music, for all its idealism, also demanded serious business skills. And I'm not sure if it's changed much – young artists are pressured to spend more time developing their social media presence than their sound. But the strange, bittersweet, and wonderful life of Kat Rocket carved a path for other 416 slackers – such as their former members who tour the world with Broken Social Scene and Danko Jones – to finally get their shit together.

GHETTO CONCEPT
Certified Motion
1992–

Nineteen ninety-four was a rough year for Toronto hip-hop. Just three short years after the first wave of local rap artists broke out big, they hit a sophomore slump. Maestro Fresh Wes released a disappointing third LP. Dream Warriors' second album didn't hit the sublime heights of its predecessor. Main Source's follow-up to *Breaking Atoms* was shelved after the group broke up. Michie Mee parted ways with L.A. Luv but soon resurfaced as part of the alt-rock project Raggadeath. Community members blame the slump on major-label and mainstream media indifference. But when the industry drops the ball, the underground is there to pick it up.

A slinky jazz bassline and dreamy horn hook broke through in '94 to let people know that Toronto hip-hop was alive and well. 'E-Z on tha Motion' was actually the second single from Rexdale crew Ghetto Concept, after local indie Groove-A-Lot Record released 'Certified' in 1993. The records won back-to-back Juno Awards for Rap Recording of the Year.

Ghetto Concept were there at the start of Toronto hip-hop's second wave, a movement that was gritty, DIY, and underground. I spoke to co-founder Kwajo Cinqo over the phone from his current home in Los Angeles to find out more about how they made it all happen.

So where did you guys grow up?

I grew up in Rexdale in the west end of Toronto, and my partner, Dolo, he grew up in the Lawrence and Allen area, which is what they quote unquote call the 'hood, you know, or the ghetto.

How did you meet?

Everybody used to come converge at Eaton Centre on Saturday in the afternoon, probably around six o'clock, before we'd go to a club called Focus. So while we were waiting for Focus to open, there would be rap ciphers. When I heard Dolo spit in that cipher, I was like 'This dude is the nicest rapper I've heard out of Toronto.' You know, he's like fire.

Whose idea was it to start making music together?

I got an offer to open up for Brand Nubian, at Hollywood Nightclub on Danforth Avenue. That was in 1992. From meeting Dolo in those ciphers downtown, I was like, 'Damn that dude's nice. I'mma make him come and rock with me on stage.' So then we started practising to get ready for that show. It's not like we ever sat and said, 'Oh, let's create this thing Ghetto Concept,' right? It just happened. After that show everybody was like, 'Yo, y'all ripped it.' Good feedback. And then we just continued making songs and working together.

How did you start making your own beats?

Initially we were working with Da Grassroots' Born Swiff, rest in peace [Swiff LaRoc died of cancer in 2018]. He connected us with our first record deal with Groove-A-Lot Records. And he was also our producer. He recorded the first Ghetto Concept demos in his bedroom. Those first couple songs that people heard from us – 'Hard Copy' was one of the first beats I personally made myself, and then 'Certified,' I got the loop from my dad. I got the sample and then I gave it to Swiff and then him and Da Grassroots produced that record. They really mentored me. And then I started going in and making tracks and made the majority of the Ghetto Concept material that came out.

So you were digging into your dad's record collection?

Yeah, yeah. My dad has a lot of records. It was funny because even that song 'Certified,' my dad would never give me the actual vinyl, so he would only let me make a tape of the record. The fidelity would have been a lot higher if we could have used the vinyl! My dad has hundreds and hundreds of records, so that's where my ear comes from, he was always playing good music in the house.

And is that where the jazz influence came from?
Yeah, jazz definitely – my dad had a lot of jazz. But a lot of people were using jazz samples at that time – Pete Rock, Premier, Large Professor, and all those guys – that was the sound of that time.

What was it like winning the Juno for 'Certified' in '95?
The record came out and it was very well received all over North America. You'd go to the club and you'd actually hear people playing it. People didn't expect us to win, we weren't on a label, we were really out of pocket. No major support. We were up against all the heavy hitters. We were just going to go have some drinks and chill. And as soon as we sat down, they were announcing the rap category. And then they said 'Ghetto Concept.' It was a major, major upset for a lot of people, but for us it was a victory for the 'hood. And it felt great.

And then you won the next year as well.
Yeah! So that was another complete surprise, because we were like, 'Damn, they ain't going to give it to us again.' But again, that song, 'E-Z on tha Motion,' is now regarded as a classic. I remember when I first heard the sample, Attic [of Da Grassroots] played that beat out of his car. And instantly, as soon as I heard the beat – you know that's a hit. We need that. When we released it, it was instant. All the media, all the radio, and the video came out while we were on tour. We were doing the first *RapCity* tour with k-os and the Rascalz. We toured across Canada and we went hard. So again, we showed up at the Junos – as soon as we sat down, they called us up again.

Was it frustrating to get that level of recognition, but then not have the support from major record companies or from mainstream radio?
Ten million percent. It didn't make sense. You know, I've got to give props to Mike McCarty from EMI Publishing. He was the one really invested in Ghetto Concept. They'd seen the buzz that we had in the street. They came in and gave us a publishing deal. We put out of the majority of our records through that venture. That's what allowed us to operate at a major level. We were on platforms like MuchMusic, we were playing the game with the majors, but in reality, that stuff was done out of our bedroom. It was literally

us in the basement grinding. It's a blessing that we were able to touch so many people.

For their early singles, Kwajo and Dolo were joined by a third member, DJ/rapper Infinite. He parted ways with Ghetto Concept after 'E-Z on tha Motion,' and the group took a hiatus before releasing their self-titled debut album in 1998, on their own label, 7 Bills Entertainment. They reached their commercial peak in 2001 with 'Still Too Much,' an all-star jam featuring Maestro, Kardinal Offishall, Snow, and others. After releasing their last single in 2004, the members focused on other projects, with Kwajo producing and scoring tracks for TV and movies. The classic mid-nineties lineup reunited in 2011 to perform at CBC's Hip Hop Summit.

QUEEN WEST: THE (COUNTERCULTURE) ESTABLISHMENT DIGS IN 1995-97

Formerly counterculture central, Queen West becomes home of the
Canadian music industry establishment with the launch of the
North by Northeast (NXNE) club-crawl festival

Three hundred bands! Twenty venues! Only twenty-nine dollars for a wrist-band! The inaugural North by Northeast festival landed in Toronto June 15–17, 1995, and you can't fault the organizers for bombast; the fest was long overdue. Though the Jazz Fest and Afro-Fest had been thriving since the late eighties, pop-aligned music festivals had been a non-entity inside city limits since the last Police Picnic, twelve years earlier.

Riding the slipstream of South by Southwest, which had been steadily building an annual buzz in Austin, Texas, the festival format consisted of a 'club crawl' of showcases for mostly unsigned artists looking to 'expose their band to the world,' along with an industry conference. It was a format that had worked well for the New Music Seminar and the CMJ Music Marathon in New York. A similar festival, the 'Independents,' had been attempted in Toronto in 1988, but it never came back for a second year.

Michael Hollett (co-founder, NXNE and *Now Magazine*): *I'm very close with the folks who started SXSW, some of my best friends. We met through our alternative newspapers, me with* Now, *them with the* Austin Chronicle. *I remember them telling me that they were going to start a music festival in Austin and I thought that was charming. Once it started – and took off – we noted many of the same qualities that made Austin such a good home for SXSW existed in Toronto – great live music venues, lots of them, and a dynamic local music scene.*

In essence, North by Northeast wasn't much different than Canadian Music Week, which had launched two years earlier, though NXNE claimed to be more 'about the music.' The lineup included local heroes 13 Engines, African drum group Muhtadi, Andrew Cash's new band Ursula, and edgy international acts like Poster Children. It was a wise move to schedule the festival during the fresh warmth of mid-June, in contrast with the late-winter CMW. For their first edition, NXNE's programming team selected their talent from a pool of over 1,600 demo tapes, all of which came with a ten-dollar submission fee.

Yvonne Matsell (club booker and co-founder, NXNE): *I was doing all the listening and booking and remained doing that for many, many years. With all my contacts and musicians that I had worked with over the years, I was able to maintain integrity for the festival. I was still booking Ultrasound, then Ted's, then later the El Mo, all while still being a single mom!*

But the new festival wasn't welcomed with unanimous applause in the music community. For many local bands working these same clubs week after week, the submission process was the source of some eye-rolling. Who wanted to pay for the privilege of playing the same clubs you could get booked into on your own, for the cost of lifting the phone? And why would audiences pay big-ticket prices to see those same acts you could see any night of the week, any week of the year?

The notion that your band was going to get 'discovered' and signed at either NXNE or CMW was considered snort-worthy. One high-profile group put up posters for their showcase that said '_____ play WeaselFest!' The truth was, if you weren't scheduled into a high-profile club the record company 'weasels' weren't likely to see you. An unknown band might end up playing at seven p.m. at a falafel shop alongside a bunch of random other bands with whom they had little in common. And despite the supposed major-label feeding-frenzy around indie music, hardly anyone from the local community had actually been signed.

There was also the matter of the association between the festival and *Now Magazine*, which put the paper in the awkward position of trying to provide objective reporting on an event it was involved in promoting. But when it came to boosting the local scene, the strategy worked. Getting on the cover of *Now* was already considered a pinnacle of Canadian success in the mid-nineties, and for Kingston, Ontario, band Weeping Tile – an earnest roots-rock quartet led by engaging singer/songwriter Sarah Harmer – seeing their faces all over town that week in June '95 must have been cool, though they had already been signed to an American major label at that point.

It's worth noting, however, that NXNE overcame these early hiccups, and by the late 2000s the festival became one of the most beloved events in the local music community, especially under the programming aegis of Crispin Giles and Cheryl Maciver.

More than half of the inaugural NXNE's twenty-three venues were located on or near Queen West, a sign that by the mid-nineties, the former new-wave 'rebel zone' (as Lorraine Segato dubbed it) had become the centre of Toronto's and Canada's music industry establishment. The Horseshoe Tavern, in particular, had become the premier schmooze spot for A&R reps looking for the next big thing – and a slew of Canadian rock hopefuls such as Waltons and the Watchmen were discovered there. It was around the 'Shoe's front and back bars that the Canadian music industry began to find itself, as well.

Steve Jordan (founder, Polaris Music Prize; former A&R, Warner Canada): *The 'Shoe was artist-friendly and curated by folks like Craig Laskey, Jeff Cohen, and Amy Hersenhoren, who were genuinely into the music and presenting artists that went beyond just the commercially viable. The sound was always decent. It's like the place itself was a trusted filter. And if it was just Bonnie Fedrau (EMI), Dave Porter (A&M, then Universal), and me, then you knew you had to pay close attention.*

Earlier in 1995, the Horseshoe launched a weeknight tradition that would fit in right next to Elvis Mondays amongst the rites of passages for Toronto bands: on Tuesday, April 18, the first Nu Music Nite took place, booked and hosted by Dave Bookman, journalist, CFNY (and later Indie88) radio host and frontman of college-rockers the Bookmen. 'Bookie' brought his love of flannel-clad indie-rock to the stage; the inaugural show featured two then-buzzy groups: Radioblaster, a sugary indie-pop trio, and Scratching Post, a metal-influenced power-pop band – both on local indie label Squirtgun Records. With no cover, it was a great night out for broke music fans. But it traded Elvis Mondays' creative chaos for a more organized, business-like approach. Given the sheer number of would-be rock stars dropping by clutching demo tapes, this was a smart move.

The Horseshoe had begun expanding its market reach, with new in-house bookers Jeff Cohen and Craig Laskey starting a promotion company,

Surf garage punks Suckerpunch were the coolest kids on the Queen Street strip.

Against the Grain, with the aim of presenting more touring acts. For local bands, success on a Nu Music Nite — in terms of bringing people out — could lead to higher-profile bookings later in the week, or a coveted opening slot for a hyped out-of-towner.

A few doors down from the 'Shoe, the Rivoli was the go-to spot for CD release parties. In 1995, you could still see bands like MAdE or Len play there for fifty people, when the latter, before 'Steal My Sunshine,' were a anarchic lo-fi indie band who put out tapes in red fun-fur packaging. Much-Music VJ Sook-Yin Lee could regularly be seen singing her offbeat pop at the Riv, later backed up by the Chevrons, including bassist Cindy Beattie of Suckerpunch and drummer Justin Peroff (pre–Broken Social Scene). Suckerpunch themselves ruled the mid-nineties Queen West scene with their dead-cool garage/surf-punk, handsome brothers Chris and Sean Dignan a recognizable sight strolling down the street with slick retro pompadours.

Sean Dignan (drums, Suckerpunch): *The scene back then was dense – everybody lived and gigged within a ten- or twenty-minute walk along Queen, which for a big town made it familiar and supportive, as one sees in smaller cities. It's what Toronto has been as a home for music and culture; bringing other circles into a bigger and hopefully growing circle.*

Rivoli regular Bob Wiseman wasn't much of a friend of the music industry. Though he left Blue Rodeo as keyboardist in '92, he had been releasing solo albums as a singer/guitarist since 1989 – and on a major label, Warner Music

Canada. Mildly astonishing, given that Wiseman played outsider folk that addressed topics like corporate complicity in mass murder. After taunting David Geffen in a 1995 song, Wiseman left the majors for good.

Canadian labels wouldn't touch hip-hop in the mid-nineties, and the Rivoli was one of the few places on Queen West where you could hear it live. Plains of Fascination, who self-released a solid disc in 1996, could be seen there playing benefits for Anti-Racist Action. CKLN's *Power Move* program promoted shows at the Riv with emcees like Thrust and crews like Scarborough's Monolith, while rapper k-os played Bump + Hustle parties. And DJX's Live at the BBQ, one of the key local hip-hop nights – named for the Main Source cut where Nas was first heard – got its start at the Rivoli. With Ron Nelson moving to promote dancehall and reggae shows, X saw a void to be filled.

DJX: *The reason I did it was because I saw what Ron did. He had created a legacy of bringing artists from New York and doing shows. I said to myself, how am I going to be different from what Ron was doing? And my answer to that was to feature local artists. The concept was a showcase of Toronto's underground hip-hop scene. (Views Before the 6 podcast, 2017)*

Jonathan Ramos: *Live at the BBQ was one of the most influential and now legendary parties that featured the best DJs in the city and some of the best artists. The energy was always amazing.*

The Cameron House, meanwhile, continued its diverse booking policy established in the eighties. James Duncan and Mike Gennaro kept the free-jazz freak flag planted with the Free Music Ensemble's Saturday afternoon matinees, while DJs Malik X and Mark Oliver's sweatier acid-jazz night packed the back room on Wednesday nights. Regulars at the BamBoo in the mid-nineties included Punjabi by Nature, a seven-piece live bhangra band, and Women Ah Run Tings, a rare all-woman reggae group. And the tiny stage at the Rex could get crowded when the sixteen-piece NOJO (Neufeld-Occhipinti Jazz Orchestra) held court.

But Queen West's robustness didn't mean it was invincible. In September 1996, the Ultrasound Showbar closed down unexpectedly, an eviction notice taped to the door. Bands left without a gig included the Matthew Good Band. Creeping gentrification was starting to displace Classic Queen West and push the strip further west.

Yvonne Matsell: *Business started slipping in the downstairs restaurant. The landlords of the building started to get greedy, the club was behind in the rent, and suddenly the bailiffs closed it up. I was truly devastated!*

Steve Jordan: *Ultrasound: Toronto still has not matched this magical venue for both setting and quality of booking.*

Matsell resurfaced a few months later, with a bold new assignment at the start of 1997: she took over booking duties for the Big Bop, the purple-hued, multi-storey dance club at the corner of Queen and Bathurst. Under new management, the Bop became a multi-room live venue, with mid-level rock, pop, electronic, and hip-hop on the second floor, now branded 'Reverb,' and a more intimate, singer/songwriter room and DJ lounge, 'Holy Joe's,' on the third. Heavy metal and punk found a home on the ground floor, later renamed the 'Kathedral.'

Like the Opera House, the new Big Bop drew in a younger, more suburban crowd, with regular all-ages shows and Battle of the Bands–style showcases organized by Supernova. The chaotic, poster-stapled front of the building matched the frenetic energy of the Queen and Bathurst intersection. Grimy, leather-clad rocker types had already been attracted west along Queen by the Bovine Sex Club, a hard-rock bar that had opened in 1991.

Reverb provided another much-needed live venue for hip-hop, in March 1997 booking a fresh young emcee named Kardinal Offishall, who was turning heads with his track on Beat Factory Records' *Rap Essentials Vol. 1* comp. 'Naughty Dread' combined dancehall, roots-reggae and Jamaican patois with hip-hop to create a uniquely Torontonian sound. Later that year, Kardi would help inaugurate the Canadian hip-hop renaissance on Rascalz' patriotic posse cut 'Northern Touch,' alongside Choclair, Thrust, and CheckMate. Hip-hop culture began to transform the Queen West streetscape as well, as graffiti artists brought the main drag's alleyways to life. The old Queen Street weirdness pushed further west, with spots opening up between Bathurst and Niagara, like goth haunt Sanctuary: The Vampire Sex Bar; cozy resto-lounge Gypsy Co-op, where DJs Denise Benson and Vania spun chill beats and the Resinators played live dub; and La Hacienda, a brunch spot staffed by delightfully grumpy musicians, where you might catch the occasional live band like GUH on the back patio.

At the other end of the strip, poet and entrepreneur Duke Redbird opened up the Coloured Stone in 1997 in the growing Entertainment District, providing a much-needed performance space for Indigenous artists, such as blues guitarist Derek Miller and folk-rappers No Reservations. The Coloured Stone was a sanctuary amidst intensifying nightlife, with numerous nightclubs like Limelight and oz opening up in the immediate vicinity.

But the Entertainment District was threatened even before it reached its apex. Dance clubs had started to cluster in the area because they were getting zoned out of other parts of the city. In 1996, the City started pushing for residential development in property-rich Clubland. When condos and clubs began to share blocks, it would cause huge issues for the city a decade down the line.

Rave culture's growing popularity coincided with electronic music's foray into the mainstream via the Chemical Brothers and Moby, which prompted many a 'rock is dead' think-piece in the music press. But as live clubs like the Horseshoe and the Rivoli continued to thrive, it was clear that 'dance' and 'rock' could peacefully co-exist.

DJ Denise Benson brought downtempo beats further west along QSW to hangouts like Gypsy Co-op at Queen and Niagara.

Queen West's live venues had undoubtedly become a part of the Canadian music-industry establishment, but it was less of the nurturing hotbed that it was in the eighties. The dotcom boom was making some people rich, but it was hard times for artists in Ontario, as the recently elected Conservative provincial government under Mike Harris began slashing social assistance, cancelling public transit projects, and cutting arts funding. The Rheostatics summed up the local zeitgeist with their '96 tune 'Bad Time to be Poor' (''cause we don't give a shit no more'). In this climate of pre-millennial tension, the establishment was ready for a shake-up. Enter stage left a real rock'n'roll rebel.

DO MAKE SAY THINK
Highway 420
1995–

Do Make Say Think are from Toronto but have spent much of their career getting mistaken for a Montreal band – mostly due to their long tenure with Constellation Records. They're now the second-longest-running act on the label's roster, after its flagship act, Godspeed You! Black Emperor. Both groups are also now globally recognized as key artists in the second wave of the subgenre known as post-rock.

DMST's sweeping, cinematic post-rock pull in elements of jazz, dub, psychedelia, and electronica – the ultimate record-geek music. Their albums and live shows can be heady stuff – the imaginary soundtrack to everything from lying in a sunny meadow to witnessing it all get wiped out in a fiery apocalypse. Yet its members possess a healthy sense of humour.

This dichotomy at the heart of Do Make Say Think can be somewhat explained by the five core members' roots in two very different high school bands. Three of them, bassist Charles Spearin, multi-instrumentalist Ohad Benchetrit, and drummer Dave Mitchell, were members of Dead Lemmings, a Spinal Tap–inspired joke-rock band with a serious love for Metallica. Together from 1990 to '95, midtown-Toronto-based Dead Lemmings built up a small but fierce local cult following – mostly among their classmates – for their onstage antics.

Charles Spearin (bass): We had a two-headed bass player routine, where we faked a fight on stage, because we had two bassists and they got into an argument. Then they went off and came back on stage wearing a suit that I made, that was a huge pair of pants and two shirts sewn together.

Dead Lemmings played anywhere that would have them – the early-nineties D-list circuit of mostly east-end rock clubs that didn't care if the bands were underage: The Spectrum at Danforth and Main. The Marquee at Coxwell and Gerrard. Stratengers at Queen East and Leslie. If you were lucky, Lee's Palace on a Monday night.

Beyond the city limits, in suburban Ajax and Pickering, Ontario, at the same time, the other future DMSTers, guitarist Justin Small and drummer James 'Jimmy' Payment, were having a very different experience.

Justin Small (guitar): The band that Jimmy and I were in, Domestic Violence, was a straight-up death metal band. We sang songs about the devil, and it was supposed to be not-funny. And unfortunately, if you hear the first demo that we did, it's unintentionally funny because my voice isn't really pubertized into 'scary voice.' Our one claim to fame was we had the first release on Toronto metal label Epidemic Records' cassette-only imprint Plague.

Through their affiliation with pioneering industrial/metal project Malhavoc, Domestic Violence played a few gigs downtown at the Apocalypse Club, but due to a lack of wheels were mostly stuck in the 'burbs. Playing sporadic gigs in community centres and basements, they were part of the short-lived early-nineties all-ages scene in their suburban backyard.

JS: There was a vital music scene in Ajax and Pickering, but it was such a struggle. It was always a hassle to book a gig at a bar if you weren't a Pearl Jam cover band. There was one record shop and it sold only mainstream stuff. There were skinheads and shitty people and it was a horrible place to grow up.

Barely out of their teens, Small and Payment moved right into the heart of things, sharing an apartment in the Annex, directly across the street from Lee's Palace on Bloor.

CS: My Aunt Sally saw a poster for a job opening at a community theatre company in Cabbagetown. I got an interview and got the job. On the first day, we were all sitting in a circle, introducing ourselves. Justin Small, who looked a bit like a young Keith Richards, sauntered in late, wearing a Rolling

Stones shirt and radiating a kind of affable confidence that immediately put people at ease. He and I soon got along famously, bonding over Slint, Steve Reich, and Henryk Gorecki, and when I broke up with my girlfriend and needed a place to stay, he invited me to move in with himself and James.

JS: Charles and I got hired to write, produce, and perform this play, as a PR thing for cops to take to grade schools and play to Grade 2s and tell them, 'Drugs bad, cops good.' But we ended up not doing the best job – we ended up *doing* lots of drugs!' (to the author, *Eye Weekly*, April 9, 1998)

CS: In the following years, the three of us became inseparable, devouring any new, unique music we could find, buying records, going to shows almost every night, eagerly awaiting Thursdays, when the new *Now* and *Eye* magazines came out with the latest listings, and composing soundscapes on my old dusty reel-to-reel. Who knew we were about to skyrocket to subgenre pseudo-stardom? All because of my Aunt Sally's message.

A quarter century later, the former roommates still banter back and forth like siblings, rotating recollections like the albums they used to spin endlessly at the Albany apartment.

JS: The one thing that also needs to be said about us moving in together and starting Do Make Say Think was our merging of record collections. I was at this crux of buying newer records and discovering stuff like Yo La Tengo, but when Tortoise came around, it was like, 'What the fuck is this?' But it was also Charlie bringing in Pink Floyd and all that kind of stuff.

CS: Which you could have found in Ajax if you looked.

JS: Oh yeah, it was everywhere in Ajax. That's why I fucking hated it! Anybody who was like, 'Oh my favourite band is Pink Floyd,' I was like, 'Fuck you, man. It's Napalm Death or nothing!' But I remember this one night, you know the one I'm talking about, when you laid [Floyd's] *Ummagumma* on me and I got to the end and was like, 'This is a *live* record?!!'

When it came time to 'start a band,' they didn't get together to jam on anyone's songs, they made long, spaced-out home recordings, fuelled by healthy amounts of cannabis. But it wasn't long before they found themselves on stage.

CS: I brought in my eight-track reel-to-reel, a Tascam 388. That became our television set. We'd sit around and make recordings instead of watching TV.

We'd do late-night jams in the living room, rolling tape. I think I sort of pissed these guys off by booking the first gig without telling them.

JS: No, you didn't piss me off, you pissed Jimmy off. And he's louder than me. But I was very much like, 'Whoa!' I was definitely scared.

CS: That was the one thing I learned from the Dead Lemmings, is that you should just play gigs. You should just get out there and do it, just play for nobody. It was just something fun to do – way more fun than anything else. I just called up Craig [Morrison, club booker] from Lee's Palace, or maybe I walked in, and booked the gig and said, 'We're called Do Make Say Think.' The other guys didn't know that.

JS: I immediately thought it was the worst band name in the world, but I was like, 'All right, whatever.'

The band name, like their fateful meeting, originates in Cabbagetown. They were working together at the Regent Park Public School, where Spearin couldn't help but notice signs plastered all over the walls that said, 'Do. Make. Say. Think.'

CS: I thought it was kind of a strange thing to be preaching to kids, but it really stuck with me. I went in to book the gig and that was the first thing on my brain. So I said that. And Craig funnily enough said, 'I'm not always right, but I can tell by a band's name whether they're going to be successful or not. [pause] And I don't think so.'

The first official Do Make Say Think gig took place at Lee's Palace on March 11, 1996 – a Monday night.

CS: We ended up being invited to play the night before at our DJ friend Michael Markus's rave at a warehouse on Spadina. We set up in the corner of the smaller of two rooms (the 'chillout' room) and taped down keys on monophonic synthesizers and played quiet chords on guitar while deafening drum'n'bass pounded through the wall beside us. At five a.m., the raver kids would take a break from dancing and come into our room and lie around on couches.

JS: It wasn't uncommon for electronic music parties to converge with experimental music and indie-style music. Fast-forward to the next night, and here we are on an open mic night at Lee's, sandwiched between two Pearl

Jam cover bands. We play three 'drone compositions,' one of which became our hit 'Disco and Haze.' There is no encore.

CS: I think it was really electronic music that gave us the sense that there are no time constraints on music. If you go to a rave, it's the same thing all night long with no beginning and no end – it's all crossfades, DJ moves, slow mood shifts over an hour. It's an immersive thing, you kind of have to surrender to it. And I think we took that in. When we played music, we didn't want to stop because it felt like it needed to stop. On 'The Fare to Get There,' I play two notes for twenty minutes. And it was just bliss.

Do Make Say Think spent the rest of 1996 playing renegade raves and the traditional club circuit, including a residency at the Cameron House that fuelled word-of-mouth buzz. Because they went out all the time, they had built up a sizable social network – IRL, of course. And their lineup expanded from three to five with the addition of one old friend – Ohad Benchetrit, who played guitar, bass, sax, and flute – and one new one, Jason MacKenzie, a.k.a. Stumpy Godhead. Adding keyboards and second drums to their sound, Stumpy also became DMST's entry point to campus station CIUT.

CS: Stumpy hosted a free-form, unsupervised, all-night radio show on Wednesdays on CIUT called *Stage Zhow Exploritoire*, that eventually became co-hosted by Justin. *Stage Zhow* was a kind of gravitational centre around which all of our record store discoveries orbited. Any curious finds, from any genre, from any era, were played – sometimes at the wrong speed, sometimes on top of another record – to the presumably baffled (and largely hypothetical) audience.

JS: We were doing a *lot* of drugs. Acid and mushrooms. We would go in there and dose up. We had Wednesday overnight from midnight to six a.m. Six hours to get so out there. One time, we were blaring music in the studio and the station manager called and went, 'Guys, you've had dead air for like an hour!' [They had the master volume down.]

Do Make Say Think also used the CIUT basement as a rehearsal space and pop-up studio where Spearin's reel-to-reel could be synched to a digital eight-track recorder. There, they began assembling the material that made up their first album. The self-titled debut, initially released at the end of 1997, is markedly different from their later albums. Most of its minimalist pieces are based around hypnotically repetitive dub basslines, synth squiggles, soft yet insistent drum beats, and meditative space-rock guitar chords. The titles paid cheeky tribute to the places around them: 'Le'espalace,' 'Highway 420.' It's a fine record, but it sounds like a group finding its sound.

What changed everything for Do Make Say Think was signing to Constellation Records. The Montreal label raised the bar in almost every way – beautiful, often handmade packaging; an uncompromising commitment to non-commercial music; an ethical rejection of most capitalist marketing techniques; a sophisticated curatorial aura. And with the international phenomenon of Godspeed You! Black Emperor, Constellation co-founders Don Wilkie and Ian Ilavsky were suddenly able to sell a lot of records (by indie standards, at least).

JS: I went to a Godspeed/Fell Gang gig at Symptom Hall. I was destroyed! I gave a cassette I had with me to Dave in the band. He gave it to Constellation, and Don came down to see us open for Bardo Pond at Club Shanghai. We made a meeting date, and they travelled to Toronto sign a deal. There was no signature. Twenty years in, there's never been a contract!

Constellation re-released *Do Make Say Think* worldwide in March 1999, to positive reviews. But by then, the band's sound had already morphed into something heftier. The previous fall, they had gone on an East Coast tour. At a show in Sackville, New Brunswick, they blew away their new label bosses with an intense unplanned set.

JS: We came on stage and made complete nonsense noise – just relentless, relentless noise. And Don and Ian came up to us afterwards and said, 'Oh my God, guys, make a record like that!'

DMST had already begun work on their second album, evolving beyond the free-form jams into more composed pieces. Their sound had become heavier, more focused and dynamic, with the addition of second full-kit drummer Dave Mitchell.

JS: I also think we took it more seriously. Our situation with Constellation started to expand. We were part of something that looked like it might be global.

In the fall of '99, Do Make Say Think embarked on their first of many tours of Europe. The Continent's tightly packed cities would become the market that would sustain them the most over the next two decades.

CS: None of us had ever been to Europe. A lot of the guys had never been on a plane before. It was beyond exciting to be there. And then after about two weeks, you find yourself being more irritable than you can imagine, and you're like, 'How can I be so irritable when I'm in fucking *France*? Sure, it's a gas station, but I'm in France!'

JS: We took the finished version of our second record on tour with us when we went to Europe for the first time. We had recorded *Goodbye Enemy Airship*, but we hadn't released it yet and we were playing songs from it. We had a day off and said, 'Let's put our record on.' And I remember listening to the record going, 'Oh my God, oh my God. I don't know what to make of this record. What have we done?!' And not in a good way – there was a lot of doubt. But then the record came out.

Released in March 2000, *Goodbye Enemy Airship the Landlord Is Dead* was a stunning achievement. Both minimal and maximal, its songs were built around nervously looping guitar parts that could explode at any moment – to devastating effect. Two tracks were tracked at CIUT, the rest in MacKenzie's grandparents' barn in Port Hope, east of the city. With the sound of crickets chirping in the background, the songs flowed into one another, added record crackles making it sound like its own late-night radio show from after the end of the world. For the first time, nocturnal horns crept into the DMST sound. And yet it is rougher-hewn than either its predecessor or the five albums that came after it.

CS: I don't listen back too often, but now I think it's probably my favourite. All the things that I thought were mistakes back in the day, now they have some real soul in them. There's no click track, no tuning pedals, and everything's just kind of drifting in and out. And sometimes it feels like a record with the hole punched off centre. But then you step back, and it has this humanity to it.

Goodbye Enemy Airship was even more rapturously received by critics and audience. In Toronto, the band had clearly reached local-hero status, feting its release with a self-promoted concert at the Bloor Cinema. A horn section of GUH members expanded their sound, becoming a semi-permanent addition. The larger ensemble performed alongside silent films made by friend Christopher Mills, to a sold-out crowd of over six hundred.

CS: I remember Dave Mitchell looking at the lineup of people waiting to get in, that went around the corner and up the street, and saying, 'Whoa, Do Makes is for real.'

JS: I agree, that Bloor show was truly a defining moment for me. I remember seeing the lineup and thinking, 'Darn, we didn't buy enough beer!'

Do Make Say Think are now approaching their twenty-fifth anniversary. Their 2002 album *& yet & yet* showed a more melodic side, and the track 'Chinatown' appeared in the film *Syriana*. Small and Benchetrit began composing soundtracks together. Spearin expanded his career as a touring musician as a core member of Broken Social Scene and with Feist.

The affiliation with BSS may overshadow DMST, but the former wouldn't exist without the cradle constructed by the Annex's best-loved instrumentalists. Do Make Say Think's most recent album, 2017's *Stubborn Persistent Illusions*, was one of their career-best, justly recognized with the Juno Award for Best Instrumental Album.

CS: You're in a band unless you announce that you've broken up. We don't see each other for big chunks. It's not like a marriage, where you have to be together all the time. We come together, we make music, and we drift apart, but we're still a band. I think all of us recognize that when we're together we make good music, and that keeps bringing us back.

THE LAST ROCK SHOW: COLLEGE STREET RISES UP 1997-99

Upstart promoter Dan Burke shakes up the establishment and brings the creative edge of the music scene up to College Street and Kensington Market. With alt-rock bands dropped by labels, the boundaries begin to blur between indie, experimental, electronic, and hip-hop music.

Dan Burke: *It was a fucking live music town. That's all I knew about Toronto. I'd be listening to the radio – Q107, CHUM-FM, CFNY – and the announcer would say, 'Tonight! Under the neon palm.'*

O ne day in the spring of 1997, I was sitting at my desk at the *Eye Weekly* office typing faxes from promoters into my Mac Classic. An internship at the alt-weekly newspaper had turned into a full-time gig inputting their concert and events listings. Our staff news writer, Peter Kuitenbrouwer, sidled up to my desk.

'Hey, Jonny, you're up on the music scene, right?' Sure, I said. 'Okay, I want to introduce you to my friend Dan. He used to be a journalist, and he just moved here from Montreal, but he's started managing a club. He's looking for some pointers on which bands to book.'

And so I was introduced to Dan Burke. I was intrigued by this talkative, rough-hewn, older man who seemed like a hard-boiled film-noir private eye. Without any experience in the music business, he had fallen into managing a struggling poolhall and nightclub in Chinatown. Located on the third and fourth floors of a building over a grocery store, the venue had to be accessed via passenger elevator. This, combined with fish tanks and an array of shady-looking gangster characters hanging at the bar, gave the club a surreal, action-movie ambience. It didn't have a name, so Burke christened it Club Shanghai.

Dan Burke: *Being from Montreal, I had always been attracted to nightlife. And having been a journalist, I wasn't afraid to pick up the phone, get in touch with people, and put things together. I didn't know a single musician in Toronto. I knew one girl who was a singer and I knew her from AA meetings. She told me about a band called the Sinisters. And that's all I knew. So I had to start doing my research. I applied myself like a journalist.*

I came on board to help book some of the bands at Club Shanghai as part of a short-lived collective, Co-Pilot Productions, along with my friends Greg Chambers of Mean Red Spiders and Phil Klygo from Skull Geek. We didn't last long (two months tops), as it was pretty clear Burke didn't need the help. He was less enthused about arty, shoegazing indie-rock and more amped up about the revival of raw, gritty garage-rock in Toronto, especially a new, young band called the Deadly Snakes.

Burke: *I didn't like indie-rock. There wasn't much showmanship in it.*

Burke took over booking the Shanghai single-handedly, launching a twenty-plus-year career as Toronto's most irascible, unpredictable, determined, and passionate club booker. I wouldn't find out for another ten years about the incident that had ended Burke's journalism career: after he investigated a corrupt Montreal RCMP cop for *the fifth estate*, the subject of his piece fatally shot himself in the head the day before it aired, in 1992. In the aftermath, Burke became addicted to hard drugs and was sent to rehab but ended up on the street. 'After that,' he told the *Toronto Star*'s Cathal Kelly in 2009, 'I became a 24/7 crackhead, thief, criminal.' In 1997, he resurfaced in Toronto and discovered Club Shanghai while seeking a place to store his stash for his latest enterprise: a wholesale flower business.

In his new career as a club booker, Burke deployed his journo-chops, picking up the phone, connecting the dots, and seeing where it led. Bernie Pleskach from Satan's Archenemy G.O.D. wanted to bring in a band from Detroit called the Wild Bunch, so they made it happen at the Shanghai. That led him to book some friends of theirs who had a band called the White Stripes. 'You could've put the whole audience in the same cab,' he later told *Now*.

Club Shanghai may have only been a few blocks north of Queen, but its July '97 opening marked the migration of music-scene energy toward a new commercial strip: College Street. Though in some ways College was more upwardly mobile and less gritty than Queen, it was also nerdier and more, well, collegiate – which made it equally cool, in a geek-chic sort of way. Initially, Burke and Club Shanghai owner Shirley Wu saw themselves competing not with the Horseshoe Tavern but with the tiny Lion Club on the edge of Kensington Market.

Since Elvis Mondays kingpin William New took over booking the El Mocambo in '93, it had become a clubhouse for scrappy up-and-comers. In December '95, Mean Red Spiders guitarist Dave Humphreys came up with the idea for KIMfest – KIM standing for Kanadian Independent Music – a semi-annual, standalone club fest that mostly took place at the El Mo, plus one edition in Ottawa.

Dave Humphreys of Mean Red Spiders, working the door at one of many KIMfests at the El Mocambo.

Greg Chambers (Mean Red Spiders): *We all saw that artists in Canada's biggest city were overlooked by the media; music fans in Toronto had no idea a scene even existed here. CanCon rules invented a whole market of subpar Canadian artists who had access to funds for recording, marketing, and touring, sucking all the air out of the market for any artist who didn't adhere to the dominant trends ... KIMfest was an attempt to try and drum up support for the underground scene here in Toronto, which was bursting at the seams with amazing talent.*

The El Mo also hosted 'Canadian Music Waste,' a parallel fest to Canadian Music Week that gave the mainstream industry conference a sly middle finger. A community had developed around the main floor of the El Mo in the mid-nineties, especially around the weekly Sedated Sunday, organized by Steve Bromstein of the neo-psych-folk band Poppyseed & the Love Explosion Orchestra – with the help of a few friends, and plenty of cannabis.

Chambers: *The night was originally supposed to be a low-key, acoustic night, but we took the word 'Sedated' to mean something a little different. With different bookers working different nights, it was pretty easy to get a weeknight* *gig that you could put together yourself. Artists would come out almost any night of the week to meet and greet one another, and many a band was started hanging downstairs in the 'Keith Richards Lounge' in the basement.*

Sedated Sundays also started hosting regular tribute nights, which brought together indie bands of many different stripes to pay tribute to an influential artist; my personal favourite was the tribute to the Beach Boys' *Pet Sounds* album.

Babs Vermeulen (The Helens, Rocket Tits): *Those nights were easily my favourite, watching all the bands in the city come together to re-interpret our favourite songs. It felt like there was a real scene coalescing. I was, however, bothered by the lack of female representation at these tribute nights, so when Rocket Tits played the Beatles tribute, the lineup was Barbi [Castelvi from The Spy], Peaches, myself, and Leslie Feist on drums.*

Mondo Lulu (Parts Unknown): *We must have played the El Mo about fifty times. The PA kept getting smaller and the fruit flies in the bathroom got bigger, but it was home.*

New clubs created a bit of a circuit alongside Club Shanghai and the El Mocambo. Rancho Relaxo, a bizarrely stuccoed second-floor club above a Mexican restaurant on College, provided a stage for small indie bands to start out. This helped bring Kensington Market to life at night, and the unkillable Bunchofuckingoofs created one of the longest-lasting homes for punk in the Market: Planet Kensington, on Baldwin Street. One of the foulest-smelling venues in Toronto history, Planet Kensington was plenty charming – if you enjoyed friendly mohawked headbutts. It's still keeping the Market's spirit of drunk punk alive – albeit without live bands – as dive bar Thirsty & Miserable, named after a Black Flag song.

Down the street, Little Italy had become a rarefied, yuppified enclave when grad students and media professionals started hanging out amidst the cafés previously populated only by older Italian men watching soccer. An eccentric architect named Ted Footman went against the grain of the genteel background-entertainment policy of the resto-bars along that stretch of College. He started with a bar that blasted loud rock'n'roll records while twenty-somethings argued politics as gothic candlesticks melted down over the empty wine bottles that held them up.

Ted Footman: *Ted's Collision was a bit of a shock for the neighbourhood. It was all supposed to be pasta and jazz, and all very quiet.* (to Denise Benson, *Then and Now*, 2015)

Ted's Collision opened in '94, and a few years later, Footman opened a second establishment a few doors down. Ted's Wrecking Yard was a cozy two-floor live music club that booked bluegrass, rockabilly, and – as Ted always enjoyed upending expectations – the occasional classical string quartet in its main floor lounge, Barcode.

Dimly lit drinking establishments began to pop up along College all the way from Spadina to Grace. Electronic music began seeping beyond covert raves and Richmond Street nightclubs, with low-key live performances and DJ sets taking over cozy lounge spaces like the women-run 52 Inc. Lava, opened by former Rivoli booker Greg Bottrell, was loungey and retro, with a small stage. Jason Beck, a.k.a. Son (later a.k.a. Gonzales), played the opening night on September 10, 1997, and the Mod Club DJ night started there on Wednesday nights. (In 2002, Mark Holmes, a.k.a. DJ MRK, formerly of Platinum Blonde, would open the Mod Club Theatre down the street.)

Basement lounge Ciao Edie also had a retro-mod vibe, which suited the go-go *Austin Powers* era. There was also jazz-jam and live R&B club the Orbit Room, co-owned by Rush guitarist Alex Lifeson. And you could argue that Latin drag-show palace El Convento Rico, which opened back in 1992 as 'a safe haven for the LGBTQ+ community,' is really the place that gave birth to nightlife in Little Italy.

Down at the southern end of Chinatown, across the street from the Art Gallery of Ontario on Dundas Street West, a two-floor space called We'ave was opened by a collective of artists including DJ/singer Barbi Castelvi, booking live bands at first but soon leaning toward DJs. Now-mythical nights like Chicks Dig It, Mettle, and milk. made it the best place to hear cutting-edge drum'n'bass, techno, and deep house, if you couldn't stomach the cheesiness of Clubland. Early performances by Peaches, and the Social Work DJ night by Dan Snaith, a.k.a. Manitoba/Caribou, took place there before both joined the experimental jet-set.

We'ave was a regular home for proudly homegrown electronic labels like Public Transit Recordings. Founded by DJ/producer Kevin Moon (aka Moonstarr) as Toronto's answer to forward-thinking UK imprints Ninja Tune or Warp, PTR's '98 CD comp *Code 416* surveyed the best in local production across a dizzying array of genres — future jazz, techno, broken beat, down-tempo and hip-hop. Just as important was its eco-friendly, pro-mass transit ethos, baked into the label's identity. At We'ave parties, they offered reduced admission to those clutching the old-style paper TTC transfers.

Kevin Moon (Moonstarr, Public Transit Recordings): *At the time, Mike Harris was [Ontario] premier, so there was an undercurrent of activism that permeated our parties and releases. Coal plants were a big problem at that time, contributing to smog days. We threw what we think was Toronto's first smoke-free party, called Fresh Air, a few years before they banned smoking at bars. We did another event called Devolution where we highlighted the negative effects of unchecked urban development on the city.*

Electronic music collective Public Transit Recordings threw some of the most memorable parties at We'ave on Dundas. L to R: Monochrome, Moonstarr, Frankie Gunns.

In 1997, the city of Toronto was facing an existential crisis. The Mike Harris government, acting in the name of 'cost-efficiencies,' announced plans to amalgamate the six municipalities that made up Metro Toronto into one 'megacity,' governed by one mayor and city council, while abolishing the regional governing Metro body. Many rightly saw this as a Stalinist power-play to take out the hard-right provincial government's loudest political opponent: Toronto city council and its left-leaning mayor, Barbara Hall.

Local opposition was fierce: the activist group Citizens 4 Local Democracy was immediately brought together by a group of greying veterans of the

Stop Spadina and seventies civic reform movements. They held a March 1997 referendum that found 76 per cent opposed to amalgamation. Harris was unfazed. The City of Toronto Act passed into law, and Metro Toronto ceased to exist as of January 1, 1998. Hall lost the first megacity mayoral election to former North York mayor Mel Lastman. The goofy furniture salesman became Toronto's *first* mayoral embarrassment during his half-decade in office; his numerous facepalms including racist jokes to the press before a trip to Kenya.

Toronto indie-rock was going through its own identity crisis. Just five years after the heady post-Nirvana dreams of global domination and Converse-hopping all-ages shows, many of the Canadian bands snapped up by major labels during the nineties were getting dropped, their underground cred and campus-radio play failing to translate into sales. Most of them didn't survive long after that: Change of Heart released a heavier guitar-driven album, *Steelteeth*, in '97 on Virgin, but after the hoped-for commercial breakthrough failed to happen, a burned-out Ian Blurton ended COH's sixteen-year run as Toronto's hardest-working band.

Blurton: *It was over. The record sold really badly. It was the worst-selling record in three records. With twenty times the amount of money put into it. Probably even more, actually. We did the Roadside Attraction with the Hip, and then we went out on our own, and it was just a really bad tour. We went into a record store and they said they'd tried to reorder our record but it had been discontinued or deleted. It was like, why? What are we doing? We are out on the road promoting a record that you couldn't get.*

One of the few to sign directly to an American major, hHead's experience with IRS Records ended unceremoniously when the label went bankrupt. But it was over the course of several semi-disastrous, barely attended US tours that they realized they weren't going to break big.

Brendan Canning: *It was a very short relationship. You get a bit of money, go on some shitty tours. We did a tour with the Goo Goo Dolls right before they broke. Some shows were all right. But you know, at the same time – we just weren't the best band.*

Resigned about their prospects and sick of pointless touring, the one-time grunge hopefuls chose to move on to new projects and sounds. Noah Mintz started the folk-poppy Noah's Arkweld with a young Calgary transplant named Leslie Feist, while Brendan Canning began playing with quirky art-pop singer/songwriter Spookey Ruben, who had a brief moment of international hype after signing with US-based TVT Records.

My friends in MAdE released just one album on Universal in 1997 before the whole deal and band fell apart acrimoniously. A group of sarcastic, sloppy Pavement lovers, they weren't the kind of band that belonged on a major to begin with.

Simon Bedford-James (MAdE): *It was a dreadful experience, so many stupid mistakes were made. The original mix was very 'mid-fi' sounding, so the label didn't want to put that out. They wanted to get a 'name' mixer, so a fortune was spent on 'remixing' and it still sounded fairly awful. They also spent a fortune on making an expensive, incomprehensible video that for some reason was shot on the roof of Western Hospital. It was an absolute train wreck that I don't think got played more than once and that, added to the already dodgy remixes, pretty much sunk our chances.*

Some groups did survive, even thrive, on major labels, usually by changing their style, such as Treble Charger, who abandoned slacker indie-rock and Sonic Unyon for peppy pop-punk and RCA. Another former Unyonite, Hayden, was one of the few genuine success stories of the era. Signing to US-based Outpost/Universal for his '98 album *The Closer I Get*, the indie-folkie shifted a respectable number of units – thanks in part to his appearance on the soundtrack of the Steve Buscemi film *Trees Lounge* – while staying true to his sound. Even he couldn't escape the slaughter, as his label dissolved in 1999, but the financial settlement set him up nicely.

Dave Bookman (CFNY, Horseshoe Nu Music Nite): *You had a lot of the old guard trying to market a new product they didn't really understand. As soon as the major labels see that all these weird alternative bands can't play live and don't know how to do interviews, what do they do? Just like their classic-rock brethren before them, they went and signed pretty boys like Moist and Our Lady Peace – these fake alternative bands that were massively success-ful in Canada, but really no different than the hair bands of the eighties. They just had modern mall-ternative clothes.* (to Stuart Berman, *This Book Is Broken*, 2009)

It was obvious the standard narrative was no longer working – start playing around locally, release an indie tape or CD, get featured in *Now* or *Eye*, make a video to get on Much, go out on tour ... and hope the buzz lasts until one of the major labels offers you a deal and you can finally quit your day job. You could start to feel the exhaustion at local shows – bands weren't trying anymore, and audiences weren't responding.

★

But just as nature abhors vacuums, healthy local music scenes make opportunities out of apathy. In the late nineties, some of the bands championed by Dan Burke decided to upend the standard model and find new ways to reach a global audience without the support of the traditional Canadian music industry.

Toronto kids to the core, the Deadly Snakes began playing tiny bars like the Lion Club while still attending high school in the west end. Captivated by the scuzzy, lo-fi American garage-punk scene, the Snakes brought back a sense of rock'n'roll danger to the often asexual indie music scene. They were anarchic and fun, but were also solid tunesmiths. In a time when civic pride was low to non-existent – even after the Blue Jays' back-to-back World Series wins and the start of the Raptors – the gang defended their home turf. Their band shirts read 'The Deadly Snakes – Toronto,' and they penned a tune that summed up Toronto's ambivalence about itself: 'I Don't Wanna Have to Hate This City.' If the band was a movie, it would be about a fifties youth gang who suddenly had to save the day.

Garage-rock had some history here, going back to the Ugly Ducklings in the sixties. Since the early nineties, the subgenre's small but fervent following was held up by people like Craig Daniels, vet of thirteen bands including the Leather Uppers, the Stinkies, and the Exploders.

Craig Daniels: *Toronto might not be as known for garage-rock as other cities, but people are open to it and respond to fun, crazy rock'n'roll when it happens. When I started playing with the Leather Uppers, we felt bad self-important grunge copiers of the day were a big joke (e.g., I Mother Earth) and set about being an antidote to that.*

While the Deadly Snakes were a loosely organized collective, their main rivals in Toronto's late-nineties garage-hype renaissance were the opposite. Danko Jones were a tight, no-fat power trio. They were a band *and* one guy, their eponymous frontman, who had stage presence, speaking to the audience directly – part James Brown showmanship, part stand-up comedy routine. Eschewing baggy plaid, they had dress sense. Their lyrics dealt with sexuality, embracing cock-rock tropes while attempting to avoid its misogyny.

Danko Jones: *We came out of the cannon with attitude – like, 'We've been around the scene long enough, and we know what's going on, and everyone sucks!' We didn't have anyone in our corner – we didn't have a manager, or a record label; we wanted to make a splash and we did. We told everyone from the scene, 'We're not even going to play Toronto!' And that lasted for two shows.* (to Stuart Berman, *Too Much Trouble: A Very Oral History of Danko Jones*, 2012)

Turned off by the lameness of the Canadian music industry, Danko Jones had their sights set on joining the American indie elite. They befriended the likes of New Bomb Turks, Blonde Redhead, and the Make-Up, and began playing shows south of the border before they even had a record to promote. In '97, Jones declared the band would never release anything and would go on live reputation only. But that was just classic media manipulation, and they released their first EP on Sonic Unyon before signing to Swedish imprint Bad Taste Records, ultimately finding their biggest fanbase on the lucrative European festival circuit.

The Deadly Snakes, meanwhile, found their way onto a hip American indie label. In 1999, they released their debut album, *Love Undone*, on prestigious Olympia, Washington, garage-rock imprint Sympathy for the Record Industry, by connecting with their hero Jack Oblivian of Memphis band the Oblivians.

The retro-rock revival hit the mainstream in the early 2000s with the White Stripes and the Strokes, but Danko Jones and the Deadly Snakes didn't really benefit from being ahead of the curve. After the turn of the millennium, Canadian indie music steered away from garage-punk primitivism and toward subgenres that had been considered uncool since the early nineties: shoegaze, dream-pop, space-rock, and twee indie-pop. But I'd argue that the Canadian collective-band craze of the early twenty-first century had its roots in another nineties music movement, and that's post-rock. Sprawling, cinematic instrumental music inspired by the boundlessness of electronica and rave music, the subgenre's pre-eminent Toronto export also made the leap across the pond: Do Make Say Think.

★

By the end of the nineties, electronic heads whose taste had evolved beyond the basic food groups of house, techno, and drum'n'bass were feeling alienated. Along with his friend Greg J. Smith a.k.a. DJ ether.mann, laptop musician Neil A. Wiernik, who ended up recording for Noise Factory in the early aughts as naw, started a night called clonk circa '98.

Smith & Wiernik (clonk): *We had a similar interest in what we called 'bleeding-edge' electronic music, outsider techno or the stuff that sat on the margins within the larger electronic music scene. We described this marginal music as 'post-rave music' – glitchy, dubby, minimal music. We felt this sound was not represented in Canada, never mind Toronto, but knew it was important and needed a venue. We decided to create a monthly club event that featured this music in an immersive space that would include visual art installations.*

Clonk booked respected international acts like Monolake and Rechenzentrum, Montreal heavy hitters Akufen and Deadbeat, and locals including Tomas Jirku, Mike Shannon, Blotto, and Zuzanna Grimm. Their main home base was Area 51, a bizarre basement bunker at King Street West and Portland, also home to like-minded nights like wabi. Though that stretch of King has since been swallowed up by the increasingly moneyed Entertainment District, back then it was still an outpost.

With Richmond Street commercialized and threatened by residential development, the more mainstream club scene also began to spread out to new corners and new formats. NASA Dance Pub was a fun, sci-fi themed lounge at Queen West and Bathurst where bona fide geeks could play vintage video games, sip on pints, and listen to house music. Likely Toronto's most popular dance genre, house had a more serious home at Industry, where DJs like Kenny Glasgow and Matt C held court. Opening up in '96, Industry was remote, on an empty, post-industrial strip on King Street West, at the edge of the pre-Liberty warehouse district. The more soulful side of the house scene could be felt at Roxy Blu, one of the warmer, cozier dance spots in the city, located near Adelaide and Spadina. Regular DJ nights there included Movement, Garage 416, and Hot Stepper's Bump N' Hustle.

Homegrown house music producers like Nick Holder exported the sound of Toronto to the rest of the world – his '99 collection *From Within* featured jazzy beats, African rhythms, and some nice Billie Holiday samples. Likewise, Toronto had begun to cultivate a local identity for jungle and drum'n'bass music, with DJ/producers like Mystical Influence cutting now-classic tracks like 'Dub-Plate Pressure.' Back in Clubland, d'n'b found a home at System Soundbar, which opened in 1999 at Peter Street and Richmond. System brought rave music into a controlled, nineteen-plus environment at a dark time for the rave community, after a handful of drug-related deaths brought unwanted media attention to the subculture – along with a police crackdown.

★

Back in the rock scene, in the summer of '98 College Street benefitted from the takeover of a former establishment stronghold. Dan Burke had attracted enough noise with his booking roster to get headhunted just shy of his first anniversary at Club Shanghai by the management of the El Mocambo. Though William New had kept the main floor alive for locals, the larger upstairs room was often dark, and the venue's finances had been shaky for years. After a blow-up with owner Shirley Wu, Burke bailed on the Shanghai. His first show at the El Mo promoted Atlanta garage-rock band the Subsonics, on June 30, 1998.

Burke: *On a Monday upstairs. People were terrified of doing shows upstairs. Anyway, it picked up speed, because I brought in people like the Brian Jonestown Massacre, from my time at Shanghai. It wasn't long before I was running the whole place.*

Burke was intent on returning the El Mo to its former glory, recalling the allure of its neon palm sign from his visits to Toronto as a youth. And as a real rock'n'roll believer, Burke couldn't pass up the chance to book the stage once graced by the actual Rolling Stones.

Burke: *I'm a Montrealer and I couldn't give a fuck about Toronto – back in the seventies, we were a way cooler city. I knew nothing about Toronto. The one thing I did know about Toronto was the fucking El Mocambo. The Stones, Maggie Trudeau, Keith Richards, Love You Live … Fuck, that's interesting.*

Burke had begun to perfect his booking model while at the Shanghai – digging deep into booking agents' rosters to take a chance on visiting acts that other local promoters and venues wouldn't touch. He knew how to hype things up in the press, and got the local papers covering legions of obscure acts like they were the Next Big Thing, including New York's Toilet Boys, Japan's Zoobombs, and Germany's Chicks on Speed.

And Burke was also business-savvy enough to bring a cash cow or two to the El Mo: DJ night Blow Up, running since 1994 at a series of ever-larger pubs and clubs, was right on top of the Brit-pop/mod revival. DJ/founder Davy Love capitalized on Toronto's Anglophilia, and soon the El Mocambo's upstairs was awash with Union Jacks, Fred Perry shirts, and miniskirts.

Burke's bold band bookings quickly built the El Mo's reputation – and finances – back up over '98/'99. William New was out in early 1999, ironically moving on to book Burke's original competitor, the Lion Club. The El Mo hosted a series of fundraising shows to relight its historic neon palm sign, raising $22,000 to create and erect a replica of the original, which was too damaged to safely hang over the Spadina sidewalk. Burke thought this might generate some excitement and stir Toronto out of its indie-crash apathy.

Burke: *Jim Eng [then-owner] came up to me and it was his idea: 'Do you think we could light the sign up?' And I said 'Oh, fuck yeah, brilliant!' And I thought, I can create shows around this. You know, get everybody on side, rally the troops. Not that people gave a fuck, which really ticked me off. People aren't so deep, they don't get the fucking depth of history. Nobody gives a fuck.*

Undeterred, Burke also began hosting an ever more ambitious series of mini-festivals at the club, starting with the Rock'n'Roll Landmark Series in August '98 and culminating in the Last Rock Show in December '99, headlined by Danko Jones and the Sadies.

I don't know if Dan knew how prophetic a name it would be.

With ever higher-profile bookings, Burke was making waves in the local club scene. At the time, he was determined to destroy the competition, primarily the Horseshoe Tavern but also pretty much the entire Queen West establishment.

Burke: *They were the enemy. I didn't like any of them. But that would be the same way I would be in hockey or baseball or football. They were my competitors. I was out to defeat them.*

Ironically, today the Horseshoe is one of Burke's regular venues, and he considers 'Shoe booker Craig Laskey one of his closest personal friends.

One high-profile Toronto band pulled in by Burke's passionate promotion was the Sadies. Led by brothers Dallas and Travis Good, with the whip-tight rhythm section of Sean Dean (ex–Phleg Camp) and Mike Belitsky, the Sadies were early adopters of the 'alt-country' movement that swept through

American indie music in the nineties. They released their debut album, *Precious Moments*, in 1998, on an American indie label, Bloodshot Records. The Sadies were another healthy indicator that Toronto indie artists were breaking through the invisible force field around the city. But the city was still holding some artists back.

I first saw Merrill Nisker cease to be Merrill and become Peaches at some point in 1999 at a show on the ground floor of the El Mo. But it was a shocking metamorphosis. 'Merrill Nisker' was a quirky indie-folk singer ... right? She'd played in an acoustic trio named Mermaid Café in the early nineties, and under her birth name, self-released an album in '95 called *Fancypants Hoodlum*, on which young Merrill deconstructed pop hits like 'Kung Fu Fighting' in a funk-rock style.

But shortly thereafter she started a garage-punk band called The Shit, along with friends including Jason Beck (who was also a Warner recording artist under the name Son), in which she began to test out some sex-positive lyrics. At Peaches' early gigs, Merrill played solo with just a Roland MC-505 Groovebox sequencer, rapping sex rhymes along with minimalist beats, occasionally strapping on a guitar for a more post-punk vibe. I fucking loved it.

Peaches and her crew had had enough of this city. Self-reinvention was in the air – Nisker borrowed the name Peaches from Nina Simone, and folkie Merrill was an instantly distant memory. Like Danko Jones, Peaches talked about sex, but through a lens of female empowerment that was revolutionary and refreshing. No one *anywhere* had heard a woman say 'fuck the pain away' in a song, and Peaches knew her message needed to be heard everywhere.

Released from his Warner contract, Jason Beck crossed the pond, moving to Paris and then settling in Berlin, reinventing himself as Gonzales and steering away from the stoic alt-rock of Son toward arch electro-lounge music, releasing critically acclaimed discs for über-cool German label Kitty-Yo starting in 2000. He now makes solo piano music for the upscale concert-hall set (and many a work-focus Spotify playlist) under the name Chilly Gonzales, now an esteemed senior artist in Germany.

Peaches and Gonzales succeeded in part by moving away from the standard 'band' model, instead creating a loose collective of independent solo artists, inspired more by the DIY self-reliance of electronica DJs than the gang mentality of rock music. Their extended crew included Taylor Savvy, Mocky, the World Provider, and Feist.

After moving to Toronto from Calgary, Leslie Feist began woodshedding her own songs, eventually self-releasing the beautiful indie-folk album *Monarch (Lay Your Jewelled Head Down)* in 1999, to a brief blast of local buzz. Though Feist the solo artist was more traditional in sound, she had an alter ego, Bitch LapLap, who guest-rapped on stage with Peaches. The two shared an apartment above the feminist sex shop Come As You Are on Queen West, where there was a pretty raging after-party in July 2000, when Peaches held her farewell to Toronto at Ted's Wrecking Yard as part of an early Wavelength series show. Peaches moved to Berlin, never looked back, and certainly never *moved* back.

Merrill Nisker (Peaches): *I've been in Toronto making music a long time, so what the fuck? If they like me there [Berlin], Canada will like me more.* (to Ben Rayner, *Toronto Star*, March 16, 2000)

Peaches and Gonzales brought sex and electro-rock swagger to Toronto before decamping to Berlin.

Feist eventually joined this exodus, relocating to Paris for the incubation of her second album, 2004's bossanova-infused *Let It Die*, which marked the massively successful relaunch of her solo career. One could read the Peaches/Gonzales crew's middle finger to Toronto as a repeat of the sixties flight of Neil, Joni, and the Band, though in setting their sights on continental Europe instead of the Anglospheric rock capitals of the US and UK, it seemed more like something out of the Jazz Age – Peaches took her name from Nina

Simone, after all. A giant transatlantic magnet for bohemians and artists, Berlin attracted others from Toronto, including electronic musicians Adam Marshall and Tomas Jirku.

What the exodus really represented was Toronto's creative artists turning their back on the Canadian music industry. Which had effectively turned its backs on them; the domestic majors could turn a profit off cookie-cutter modern rock acts, but they had no idea what to do with Peaches.

Adding to the sense of doom in the Canadian indie-music underground, Montreal-based distributor Cargo Records went bankrupt in January '97. Its failure was attributed to bad business practices as much as to the downturn in interest in guitar rock – this was still several years before MP3s gutted the music industry; physical distribution was still paramount. But the demise of Cargo ultimately opened up the field for new competitors like Sonic Unyon, Outside, and Fusion III to strengthen domestic music distribution.

And there were a few other signs of hope deep in the wintry Toronto underground: though Phil Klygo folded Skull Geek in late '97, holding a 'Burial' show at Club Shanghai, he teamed up with music biz veteran Mark DiPietro to launch a new indie label, Teenage USA. None of the Skull Geek roster followed, however – Slowgun, Smallmouth, and Secret Agent all called it quits in 1998. Pecola, meanwhile, decided to release their swan song, 1999's bluesier full-length *The Mexican*, on tiny Kosher Rock Records, run by Alex Lukashevsky, then of the band Fell Gang and later Deep Dark United. Pecola frontman Jamie Fleming fully indulged his blues id with his 2000s band catl.

For their initial roster, Teenage USA pivoted away from angry post-hard-core toward dreamier indie-pop and space-rock sounds. Mean Red Spiders and Neck were two of the label's first CD releases in 1998, and both discs benefitted from a massive, enveloping sound light years beyond the lo-fi recordings most of our peers had been outputting until then. These enhanced production values were the creation of a genius engineer named Dave Newfeld, who owned a studio called Stars and Sons, a few blocks down from the El Mocambo, where Teenage USA held many of its regular showcases.

Greg Chambers (Mean Red Spiders): *Dave Newfeld came out to a gig one night at the El Mo. He was the first person I met who used digital recording* *with Pro Tools. At the time, if you were a true recording artist, you recorded to tape, which I thought was pretty ridiculous considering the freedom digital gave you. We were already recording our first album, to tape, when I asked if he would be interested in recording us. I believe he had not really recorded a full band, before so it was something new for the both of us.*

Mean Red Spiders, sonically indebted to My Bloody Valentine and Stereolab as well as the psych/garage scene, were at the edge of the second wave of shoegaze, which, after being left for dead in Britain, was seeing an unexpected revival in North America and would heavily influence the sound of twenty-first-century indie music (Alvvays, Beach House, Tame Impala). Neck were also MBV-mad but applied their wall of sound more to punky, Buzzcocks- and Beach Boys–inspired speed-pop. They had been feverishly releasing indie tapes packed with home-recorded songs since '93 – making them Toronto's answer to Guided by Voices. Newfeld's meaty production made *Uncrated Distant Star* into an instant indie-rock classic. (Disclosure: I later joined Neck, then renamed Christiana, on bass from 2001 to '03.)

Dave Newfeld (Stars and Sons Studio): *It was an important experience working with MRS and Neck. There was a lot of excitement, youth, exuberance, and experimentation infused into the process.*

Newfeld's work on the MRS and Neck discs was ultimately a bit of fortuitous guinea-pigging – a chance to perfect the sonic techniques he'd deploy to considerable success four years later, on Broken Social Scene's 2002 break-through *You Forgot It in People*. The Spiders would name their second album, *Starsandsons*, after Newfeld's studio, and BSS would follow suit with a similarly named track on *YFIIP*.

Teenage USA also signed Elevator, Rick White's post–Eric's Trip band, which found him drawing heavily on psychedelic stoner-rock after relocating to Toronto. The label would find financial success with sugary pop-punk band the Weekend (who are the reason the Weeknd styles his name that way) and indie folk crew Great Lake Swimmers, who would follow Klygo to his new label, weewerk, in 2003.

Former Slowgun guitarist Liz Hysen started a new project, Picastro, performing her sombre, quiet songs on acoustic guitar and violin, joined by a rotating cast of collaborators, making Picastro a predecessor to indie music's 'bandonym' craze – a phrase coined by Toronto *Globe and Mail* critic Carl

Wilson. With most of her like-minded 'slowcore' peers coming from south of the border, Hysen began inviting artists like Elliott Smith and Smog to town to share bills with Picastro.

Liz Hysen (Picastro): *No one was bringing in bands from Drag City or Kranky Records or that scene. I felt completely isolated as a person making quiet music in this city, so I had to bring in musicians that I wanted to see in person.*

Most memorably, Hysen shared a bill with future indie superstar Cat Power (a.k.a. Chan Marshall) in 1997 at the Cameron House, for a crowd of less than fifty. Picastro finally released their debut album, *Red Your Blues*, in 2002. They became an international cult phenomenon but are still mostly forgotten at home, despite the long-term membership of award-winning composer/violinist Owen Pallett. I suppose Canadians aren't that cool with being sad.

Ted's Wrecking Yard wasn't really much of a venue for its first year. It had a cool, unpretentious vibe, but Ted seemed to book the same three bands over and over again. He needed help, and thankfully he knew it. And it came along at just the right time.

Space-rockers Mean Red Spiders were part of the second wave of shoegaze in the late nineties.

In mid-1998, Yvonne Matsell found herself a free agent when the owner of the Big Bop decided he didn't need the help of a booker. The weekly papers deemed this regime-change newsworthy.

Matsell: *As soon as the press wrote about me leaving, I got a call from Ted. I went to meet with him and we hit it off. The room was upstairs and quite dingy. I got Ted to change the PA with my sound guy's help. I always kept on a bunch of great sound techs, who were willing to follow me wherever I went, as they knew they'd be mixing good bands.*

Suddenly, Ted's Wrecking Yard was the best-sounding small room in the city. It was also the coolest-*looking*: black walls with tire tracks painted across them, a bar that was a rough-cut slab of granite, candles on tables. Not yet plastered in band stickers or ugly beer ads like most rock clubs, it felt downright *classy* in comparison. I still get defensive when anyone reminisces about what a dive Ted's was.

Matsell: *We had a real gritty feel in that room, which the majority of people felt quite comfortable in. Only one of the two washrooms worked ... the bartenders also loved music and seemed to add to the ambiance. A great group of people worked there. Ted Footman was a total character. I loved him as a person, though he drove me insane at the same time. I banned him from his own club for a month for disrupting one of the shows when he was really drunk!*

Yvonne brought along her hefty Rolodex, and her bookings showcased the wave of indie singer/songwriters that Toronto continued to champion in the decade since roots-rock first conquered the club scene: Sarah Slean, Mia Sheard, Andy Stochansky, Jason Collett, Ottawa's Kathleen Edwards. And there was the occasional rock show at Ted's Wrecking Yard in '98/'99, including a very fun Deadly Snakes / Dodge Fiasco show promoted by *Eye Weekly*.

My role at *Eye* continued to expand my horizons. Through assembling the club and concert listings, I got exposed to a wider world of music beyond indie guitar rock. I danced to drum'n'bass and had my face melted by electro-experimentalists Pan Sonic at We'ave. I experienced the deafening silence of free improvised music at the Ulterior series at the Victory Cafe and CCMC's Tuesday nights at the Music Gallery. I checked out local hip-hop emcees like Eternia and Mindbender at the Comfort Zone, below the Silver Dollar. I lined up for fire-hazard warehouse raves and saw legends like the Jungle Brothers and the X-Ecutioners up close. I watched Sook-Yin Lee play toy instruments and the Rust Brothers cut up records at *Exclaim!* parties.

At the tail end of the nineties, the sense of collectivism and mutual support was heartening, given how cutthroat and competitive the music business could be. The DIY spirit was alive and well.

Artists in the electronic sphere were starting their own record labels and making things happen for themselves, like electro-pop/IDM (intelligent dance music) artists Solvent and Lowfish and their Suction Records imprint, or the collective of techno/breaks artists that co-founded Public Transit Recordings. There was also the *Trails of Smoke* compilation, released in '98 by a collective of global beat crews including Excalceolators and Combustion Lente.

Small World Music began presenting concerts in 1997, becoming the backbone of the global music community in Toronto, a town that likes to brag about its cultural diversity but doesn't always reflect that on its stages. Toronto's Latin music scene was on fire as well, with groups like Cuban *son* players Klavé Y Kongo packing places like Portuguese bar Cervejaria, at College and Ossington, and DJ Alvaro C (formerly of Project 9) running Mambo Urbano Wednesdays at the Rivoli, later expanding it to a full horn-and-percussion band, the Mambo Urbano Orchestra.

Global grooves came to the dance floor at the Movement parties at the Rivoli and Roxy Blu, started up in '98 by a collective of vinyl nerds from diverse backgrounds – Aki, Dee Jay Nav, Jason Palma, John Kong, and A Man Called Warwick – who didn't want to be relegated to background lounge music. With strength in numbers, the Movement crew pooled their considerable (and considerably deep) record collections to play music no one else was playing, and packed out clubs with crowds that reflected Toronto's diversifying demographics.

Other new, long-overdue nights started up, like the Ambient Ping, the live ambient/electronic/soundscape series that got going in '99 as a weekly Tuesday night at various spots in Kensington Market. Those venues are all now gone, but the Ping is still a thing, likely Toronto's longest-running music series.

By 1999, the city and its music scene had grown so much that we were on the cusp of a true independent music renaissance – and the volume of quality records released just that year reflect that: Da Grassroots' *Passage Through Time*; crucial second-wave rap discs like Choclair's *Ice Cold* and

Saukrates's *The Underground Tapes*; bedroom popster Jim Guthrie's debut *A Thousand Songs*; Leslie Feist's solo indie-folk debut *Monarch*; and post-punkers Parts Unknown's *Airshow*, among others.

Looking over this list makes me nostalgic, not because the music was better back then, but because people actually *bought* these records. At the time, the industry was worried about people burning CDs. Ultimately, it brought its destruction upon itself. In 1999, Napster was set loose upon the Internet, and the digital genie was let out of the bottle. Music was free, it was suddenly easy to share and promote, anyone could find out about any band or any record made anywhere in any time – and musicians would no longer get paid. Not off their records, at least.

Back in the early nineties, techno-pessimists predicted the Internet would keep us all isolated in our bedrooms. In the twenty-first century, the opposite happened: people longed to be together. And in music, across all genres, the most important thing – or at least your biggest moneymaker – became your live show. With so many places to see and hear live music, Toronto went into Y2K with a huge lead.

DA GRASSROOTS / LAL
Let's Just Create Our Own World
1991–

Da Grassroots.

What makes Toronto a great place to make music? Until recently, affordability seemed to be the biggest factor, followed closely by walkability and cultural diversity. But I don't think you can disqualify the density and quality of our record stores. In North America, Toronto may be second only to New York for crate-digging. In the nineties, vinyl was thought dead after the CD took hold, but quickly became both the conduit to underground credibility and the transmission source for new musical ideas, through DJ culture and the sampling revolution.

In Toronto, record stores like Play De Record and Starsound became hubs for the hip-hop scene; for electronic music, it was Eastern Bloc or Traxx. For old rock and soul records, you went to the Vinyl Museum or Driftwood; for jazz or indie stuff, it was Vortex Records or She Said Boom. Before streaming algorithms chose your new favourite band for you, you'd walk into Rotate This and ask the staff what was hot. DJs and musicians worked behind the counter.

Record shops allowed Toronto's music-makers to expand their minds and widen their influences – and in the case of Da Grassroots, it's where they dug up the raw materials for their sound.

Da Grassroots were the sonic heart of Toronto hip-hop's second wave, which brought hip-hop back from major-label boardrooms to the apartment buildings and high-school steps of the suburban neighbourhoods where it originated – Rexdale, Scarborough, Jane and Finch, Brampton. (For a window into this era, check out the 1994 documentary *Make Some Noise* – which features a freestyle rap from none other than a visiting Mos Def.)

Nicholas Murray (Da Grassroots, LAL): We were all crate diggers. We would scour record stores and our parents' collections. The generation before us kind of embraced that – but we *really* embraced it and took it to another level.

Da Grassroots released only one album, but it's considered one of the city's essential hip-hop records. You can't find it anywhere, unless you want to shell out two hundred dollars on Discogs, but you can listen to the whole double album on YouTube. The twin boogeymen of sample clearance and the collector's market have only increased its mystique over the two decades since its release in December 1999. *Passage Through Time* was a prophetic title.

Nicholas Murray, a.k.a. Murr, a.k.a. Calibre, is the link between Da Grassroots and LAL, as a member of both groups. While Da Grassroots were rising up from the underground circa '94, Murray met his future life and creative partner, Rosina Kazi, vocalist in LAL. They worked together at a record store, naturally: in the dance department of the HMV Superstore on Yonge Street, known as the Bassment. Both resided in Brampton, but their worlds already revolved around downtown and its access to record shops. Like most suburban youth, they'd been coming downtown on the bus since Grade 6.

Born in Barbados, Murray moved to Canada at age six, his family first settling in Scarborough, then Rexdale, then finally Brampton – the municipality northwest of the city that's home to the country's largest South Asian community. Murray got into hip-hop through listening to Ron Nelson on CKLN as a kid, and first heard electronic dance music by going to 23 Hop with his older brother. He started experimenting with turntablism together with a Rexdale-based friend, Howard Nicholson, a.k.a. Born Swiff.

NM: At some point, my brother bought a Roland s-330 sampler and we would sneak into his room while he was at work and make beats.

Connecting with an emcee named Mr. Roam, the pair started a group named Born to Roam. They worked with a producer who would soon become a mentor to them and the next generation of local hip-hoppers, and eventually a Toronto music legend: Noel Campbell, a.k.a. Gadget, who in the 2010s produced Grammy-winning records for Drake and his OVO Sound label.

Around this time, Murray and Swiff met the third member of what would become Da Grassroots – Roger Perryman, a.k.a. Mr. Attic, from Jane and Finch, who got his moniker from a neighbour who teased him for keeping his substantial vinyl collection upstairs in his bedroom.

NM: Initially we started recording music at Howard's apartment at Finch and Islington, where he lived with his mother and his two sisters. But then we started recording music with Gadget in the basement of Trebas.

Trebas Institute, a private post-secondary college aimed at aspiring entertainment industry professionals, had a few recording studios at its original location near Queen and Parliament, which became a hub for Toronto's hip-hop community in the nineties. Out of these sessions came 'the' Grassroots' first twelve-inch, *Drama / Living Underwater*, featuring rapper Elemental, released in 1995 on their own DIY label, Black Employed Records. It hadn't occurred to the group that they could just go press it themselves – until Gadget suggested it.

Born Swiff: Everything was brand new in terms of that mentality, because it was the simplest idea, but it seemed so foreign. So Gadget says, 'Yeah, you can just go to the pressing plant, press it up yourself, make a label.' So Attic looks at me, I look and him, and say, 'Yo, it's income tax time, I got a G-note comin' in!' (to *Views Before the 6* podcast, 2018)

Consigning their first run at Play De Record, they quickly had to do a second pressing. The record started generating interest in the US and Japan, with Swiff doing international business through the fax machine next to his bed. It also led to some unwanted attention: a cease-and-desist from an identically named rock band; a blessing in disguise, as it resulted in the group styling their name as the more distinctive 'Da' Grassroots.

Over the next few years, Da Grassroots would keep making tracks in the Trebas basement, hanging out until four a.m., with a rotating crew of guest emcees: k-os, Thrust, Arcee, Choclair, Saukrates; old friends Ghetto Concept, Mr. Roam, and Elemental. It became something of a community drop-in.

NM: People just came through and started recording. It was only after a while that we were like, 'Hey, we should probably do something with this stuff.' It wasn't our intention at the beginning to make a record.

The group members didn't share an equal level of enthusiasm for running a label on top of making beats, and they began to seek out a bigger platform. Mr. Attic had a connection with a Seattle-based underground hip-hop label, Conception Records – who jumped on the demo they sent. An hour-long double vinyl opus, *Passage Through Time* was released in December 1999 to immediate critical acclaim. It was clear that this was an album with a uniquely communitarian approach.

Rosina Kazi (LAL): It was the first album that brought together a lot of different emcees from that time like that. You didn't really see that, people were pretty camped out.

NM: It was pretty special in that way. It brought everybody together.

Passage Through Time's classic jazz-album artwork also explains some of its crossover appeal. In spite of the opportunity to reach a wider audience, however, the group maintained a low profile. They only played a handful of live shows to promote the release, including an incredible March 2000 *Exclaim!* party set at Reverb. Their debut ended up being their denouement.

NM: A lot of the sentiment after the record was, 'Why aren't we doing better?' We've won Junos, there's people that haven't won Junos that are doing better than us. We didn't really understand the whole 'you have to perform, you have to tour' thing. We were just a bunch of crate diggers that had a random amount of rappers around us – not to say that wasn't powerful, but there was just no scene for it.

The prohibitive cost of sample clearance partly explains why Da Grassroots never followed up *Passage Through Time* – and why the album itself has never been reissued, in spite of continually growing demand. But another factor is that, within a year of its release, Nic Murray was busy with another musical project: LAL.

RK: We were hanging out so much that we fell in love. We'd be going back and forth to Brampton and it just happened organically. And then I lived downtown because I was at university and he wouldn't leave. I was like, 'Either pay rent or get out of here!'

Rosina Kazi had been singing since she was a kid coming up in Brampton. Working in the Bassment at HMV blew open her musical horizons. One of her earliest champions was Born Swiff. Getting involved in the local R&B/hip-hop scene, she helped organize the Honey Jam, an acclaimed showcase for women artists founded by promoter and writer Ebonnie Rowe, where she performed her first solo show – on the same night that Nelly Furtado was discovered.

RK: I had gotten an Ensoniq -10 via my father – and my father never bought me shit. But I kind of begged him to buy me a sampler. So then I started producing, and then Nic and other people would show up and produce on it.

Through university friends, Kazi made friends with Kevin Moon a.k.a. Moonstarr, and Mano Narayanan, who were running the uber-DIY, Toronto-centric electronic music label Public Transit Recordings. Kazi gave one of her early recordings to Moonstarr, who included it on PTR's first release, the *Code:416* compilation, under the artist name Rosina.

RK: As soon as I met Kevin, I was like, who is this? He reminded me of Nic so much, but from an electronic sort of music place. And I dragged Nic over that same day. 'You need to meet this guy.' And then they went into a room and nerded out for hours, while I sat outside.

Having access to Moonstarr's synth collection opened Murray's eyes to new sonic possibilities – as did access to other new cultural inputs, now that the couple was cohabiting on Borden Avenue, right on the doorstep of Kensington Market.

NM: Now that I'd moved downtown, it was in overdrive because I had access to record stores all over me. It was just like, 'Whaaaat?' I was buying records all the time, to a fault, actually, before food sometimes. It was just madness. Since I didn't have to go home to Brampton with these records, I could just literally go to She Said Boom, buy a record, and go around the corner and make a beat. I was living the dream, so I was very prolific at that point.

At first Murray was reluctant, but eventually Kazi cajoled him into making tracks with her. The new project was a bit of a departure from his hip-hop roots – downtempo beats, burbling synths, dubby basslines, and soulful, questing vocals speaking out against social injustice. After a long gestation, LAL feted the release of their debut album *Corners* in November 2000 at Lee's Palace.

RK: *Corners* had this dub thing, this trip-hop thing. But I was also influenced by Asian Underground music at that time. So that's a whole other thing, the first time I had heard a South Asian influence over really progressive, electronic stuff. When we started making music, there was this interesting attempt to bring all those worlds together.

LAL.

Though veena and harmonium appear on a few tracks, the influence of traditional Indian music is minimal on *Corners*. It's a subtle record, one that reveals itself layer by layer – a chill streetcar ride through a slowly evolving Toronto cityscape. The South Asian influence came more to the forefront on later records, after LAL began to incorporate more live musicians, such as bassist Ian de Sousa, drummer Rakesh Tewari, and guitarist Nilan Perera, and spending more time visiting India to connect with Kazi's family roots – and Murray's; though his parents are Bajan, his grandfather was from Bombay.

RK: I think because my personality was so huge, the South Asian influence was what got focused on. But Nic's Blackness was very much erased in some ways.

NM: But that's how the grant was filled out.

LAL remain active twenty years after the release of *Corners*. In 2018 they released their fifth album, *Dark Beings* – their first to be nominated for the

Polaris Music Prize. Over the years, their work became more socially engaged and activist-oriented. They reside together in a loft space on Sterling Road, a former industrial strip that's rapidly gentrifying, where they run a community space called Unit 2. The space hosts various inclusive and accessible events, such as the Bricks and Glitter Festival, aimed at supporting queer youth, BIPOC, and other marginalized groups. Kazi and Murray are considered mentors by the next generation of artists, who rightfully look up to them for walking the walk for so long.

RK: So much of my perspective and how I deal in community came so much from the early hip-hop and R&B and electronic music communities. But also tapping into the indie-rock community, working at the Women's Bookstore for a long time – and queer culture, which is fully DIY in so many ways. And we're losing it. The city is just drastically losing space and artists. I used to be frustrated and angry and bitter. But I'm no longer like that. I can either choose to hold on to that shit and die being like that, or I can be like, fuck it, let's just create our own world.

THE FIRST WAVELENGTH: BEGINNINGS AT THE ENDS 1999-2001

The author co-founds the artist-run Wavelength collective to celebrate the diversity of underground music, helping transform Toronto music at the start of the millennium, alongside a handful of other new institutions – while other eras come to an end in a rapidly changing city.

The rays blazed down and a lot of indie-rockers got a sunburn that afternoon. Okay, not a *lot*, probably a dozen. The first and only Harmony Picnic took over Cherry Beach for the afternoon of July 24, 1999. My old university friend and occasional bandmate Duncan MacDonell had the idea of staging an all-day festival down by the lake, at one of the prettiest, most forgotten spots in the city. We musicians spent our lives trudging concrete sidewalks to get to smoky clubs, seemingly unaware of the fact that Toronto is on a big body of water.

Duncan had the idea of 'taking it to the people' and staging a ten-band music festival down at the beach. He intentionally chose a name that would fly under the radar as a 'family-friendly' event. But instead of doing it guerrilla-style and getting shut down, he complied with the red-tape-mad City of Toronto and spent his own money on permits, insurance, and renting a generator. Someone lent us a sound system. All the bands played for free, for the love – and the experience.

Duncan MacDonell (a.k.a. Doc Pickles): *I wanted to do something nobody had ever done before. The people at City Hall were bewildered that I was trying to put on live music but didn't have any plans to make money. I was prepared to spend my own savings to make it happen. There were to be no alcohol permits,* *no merchandise sales, no admission of any kind. Police came by the day of the show and carefully inspected the permit.*

The bands that played the Harmony Picnic were made up mostly of 'our scene' going back to *Leisure Terrorists* – and we mostly played for each other. The show was fun, a beach party plus bands. If it had happened today, it would have been a pop-up marketing activation. Instead, it was all about community. It didn't 'introduce the next wave of Toronto bands you are going to fall in love with!!!' or any other lofty goal. What it did do was solidify a sense of camaraderie among our little group.

Decoy were one of ten local bands that played the Harmony Picnic at Cherry Beach in 1999.

February 13, 2000, was a much darker and colder night. My strongest memory is our panic to get the first issue of the *Wavelength* zine off the photocopier at Kinko's on Bloor in the Annex and down to the venue on College Street in Little Italy in time for doors. Somehow, we made it.

That night, our recently formed collective, Wavelength, launched our monthly print zine along with our weekly Sunday night pay-what-you-can concert series. Mean Red Spiders and Neck were the first bands to perform at the very first Wavelength show at Ted's Wrecking Yard. The series is now closing in on its 800th edition. Most of the Harmony Picnic bands had members at the first planning meeting for Wavelength, which took place

September 13, 1999, at the Green Room at the Annex. After Cherry Beach, Alex Durlak (from the Connoisseurs) and I had got drunk on my porch and decided, 'We need to form a collective!' (Alex now co-owns Idée Fixe Records, who have released brilliant albums by Jennifer Castle and the Cosmic Range.)

In some ways, the whole Wavelength project was an act of problem-solving: How would we get Toronto independent music out of that same old trap, that familiar old plateau or force field? Bands like Neck were beloved in our circle of friends/bands, but it was frustrating to see them fail to garner more widespread renown, despite a slew of releases packed with great songs. The mythological arc of Guided by Voices – the underground band that did it for the love, in isolation, for years, until *one day* the press and the industry discovered them – always seemed to elude Toronto bands, and it was becoming mildly infuriating. We had to make that 'one day' happen ourselves.

But it wasn't just about our bands. We debated this at length: was it going to be about promoting 'our circle' or expanding our circles to include the rest of the music scene? Diversity was a guiding principle from the start. Why not book a free-jazz trio alongside an ambient electronic project, or a hip-hop emcee alongside a punk band? By match-making groups from different corners of the scene that didn't know each other, we helped enlarge that scene and build bridges between disconnected parts of the community in the days before social media.

There was so much to champion in the Toronto underground. Minesh Mandoda and Derek Westerholm (then both of Parts Unknown) were hosting *No Beat Radio* on CIUT and hearing all kinds of amazing yet obscure music coming out of the city's bedrooms and basements – the FemBots, Zebradonk, Headphone Overtone … the list was huge.

The Internet was still very new. Everyone was amped up by the promise of it, but it hadn't delivered yet. You could go online and read about new bands, for example, but you couldn't *hear* them there yet, unless you were a Napster whiz. Websites were making it easier to access information, and email was allowing people to stay more effortlessly connected. This created a hunger for new experiences, new creative expression, and new modes of discovery. But social media – addictive, toxic, and all-consuming – was still half a decade away.

So we started a monthly zine, as well as a basic website. The *Wavelength* zine functioned as the program guide for our weekly live music series, featuring interviews with the bands that played – which we could do via email, a new time-saving prospect – as well as music scene news, poetry, comics, and other fanzine fare. The zine lasted in print only until 2005, so today Wavelength is now better known as a concert series. But in the early days, zine and series were of equal importance. It was essential to us to document the ground-level happenings in the music community.

Our weekly show series aimed to fill the hole left by Sedated Sundays and Elvis Mondays, both of which had by then been booted from the El Mocambo. We chose Sundays – a night of the week generally free of competition – and adopted the format of a night called ° ('Degrees') that two of our co-founders, Greg Chambers and Minesh Mandoda, had briefly run at the Lion Club in '99: two bands and a DJ.

The question was, where would we hold it? I'd built up a rapport with Yvonne Matsell from adding her show listings to *Eye* every week, and I knew her folk-music weekly on Sundays was coming to a close. I suggested Ted's Wrecking Yard to the brand-new Wavelength crew and pitched it to Yvonne, and she was into the idea.

The first few weeks of Wavelength started slowly, with maybe thirty or forty people at WL #1, but it grew steadily Sunday after Sunday. By WL #5, with Parts Unknown alongside all-female garage-rock band the Hassle and guest DJ Solvent of Suction Records notoriety, we had a healthy-sized crowd. A positive buzz slowly built – though there were plenty of dead nights in the early days.

The city had grown since the encouragement of downtown residential development, and it was starting to feel less like a small 'town disguised as a city,' to quote Kat Rocket. With so many more people living downtown and working in the growing cultural industries, there was a potential audience, and we just had to let them know that this community existed. The social element was just as important as the musical element. We didn't want to be gatekeepers, we wanted to 'take it to the people.' Independent music didn't have to be a snobby secret society. Wavelength was, in many ways, aimed at the casual music listener who *wasn't* in a band or part of the scene. It was intended to be a friendly space where everyone felt welcome. In hindsight, though, as a predominantly white, heterosexual, male, settler-run collective, we didn't yet have the sophistication to think more about the experience of women, queer people, and BIPOC.

We also made our series Pay What You Can (PWYC), with the idea that no one would be turned away. We paid the bands from the door take, and sometimes they'd get better paid than at shows with the standard $5 cover, The vibe also benefitted from the addition of General Chaos Visuals (a.k.a. Stephen Lindsey and Eric Siegerman), who had been doing hand-painted, psychedelic, 'analog' projections for Mean Red Spiders and the Ambient Ping. Their light shows instilled a sense of radiant calm in the crowd.

Starting our new enterprise at the start of the new millennium felt very fitting. Change was in the air, and the formerly apathetic Gen-X was founding all kinds of new institutions. Artscape had opened the Gibraltar Point Centre for the Arts on Toronto Island. Community-minded Three Gut Records started up after its first release, by Jim Guthrie, came out in '99, and the Hidden Cameras – more participatory art collective than band – played their first show. Indie-rock activist Dave Meslin (who played with the Cameras) and cartoonist Matt Blackett co-founded the Toronto Public Space Committee, later spawning *Spacing Magazine*. Author Sheila Heti launched the 'non-expert' barroom lecture series Trampoline Hall. We were lucky to be in the right place at the right time, and to be part of what turned out to be the beginning of a new cultural 'renaissance' in Toronto.

Will Munro, a visual artist and hardcore punk kid who had volunteered at Who's Emma? and had been introduced to Dan Burke through members of the Deadly Snakes, had come up with the idea of doing a queer-oriented rock'n'roll DJ night as an alternative to the dominance of house and disco on the LGBTQ+ dance floor, and bring back some of the anything-goes spirit of Dyke Nite at the Boom Boom Room.

Munro was intrigued by the El Mocambo and its sleazy rock-club legacy. Burke was skeptical at first – he didn't think the queer crowd would venture past the Village – but he gave them a Friday night. The first Vaseline party took place January 28, 2000. The night was revelatory and revolutionary. People of all different orientations came together and danced to Sonic Youth and Joan Jett. Some danced on the pool tables. The night exceeded Burke's low bar-sales expectations, and Vaseline became a monthly at the El Mo. A year later, after a cease-and-desist from the lube's manufacturer, it had to change its name to Vazaleen.

THREE GUT RECORDS

One afternoon in the spring of 2000, strolling down 'Classic' Queen West near the MuchMusic building, I spotted Tyler Clark Burke, a graphic designer at *Eye*, with singer/songwriter Leslie Feist. The two women appeared to be stringing a clothesline between two skinny trees on the sidewalk. 'What are you guys doing?' I said. 'Oh hey, we're promoting a show,' said Tyler.

That show was coming up on April 22, a Saturday night, at Ted's Wrecking Yard, Wavelength's Sunday night home. One of the most exciting things happening at the club was the crossover with Three Gut Records, the label Burke had recently helped bring into the world. All the Three Gut bands played Wavelength at one point or another, and they were always amazing nights. The show promoted with the clothesline was co-headlined by Feist and the label's newest act, Aaron Riches & the Royal City All-Stars. And Burke's promotion strategies were far from the usual.

Tyler Clark Burke (Three Gut Records): I would print 500 posters with just an image, no details, and we would blanket the city. A week later, we'd cover all those images with nearly identical graphics, except the second round had all the details for the show. I made up a fake romance in *Now*'s 'Missed

Miss Barbrafisch (Vaseline DJ): *Vaseline was our fantasy event that actually materialized. It was rockers, punks, metalheads, and misfits, weirdos of all stripes and genders. It was inherently informed by the identity politics of the '90s, but without the anger. Vaseline was positivity and perversion and great music and great people.* (to Denise Benson, *Then and Now*, 2015)

Will began DJing at the third Vaseline, soon adding Super-8 films brought in by artists like Scott Miller Berry, as well as live acts. Peaches performed at Vaseline in June 2000, at one of her last shows before splitting for Berlin, while she was in the process of recording her debut album, *The Teaches of Peaches*.

Peaches: *I'd been performing as Peaches for about six months before I played that Vaseline. I remember thinking, when I was making my album, about how the queer scene and rock scene and electro scene didn't really get together. And when I was making that music, it seemed like the quintessential, perfect representation of Vaseline in 2000.* (to Sarah Liss, *Army of Lovers*, 2013)

Connections' personals that built up for weeks to reveal the next show. And when I met Leslie, I came up with Project Envelope. This was when things really took off. I printed small show invites, put them in hundreds of envelopes, stamped 'OPEN ME' on the outside, and strung

Guelph's anthemic rockers the Constantines signed to Three Gut Records after playing Wavelength at Ted's Wrecking Yard in 2001.

them all over the city. I was strategic, though. I hit media, record stores, and offices known to contain music industry-ish people. I think within three days we had a lawyer and distribution.

The Ted's show was packed, and it was wild to see a room full of rapt people sitting down, listening intently to such quiet music. Leslie Feist was an incredibly delicate performer in those days, and Aaron Riches was a heartfelt folkie with a deep social conscience. Coming out of the DIY hardcore scene in

At the March 30, 2001, Vaseline, another Toronto band played their fourth-ever gig. The Hidden Cameras was the brainchild of Joel Gibb, a zinester and bedroom singer/songwriter from Mississauga, who in 2000 self-released a gorgeous, heart-stirring collection of lo-fi, glockenspiel-laden indie-pop entitled *Ecce Homo*, amazingly homemade on a four-track. The Hidden Cameras' very first gig took place December 28, 2000, at West Wing Art Space, a gallery way out in Parkdale.

Joanne Huffa (writer, zine-maker): *I met Joel when he was a teenager selling his zine,* Glamour Guide for Trash, *outside of a Toronto radio station. He was an eager, hilarious, opinionated kid – I adored him. Years later, he channelled all that brashness into the Hidden Cameras. Their first show was pure joy, the kind that wasn't easy to find in the city in those days. The West Wing Art Space was also an exciting venue, mostly because it was run by young artists. It's not overselling it to say that those early Hidden Cameras shows united all the Queen Street queer folks, art makers, and weirdos.*

Guelph, Ontario, he had released two solo albums on DROG (Dave's Records of Guelph) and finished his third, a collaboration with a fellow Guelphite, bedroom-recording boffin Jim Guthrie.

It's with Guthrie, and Guelph, that the Three Gut story begins. A group of exiles from the adorable college town west of the city – including Guthrie, Riches, Burke, and members of Guelph's then-best-known indie-music export, King Cobb Steelie – moved into a shared house in Toronto, just steps from MuchMusic and Queen Street. In 1999, Guthrie asked Burke if she would help him design the cover for his first solo album, *A Thousand Songs*.

Burke: He told me he wanted to come up with a name for a fake record label for the back, but he wasn't sure what to call it. He kept telling me funny stories as we worked, including that he used to be called Jim Three-Gut (an inversion of sorts of Guthrie), and we both realized *that was the name*. And for some reason, I decided to spend the next day making an elaborate logo for his fake record label, and when I showed it to Aaron, he got so excited. We became a label with a logo, some bands, no money, and no records.

Guthrie's *A Thousand Songs* became the first Three Gut record, its release celebrated August 23, 1999, at the Rivoli, along with Leslie Feist's *Monarch*. Though Feist never released anything on Three Gut, she was a close friend and supporter of the label, and joined Riches on stage as a band member when he decided his solo project would become a group. Though the original tapes for Riches's new album were destroyed, the re-recorded album

In addition to art galleries in deepest Parkdale, some of the earliest Hidden Cameras shows took place in churches, like the Church at Berkeley and Church of the Redeemer. In a city with a live music scene so long dominated by bar culture, this was lofty – and revolutionary. The Hidden Cameras kicked off the trend toward 'alternative venues' in the 2000s.

Churches also suited the Hidden Cameras' reverberant, consonant pop sound. Gibb has an affecting baritone, and his lyrics swung from wry observations on queer identity and religious faith to ecstatic, optimistic declarations like 'I Believe in the Good of Life.' This, combined with the band's extravagant stage shows, which included masked shirtless young male go-go dancers – making for a wonderful dissonance within a place of worship – led to the description 'gay church folk music,' a lazy bit of journalistic shorthand that became the second Three Gut release, *At Rush Hour the Cars* by Royal City, in August 2000.

Though it drew on elements of folk and country, Royal City wasn't roots-rock. It was a new kind of indie music that drew on folk forms and was quiet, intimate, even ambient – but it could also explode. Their cover of Iggy Pop's 'Success' (as 'Here Comes Success'), with its call-and-response group vocals and Riches's voice rising to a scream at the end, helped set the template for the collective indie-rock later perfected by the Arcade Fire.

Though they put out quiet music, Three Gut threw raging parties, such as the near-legendary 'The Aliens Have Landed' party, in which thousands of people walked through the loft space Burke shared with other visual artists, waiting for a giant UFO to land in the middle of the courtyard of the warehouse complex on Portland Street (now demolished for condos).

Burke: Our resources were quite limited at first at Three Gut, and while other bands wanted us to sign them, we didn't really have much – initially – to offer beyond a lot of love and a home-cooked spaghetti dinner.

Spaghetti helped sign the Constantines, the Guelph/Toronto post-hardcore quartet who helped make Springsteen a cool influence again with their blue-collar punk anthems. The Cons' critical championing by Stuart Berman in *Eye Weekly* helped create a massive buzz that brought the band to Sub Pop Records – and things really took off for Three Gut in 2001. Lovely records by Gentleman Reg, Cuff the Duke, and Brooklyn's Oneida were to come.

has followed them ever since.

Another 2000 bedroom-based indie-pop release that made waves was *The Method of Modern Love*, by the Russian Futurists, a.k.a. Matthew Hart, who was just as influenced by the Magnetic Fields as he was by hip-hop. Hart combined cascading Casio synth lines and winsome vocals with blunted or bouncy beats to memorable effect. He deserves more credit for being one of the few artists to have successfully combined the three major pop music movements of the modern age: indie-rock, hip-hop, and electronica. Members of Hart's live band went on to play with Manitoba, a.k.a. Caribou, now one of Ontario's most beloved electronic music exports.

But while some brave new eras were beginning, others were coming to an end.

Indie-pop collective the Hidden Cameras turned Toronto concerts into joyous celebrations in the early 2000s.

August 1, 2000. While shrill breakbeats blasted over a mobile PA, a group of shirtless, big-panted teen boys ran grinning into the fountain. Within minutes, hundreds of kids were wade-dancing beneath the arches. It was the only bad behaviour of the day, as far as anyone could tell. Between 15,000 and 20,000 partiers had congregated at Nathan Phillips Square to send a message to City Hall: dancing is not a crime.

The iDance Rally was organized the Toronto Dance Safety Committee, an activist organization struck in response to a crisis within the rave community. It was a true gathering of tribes amongst rave music's fractured subgenres. Tough junglists danced alongside colourful candy ravers and listened to speeches by sympathetic politicians, including councillor Olivia Chow, who had become dance music's biggest civic champion. Star DJs like Derrick Carter and Miss Honey Dijon had travelled in from the US at their own expense to spin for the crowd at the free party/protest.

iDance was scheduled on the eve of an important vote. Earlier that year, Toronto city council had enacted a ban on raves on City property – as well as any party playing loud music past three a.m. – after a police raid of a legal rave at the CNE resulted in mass arrests. Police chief Julian Fantino and Mayor Mel whipped up a sixties-Yorkville-worthy moral panic in the press.

Public concern was amplified by the ecstasy-related death of Ryerson student Allen Ho at a rave the previous fall. Ho's was the third E-related death in Ontario in the previous year, and the first to provoke a public inquiry, the results of which were anxiously awaited by the rave community, which had gone into 'a tailspin of pessimistic self-examination' over the safety of its events, according to Ben Rayner, who was not just the *Toronto Star*'s new pop music critic but also a certified raver himself. Despite the authorities' bellicose rhetoric, the Ho inquest agreed with the recommendations of the Dance Safety Committee: fund drug education and require event promoters to meet minimum safety requirements, such as free water and ventilation.

The iDance Rally was a success, and city council voted fifty to four in favour of overturning the civic rave ban. But the downside was that the new safety regulations required rave promoters to hire a hefty number of paid duty police. This had the ironic effect of driving some raves further underground, due to expensive and buzz-killing security compliance, while others were forced out of business entirely. Many viewed the events of 1999–2000 as the end of the innocence for the rave scene, as electronic dance music was shoved back into licenced nightclubs. As an alternative, Promise began hosting their community-oriented daytime dance parties at Cherry Beach, a tradition that continues to this day.

Just a few weeks before the iDance Rally, electronic musicians of a different stripe gathered to mark the end of another era. Guerrilla Gallery: Audio Survival was a two-day festival bringing together the leading edge of live experimental electronic music, a range of abstract sounds emanating from laptops, analog synths, and oscillators. It should have been festive, but instead it was a funeral. The July 21–22, 2000, event marked the final concerts at the Music Gallery on Richmond.

Just a few short weeks earlier, the long-running avant-garde music space broke the sad news that it had been evicted from its custom-designed space. Though Artscape had signed the lease on their behalf, the property owners invoked an 'escape clause,' as they had plans to demolish the building to build condos – which is precisely what they did; it's now an ugly, faceless monolith.

Ron Gaskin (jazz curator): *My immediate response is heartbreak, because it's such a great space. It will be interesting to see how movable the feast is.* (to Robert Everett-Green, *Globe and Mail*, July 4, 2000)

It looked like an ignominious end to the clubhouse started a quarter century earlier by those free-form freaks in the CCMC. The Music Gallery staged its 2000–01 concert season under the 'Guerrilla Gallery' banner, presenting shows at other venues around town, and in September 2001, the MG moved into St. George the Martyr Church, back in the vicinity of CCMC's original location.

Yet another era came to a close in April, when the Gas Station recording studio was given thirty days to vacate its premises in the warehouse district, already being rebranded as Liberty Village. The eviction of a beloved creative hub received plenty of sympathetic media coverage, including a three-page spread in *Exclaim!* Proprietors Don Kerr and Dale Morningstar organized a protest outside their landlords' offices on King Street West, which turned into a spontaneous parade jam featuring various members of the local music community. But Artscape saved the day; within weeks, the studio relocated offshore to Gibraltar Point Centre for the Arts, located in a former public school on idyllic Toronto Island.

Eras may end, but the endings can be happy ones. As of this writing, the Gas Station is still at Artscape Gibraltar Point, nineteen years later.

Those early Sundays at Ted's are some of my fondest Wavelength memories, with 'I was there' instances like the first appearance of Broken Social Scene. Dan Bejar from Destroyer playing solo. That time the Constantines blew away every music critic in Toronto. And those weird and wonderful moments, like when we screened Michael Snow's *Wavelength* followed by a performance by the man himself, or the time noise artist Knurl played a toaster. And those lovely, intimate moments, sitting at a darkened table, sipping a beer over a candle flame, listening to Michelle McAdorey play songs off her album *Whirl*.

Wavelength's run at Ted's Wrecking Yard lasted for eighty-six Sundays. We've since called many other venues home, but Ted's will always be our spiritual home. We cultivated a warm, welcoming atmosphere, and the layout of Ted's, with good sightlines everywhere and lots of nooks and crannies to hang and chill, helped that to take root. And I know lots of musicians have fond memories of smoking up in the backstage 'kitchen' – which doubled as its green room.

I should have learned my lesson from the 1150 – *don't get too attached.*

★

Dan Burke: *We may survive this assault on rock'n'roll.* (to Karen Palmer, *Toronto Star*, October 1, 2001)

The first Wavelength that took place after September 11th, 2001, featured Do Make Say Think. That was monumental enough – they were the biggest band we'd booked to date, and they could easily out-stuff Ted's Wrecking Yard by then. There was a huge lineup to get in. The atmosphere inside was heavy. Our emcee, Doc Pickles, looked the elephant in the eye: 'Okay, everyone. Tuesday *happened.*'

The band's set was as intense and cathartic as you could have hoped for. But it wasn't all doom and gloom: it was DMST guitarist Justin Small's birthday, and the opening act was Deep Dark United, whose bassist, Katia Taylor, he'd begun dating at the start of the year. They'd first met when their bands played together at Wavelength's first anniversary party; they're now married.

While we were holding court at Ted's, Dan Burke had had a fantastic few years at the El Mo. He'd made the club into one of the continent's prime spots for loud, boozy, gritty rock'n'roll as well as gender-bending electropunk, thanks to the success of Vaseline.

On September 18, 2001, Ben Rayner broke the news in the *Toronto Star* that the El Mocambo's building had been sold to a businessman named Abbas Jahangiri, a figure completely unknown in the music scene. He had plans to convert the upstairs into a dance studio, which would house a small company he ran called the National Dance of Canada. The downstairs would remain a nightclub, but one with a new and unclear booking mandate – and the new owner planned to renovate it. Jahangiri's claim that he would convert the El Mo's dingy basement into a women's shelter – right underneath a rock club – seemed even more dubious.

Originally given thirty days to vacate, Dan Burke and the club's managers were given a reprieve of forty-five days. The El Mocambo as we knew it would cease to exist on November 1, 2001.

Everyone in the music scene was devastated. Well, everyone that *I* knew, at least. It seemed unthinkable that such a historical landmark could simply be wiped away. Jahangiri – a self-styled philanthropist who harboured a strange obsession with Mother Teresa, drove a giant yellow Hummer, and claimed not to have heard of the El Mo or its legendary status before purchasing the building – quickly became public enemy number one among Toronto musicians and fans.

Burke rallied his friends in the press and the music community with an online petition to 'Save the El Mo.' A public meeting was held at the club on October 3, hosted by councillor Olivia Chow.

Burke: *We couldn't do a thing. I knew that too, but I thought, why not get some publicity? Why not make a stand? You've got to try. But you can't stop a commercial transaction like that for cultural reasons, for pop-historical reasons.*

The El Mo's fate was sealed. Its cultural heritage value didn't matter when it came to private property. At least not in this case; it didn't have an official Heritage designation. Over a decade before the City would open its Music Office and declare itself a Music City, there was nothing anyone could do to stop the inevitable. The El Mo's interior – and its soul – had a date with the wrecking ball.

And the music-scene drama of the fall of 2001 was only getting started.

★

On the evening of October 24, 2001, my phone rang. A musician friend was calling from a payphone on College Street. 'Hey Jonny, do you know what's going on at Ted's? The front door is padlocked and it looks like there's an eviction notice on the door.' You ever have one of those moments when the floor just drops out below you? Ted's Wrecking Yard was closed. *Dead.*

I had heard rumours that the club was in financial trouble. But I didn't want to believe it was true. Everything about Ted's – its size, vibe, sound, and location – had contributed to the success of Wavelength. We were about to become homeless.

For the following Sunday, we moved our lineup to the El Mocambo for a one-night stand – it was scheduled to close just days later. The sudden shuttering caused a shock wave through the club scene; Yvonne Matsell had to cancel or relocate dozens of gigs that had been booked into the new year. Bar staff were left in the lurch and owed pay.

The day after Ted's closed, I got a call from Amy Hersenhoren: 'What are you going to do?' She was about a year into a new job booking Lee's Palace, which had just been bought by a new owner: the Horseshoe Tavern. The big Bloor club's new proprietors offered us a pretty good deal to move Wavelength to Lee's on Sunday nights. We were tempted, but had reservations, mostly related to the club's size. How were we going to fill a five-hundred-plus-person venue each week? Or if we didn't fill it, make it feel intimate?

We were also approached by Dwayne Slack, sound tech at Sneaky Dee's, who was starting to bring back bands. We went to take a look, but there was still a railing across the 'stage,' which doubled as booth seating on dance nights. The club also looked a lot smaller than I remembered, from all those times playing there in the mid-nineties. It wasn't ready.

In spite of our trepidation, we accepted the offer from Lee's. The first Wavelength there was November 4, 2001. The lineup included Femme Fatale, a hardcore band led by Jesse F. Keeler, who would later form the massively popular dance-punk band Death From Above 1979. About twenty people attended.

Everyone else was down the street – at the corner of Spadina and College – for the 'Last Night at the El Mo.' For that Sunday night, Burke assembled a mini-festival of acts from across the decades, with the seventies repre- sented by Spadina blues-rock- ers Mainline, the eighties by retro punks Teenage Head, William New's own Groovy Religion repping the indie nineties, and More Plastic symbolizing Burke's brief three years of millennial

Ted's Wrecking Yard, immediately post-eviction, October 2001.

garage glory. The spat between Burke and Jahangiri was only then reaching its apex. On the preceding Thursday, Burke and management had found themselves locked out by the new owner after they made public their inten- tion to take the El Mo name *and* sign to their new home. They were able to regain access in time for the final blowout. From what I heard, it was a wild mess, with Burke getting increasingly riled up. The headline-writing promoter made sure he went out in a blaze of glory.

Burke: *I got arrested leaving. I'd thrown my sunglasses [at Jahangiri]. I'd always wear sunglasses, because my hair was thinning – it was better than a hat. And it was a gesture. I wasn't trying to hurt him or anything. I don't think I hit him. I was leaving the place with my girlfriend at the time and a cop comes out, 'Dan, Dan' – really polite – 'Can you wait a sec. The guy wants to charge you. For assault.' I threw them in his direction. And I got charged with assault. I got arrested. Cuffed. I've been in jail before, but I really didn't deserve that one.*

Things continued to get strange. Burke struck a deal with the landlord of Ted's Wrecking Yard to move the El Mocambo there. It raised a philosophical question: could the 'essence' of the El Mo be physically moved? Was its identity a spiritual one, or was it tied to the bricks and mortar of 464 Spadina? With Jahangiri intent on keeping the El Mocambo name alive and reopening it after extensive renovations, there was also the prospect of two competing clubs both calling themselves the El Mocambo, only a block apart from one another. Would Burke and his team be able to 'duplicate' the El Mo's trademark grittiness down the street in Little Italy?

We'll never know.

Burke announced a New Year's Eve party hosted by Blow Up that was supposed to mark the opening of the 'new' El Mocambo. But it never happened. The move faced significant opposition in Little Italy. Ted's Wrecking Yard had pushed that community past its limit of tolerance for noise and nuisance, and more nightclubs had begun to open along the College strip west of Bathurst.

Clubs like the El Mo can't survive without the ability to serve booze, and they had to apply for a brand-new licence. Which wasn't easy to get. The local city councillor, Joe Pantalone, opposed the liquor licence application. That – combined with the building's structural deficiencies, according to Burke – resulted in a big fat red 'X.'

It was a crushing blow for the dogged promoter. His business partners from the old El Mo had already put fifty grand into the new location. And it never opened its doors.

Burke: *That was a rough one, and it was rough for me after that, too.*

The events of the fall of 2001 made it feel like the heart had been ripped out of Toronto's independent music scene. The El Mocambo was gone, and it wasn't going to rise from the rubble of the Wrecking Yard. The loss of smaller, accessible venues can leave up-and-coming artists without a place to play, to hone their craft, build an audience, and find their community. And the alternative, all-ages, DIY spaces of the mid-nineties had already all vanished. Morale was at an all-time low, and hope for a recovery seemed slim. But no one could really anticipate how much both the city and the music scene would grow and change in the first two decades of the twenty-first century.

BROKEN SOCIAL SCENE
Cause = Time
1999–

Broken Social Scene are usually described as a sprawling collective, their name a commentary on their large, fractured membership. They're also also reductively labelled 'indie-rock' — which paints over the way their sound drew on different elements of the underground nineties: post-rock, dream-pop, dub, folk, ambient electronica. The story of how BSS came together is like an explosion in reverse. Their various starting points all contributed to the band's unique sound and modus operandi. And the process of how they all met one another is intimately tied with how their sound evolved.

Broken Social Scene began in 1999 with the collaboration of Kevin Drew and Brendan Canning. Seven years older than the wide-eyed, hungry Drew, Canning was already a road-tested band vet, and BSS marked his transformation from grinning, fresh-faced hHead bassist to wise, soft-spoken elder. Canning tempered young Drew's lofty enthusiasm and arty indulgence with even-tempered experience and a focused pop sensibility.

Eight years earlier, while grungy hHead released their first cassette and took over 1150 Queen Street West, guitarist Andrew Whiteman was playing in one of the most popular bands in Toronto, soul/funk collective the Bourbon Tabernacle Choir. Kevin Drew was fourteen and had just heard Dinosaur Jr. for the first time. It was 'The Wagon,' off *Green Mind*.

Kevin Drew: That was the first time I heard a new song that I immediately related to. Chord structure, singing, everything. That changed the course of my life, because I thought, that's how I feel. That's what I want to do. But I didn't pick up a guitar till I was seventeen.

Drew attended the acclaimed Etobicoke School of the Arts, in the inner suburbs west of downtown. His schoolmates included Emily 'Metric' Haines and Amy 'Stars' Millan, seniors who later became his musical collaborators. He didn't start a band in high school, instead making droning, John Carpenter–inspired imaginary soundtracks on a friend's keyboard.

In Calgary during a demoralizing tour to promote their unsuccessful major-label debut in 1994, hHead met sixteen-year-old Leslie Feist, a stunningly talented vocalist. She looked them up after moving to Toronto a few years later. Andrew Whiteman, meanwhile, having quit the Bourbon Tabernacle Choir, dove into the warehouse district scene, forming Latin rock band Que Vida. He later saw Feist perform solo at We'ave, and the two hit it off.

In 1995, Markham drummer Justin Peroff took a break from playing in indie-rock bands to become an actor. He appeared on CBC-TV starring opposite Sarah Polley in youth drama *Straight Up*.

Justin Peroff: I didn't want the acting job because I wanted to be a touring musician. My parents talked me into it and said, 'This is a great opportunity.' I ultimately met Kevin Drew through that job. Mark Cohen, who played my best friend on the show, was best friends with Kevin Drew in real life.

KD: I met Justin and went to see him play with Kat Rocket. And immediately I was like, 'This guy can DRUM.' We started getting to know each other, and stayed in each other's periphery.

On another plane of Toronto existence, singer/songwriter Jason Collett formed folk-pop group Ursula in 1995 with ex-L'Étranger frontman Andrew Cash. And in a smoke-filled Annex apartment, Charles Spearin co-founded Do Make Say Think. While at school for audio engineering, Spearin was approached by an amiable classmate.

Charles Spearin: I met Kevin Drew at the Harris Institute for the Arts. He came up to me outside and said, 'You look like a guy who likes Tortoise.' And that was kind of it. Tortoise was the icebreaker. (to Stuart Berman, *This Book Is Broken*, 2009)

Chicago band Tortoise were revitalizing an already tired indie world with guitar-free instrumental soundscapes, part of an interconnected family of bands through their label Thrill Jockey Records. Tortoise's '96 album *Millions Now Living Will Never Die* made a huge impact in Toronto.

KD: When that dropped, that was huge. A twenty-minute song – 'Djed.' It was TWENTY MINUTES! It was the coolest thing. Being a soundtrack kid, to have instrumental music suddenly be in the forefront, it was amazing. That's what was so great about meeting Charlie, because he introduced me to Do Make Say Think.

DMST rapidly became Kevin Drew's favourite band. Even at the tender age of nineteen, he displayed the fearless behaviour that would serve him well later: instead of copying his heroes, he recruited them. Drew and Spearin started a band called Djula; they played only a few low-key gigs at Club Shanghai and the Mockingbird, where Drew worked.

But 'playing in a band' isn't where they wanted to be. Kevin and Charlie just wanted to make music. So the duo holed up at home and began recording tracks that suited that sense of cocooning. KC Accidental was what they named the project; KC = Kevin + Charlie. Meanwhile, Jason Collett was on the cover of *Now,* promoting his alt-country project Bird. Brendan Canning was playing bass with Spookey Ruben; he and Kevin Drew were still two years away from meeting.

KC Accidental self-released their first CD – originally self-titled, later dubbed *Captured Anthems for an Empty Bathtub* – in 1998. They made only one hundred copies, on sale only at Rotate This. It was pretty, meditative, and tentative-sounding. They threw a CD release party at the Mockingbird, a poolhall at King and Portland, on the edges of Clubland, not at all a regular music venue – and Drew roped in Justin Peroff to drum, alongside DMST's Justin Small and members of what would become Metric. Emily Haines opened on solo piano.

Excited about the possibilities of a larger group, KC Accidental expanded the cast for their second album, *Anthems for the Could've Bin Pills.* The Mockingbird release-party band members were joined by some eyebrow-raising additions: Big Sugar's Rich Brown, Blue Dog Pict's Keram Malicki-Sanchez, Godspeed You! Black Emperor's Jessica Moss, and Treble Charger's Bill Priddle.

KD: That was where I thought, 'Okay, I like playing with lots of people.' Charlie was like, 'What are you doing?' I just kept bringing people and bringing people. 'We gotta get this person, we gotta get this person.'

Despite the expanded personnel, it was, in some ways, a smaller, more melancholic record than the debut, but it was also more beautiful and original. It caught the ear of Joe English, a Harris instructor of Drew's. He had started an indie label called Noise Factory Records to support a Toronto glam-pop group named Nancy, Despot – but frontman Brian Gunstone passed away in late '96.

English restarted the label with the help of Drew, who assisted in the curation of a CD compilation, *Beautiful Noise (The Apocalypse)*, consisting mostly of Toronto-based ambient, experimental, and electronic projects. Noise Factory released the comp in late '99 and the KC Accidental album in early 2000. Both received an indifferent response upon their release.

If *Could've Bin Pills* has a weakness, it's that it sounds too much like Spearin's other group. Drew knew that he had to do something different to set himself apart.

KD: I was on a mission. I knew what was happening. I knew the right thing to do, and I knew Do Makes were doing something special and I couldn't do that. I had to get away from that instrumental style, because they just did it so well.

In between the release of the two KC albums, Kevin Drew and Brendan Canning finally met. There are a few different versions of the story of how they met, all involving various mutual friends and drinking in different bars on College Street. Canning had been on a journey through all the stages of grief and rebound after the breakup of hHead. In 1999, the year he and Drew met, his voice could be heard on pop radio, on the surprise crossover hit 'Steal My Sunshine' by Len.

Brendan Canning: You've got to go through some periods before you find the winning combination. hHead got me to a certain level – you make lots of friends, then you move on to another band. I could play with Spookey, then you're going to Japan or England, stakes are a little bit higher. Then you're in Len – it's like, oh this is kind of a weird situation. Then By Divine Right, okay, this is fun. But I'm still not a songwriter in this group – what the fuck, I'm not a sideman.

Before joining By Divine Right on bass, Canning thought he was done with rock music. He took his first hit of E, and decided he wanted to play house music. As the Champ, Canning became one of Toronto's most ubiquitous party DJs, spinning disco, funk, reggae, and other feel-good jams.

By Divine Right became a four-piece when Leslie Feist joined on second guitar. At that point, the band was on Sarah McLachlan's label Nettwerk Records and opening for the Tragically Hip; they spent most of 1999 on the road, and it broke them. When they got home, Canning and Feist decided they didn't want to be a part of anything with a whiff of 'Canadian music industry.'

BC: One night me and my friend Richie Cureton were hanging out on College Street. And Kevin was with Stephen Chung, a photographer friend of ours. They were going to go listen to the new KC Accidental. And me and Richie, we went back to his place and listened to the old KC Accidental. And then I started calling Kevin. I was like, 'Hey, we should do something.'

Leslie Feist: The power of Brendan and Kevin finding each other was pretty intense. They were like a complete symbiosis of each other. And personality-wise they complemented each other perfectly: Canning is so chill, and Kevin's such a sparkplug. (*This Book Is Broken*)

In addition to the temperamental equilibrium, the union of Canning and Drew represented the combination of experimental bedroom abstraction and super-connected music-industry knowhow.

In the fall of 1999, Do Make Say Think flew to Europe for the first of many well-received tours. While they were away, Spearin lent Drew his eight-track reel-to-reel, the very same Tascam 388 Portastudio that he'd moved into DMST's original Albany apartment. Canning kept coming over to Drew and then-wife Joanne Goldsmith's house in the charming residential neighbourhood of Little Portugal, then on the cusp of gentrification.

The tracks they recorded together were in the continuum of KC Accidental, if not even more ethereal and untethered to rock-band conventions. But the songs were also shorter, more concise, and for the first time, featured vocals – though often dreamy and wordless. Many of the same KC contributors came back, along with a new guest, Feist.

Another Do Make Say Think EU tour came around the following fall. Two band members were unable to commit to all the dates, so Spearin recruited his KC Accidental pals Drew and Peroff to fill in. The tour was a taxing one, with tensions running high – especially for the new recruits. Drew was by his own admission, a little green and not ready for sleeping in squats an ocean from home, harsh conditions to which DMST were already accustomed.

KD: It was just the greatest thing in the world. I loved it, but they were tough. They were tough dudes to be out on the road with. I'm just really a sensitive, little emotional kid and they were not. But that experience really helped me be in a band.

JP: Kevin and I did not get along at all during that tour. But on the flight to Europe, Kevin handed me a CDR which said 'Broken Membership.' Which is what Kevin wanted to call the project. They had just mixed or mastered the album. He said, 'Take a listen and let me know what you think.' I listened to it on the flight and I thought it was a beautiful album.

Upon returning home that fall, Kevin Drew called me up and asked me if he could do a solo set at Wavelength. We already had two bands booked for December 17, 2000, at Ted's Wrecking Yard – the Russian Futurists and Raising the Fawn – but I said yes and added him as a third act to open. He told me to list him as 'John Tesh Jr. & the Broken Social Scene.'

The show was the best-attended night we'd had to date. There was a real buzz in the room and all three acts captivated the crowd. Performing a gorgeous, blissful ambient set on his Yamaha keyboard, Kevin was joined on stage by GUH trumpeter Brian Cram – with whom he'd experienced some of those highs and lows on the DMST tour – who wandered out from backstage, his cameo a semi-spontaneous surprise.

That night was significant for a few other reasons. Drew made friends with Raising the Fawn frontman John Crossingham, who worked across the street at Soundscapes. And it marked the first appearance of the BSS name.

KD: When I did Wavelength, as John Tesh Jr. & the Broken Social Scene, Brendan came up to me after and said, 'That's the name, the Broken Social Scene.' And then my friend Ibi [Kaslik] said, lose 'the.' So then we just kept it Broken.

It also marked the start of their relationship with Ted's Wrecking Yard. What had started as a hermetic, experimental ambient collaboration between friends was turning into a band, and the coming year would be a life-changing one. A month later, on January 26, 2001, they booked a night with Yvonne Matsell and called it 'An Evening for Whatever.' The show was just listed under their names – Feist, Canning, Drew, and Whiteman – and consisted of them playing various tunes of each other's. After working through some post-DMST drama, Justin Peroff played the drums.

JP: After that tour ended, it resulted in a phone call with Kevin. He said, 'I don't think I can do this with you.' And I said, 'Oh no, you can and you will.' Basically, I talked him into keeping me around. We are both very emotional guys and we can trigger each other. I remember that phone call happening, and knowing what I was in was something so special. Not even really knowing what we were doing, just knowing that what was happening felt great.

The material they played that winter night didn't have much connection to the record that Canning and Drew had finished in the fall. That album, entitled *Feel Good Lost*, was released in March 2001 on Noise Factory Records, under the project's new name: Broken Social Scene. It's a record that may surprise fans who only heard the band later on, mostly consisting of gentle slices of post-rock and spacious, cozy layers of synth-woven ambient. A Noise Factory ad upon its release called it 'music for living in rooms.' The disc's finest cut, 'Passport Radio,' tunes the listener in to the hazy voice of Leslie Feist.

Broken Social Scene made their official live debut a month later, April 14, 2001, at Kathedral, the main floor of the Big Bop/Reverb complex, as part of *Exclaim!* magazine's ninth-anniversary party. They were at the bottom of the bill on the downstairs electronic stage, performing before Manitoba a.k.a. Caribou.

Drew: That's where it all started. We didn't play any of *Feel Good Lost*, which the whole crowd thought we were going to do. We played all original songs.

The 'big-band' era of Broken Social Scene began that spring, with new recruits including Raising the Fawn's John Crossingham, who doubled on guitar and drums, and guitarist Jason Collett, an older roots-music singer/songwriter. This was part of Drew's genius recruitment strategy – get seasoned guys who could really play, throw them in alongside younger, hungrier players, and have them feed off each other. Experience and enthusiasm created a virtuous feedback loop.

After the *Exclaim!* party, BSS made Ted's Wrecking Yard home base for the rest of the year – until its sudden October closure, that is. At one point that summer, they briefly renamed themselves Do the 95, in which they played only loud, angry, mid-nineties-inspired indie-rock ragers. Drew began to step up to the mic.

Meanwhile, Justin Peroff started a musical collaboration with friend Dylan Hudecki called Junior Blue. The pair began recording drum tracks at Stars and Sons studio, owned by producer Dave Newfeld. Impressed by the sounds Newfeld was conjuring, Peroff recommended Broken Social Scene look into the studio as a possible place to record. After seeing BSS live, Newfeld invited the band to contribute a track to a compilation he was assembling called *Pet Songs* – indeed, a collection of songs about pets. BSS went into the studio with a song called 'Mourir,' about a gerbil of Drew's that had died.

KD: I remember thinking vocally and drum-wise how cool everything sounded. To this point, I only really knew Charlie's production. I hadn't fucking heard anybody make stuff like this.

JP: That's why we ended up recording with Dave – we did this one song and it sounded cool. And he ultimately determined the sound of Social Scene in a lot of ways, definitely from a production standpoint. He's got that flavour, man.

Pet Songs never saw the light of day, unfortunately. BSS finally released 'Mourir,' then renamed 'Deathcock,' as part of a 2013 Arts & Crafts rarities comp.

In January of 2002, with their homebase Ted's shuttered, Broken Social Scene went into Stars and Sons to begin recording the album that would make them the band they are today. From a catalogue of a few dozen songs, Newfeld and Broken Social Scene carved out the fourteen tracks that made up *You Forgot It in People*. Released in October 2002, the album's astonishing production and stirring rock songs triggered a seismic hype wave that would transport the band – and Toronto – to shores once thought unimaginable.

KD: You couldn't tell at the time how magical it was. But Newf really captured that 'first thought, best thought' stuff. He really had a wonderful way of saying, 'Oh, that's a great vibe. Let's put that in there. You don't need to redo that.'

Dave Newfeld: I applied everything I'd learned up to that point, both with electronic music – sampling and synthesizers – and what I had learned about analog band-based record-making.

YFIIP's personnel included many of the same people who had been there since the KC Accidental days. But it was the affecting vocal contributions of Emily Haines, on 'Anthems for a Seventeen-Year-Old Girl,' and Leslie Feist, on 'Almost Crimes,' that brought their music to a new plane of accessibility.

KD: That's why it's called *You Forgot It in People*. It was the people that made it happen. And that's what I will say until they put me in the oven.

The album became Toronto's first smash hit record of the Internet age. Its release was heralded with rapturous five-star reviews in the local press. In early '03, then-influential US music website Pitchfork gave it a 9.2 rating, the publication's founder Ryan Schreiber breathlessly raving, 'I wish I could convey how they've made just exactly the kind of pop record that stands the test of time.' And it was made without interference from any record company.

Listening to YFIIP seventeen years later, it still sounds like a giant group hug. The 'it' we forgot is people's inherent goodness, an element of trust forsaken in the age of social media. My personal favourite Broken Social Scene tune is 'KC Accidental,' the first proper song on YFIIP. To my ears, it stands at the perfect juncture of epic and ambient, of where they came from and where they were headed.

KD: *You Forgot It in People* was more KC Accidental than it was Broken Social Scene. I said, 'This should be a KC Accidental record, musically.' It was way more in line with that than *Feel Good Lost*. But the problem was Kevin and Charlie, that's what the KC stood for. So we flipped it and said, 'Let's call it Broken Social Scene, and we'll name the first song 'KC Accidental,' to salute where this came from.'

Five or so albums later, including a handful of hiatuses, Broken Social Scene are now veterans of the festival circuit all over North America and Europe. They took inspiration from Tortoise's Chicago circle of bands, building their own family through their Arts & Crafts label, with the members getting to retreat to their various own projects – Feist, Stars, Metric, the Apostle of Hustle, La Force, etc. – and return rejuvenated.

They're the same group as they were when they started, in many ways, except now Kevin gets to make records with his hero J Mascis and go out for tacos when he's in town. And they have gracefully accepted the 'senior emerging artist' mantle, collaborating with both their elders – as Drew did with the late Gord Downie – and with the next generation. The band is now the tightest it's ever been. Like the city they call home, they've taken the life cycle of boom, bust, and renewal, and made it part of their story.

EPILOGUE: ANY CORNER OF THE CITY

Two thousand two started out as a bummer of a year. Word came down officially on January 11 that the new El Mo was a no-go. Burke had begun tentatively booking shows at another long-time Spadina haunt, the Silver Dollar Room, but his hope was to find a more permanent home up on Bloor at a massive upstairs club on the corner of Bathurst called Tequila Lounge. Burke titled his opening night 'Exiled from College Street.' But that place had all the ambience of an airport departure lounge, and its shaky management earned it a three-month liquor licence suspension, which killed his momentum. Burke went off the rails pretty badly after that.

That spring, he passed Abbas Jahangiri on Spadina and spit at his feet. He was again charged with assault, and this time it went to trial. Burke self-defended and the case was dismissed. That fall, Jahangiri's renovated El Mocambo opened its doors – its lager-soaked grime scrubbed away, the main floor bougie-fied with Chinatown light fixtures and a shiny motorcycle parked inside its front room. In an ironic twist, its new booker was former Ted's Wrecking Yard maven Yvonne Matsell.

Still, never-say-die Burke dug in at the Silver Dollar, which ended up being his longest, most storied club booking run – fifteen years of fistfights, stage invasions, and bands paid in jeans. Matsell, meanwhile, would go on to have *her* longest club run at the El Mo: twelve years, until Jahangiri sold the building in 2014. His final attempt to win over the independent music community would again be disastrous: in 2005, he bought the Internet message board 20 Hz. Its members mutinied, abandoning it en masse to create a new community-run board called Stille Post.

Jahangiri was the butt of jokes for a long time, which seemed a little unfair – despite such ill-advised business decisions, he appeared to have a big heart, and he regularly drove around Chinatown/Kensington at night to personally help feed the homeless out of his Hummer. Or did he? There was plenty of skepticism in the music community as to both the sincerity and the *existence* of his charitable efforts.

Matsell, meanwhile, made the 'new' El Mo a welcome space for funk, soul, hip-hop, and reggae. This certainly was needed after the 2002 closure of the BamBoo Club, the end of a twenty-year era on Queen Street. It's a void that sadly remains unfilled: to my knowledge, Toronto has no dedicated live venue for Black music across multiple genres.

As for Wavelength, we never really felt quite at home at Lee's Palace. Everyone there was really good to us, but there were only a couple of nights where the big room didn't feel empty. Our second-anniversary festivities in February 2002 felt almost funereal – for the first time, we did a multi-venue festival over three nights, and the other clubs we used were Rancho Relaxo and Clinton's. With Ted's and the El Mo gone, there weren't many decent small clubs left to play.

But one night that April, a band I was in played a show at Sneaky Dee's. They had finally taken down that damn railing in front of the stage. The show was super fun. The crowd pressed up front in a way I hadn't seen at a Toronto indie show, everyone mingling and chatting. The whole night, everyone asked me, 'Why don't you move Wavelength here?' I remember running into Dwayne Slack at the end of the night, and we exchanged a raised-eyebrows look and had that whole conversation non-verbally.

Wavelength made the move to Sneaky Dee's in May 2002. Attendance picked up, and Sneaky's would become the longest-running home of our weekly series, an amazing seven-year run.

Two thousand two ended up being a transitional year for the Toronto music scene – and what a transition. Broken Social Scene released their second album, their first as a proper band – also the first release for both Arts & Crafts *and* Paper Bag Records. The Pitchfork-lauded *You Forgot It in People* built a buzz like nothing else I'd heard before or since in Toronto. Their bud k-os released *Exit*, a revolutionary record for Canadian rap, combining hip-hop with elements of folk, soul, reggae, and flamenco to create a truly Torontonian multicultural mash-up.

The Watershed Year for Toronto music was 2003. With the success of bss, suddenly the eyes of the world were on us. The still-buzzing Hidden Cameras became the first Canadian group to sign to Rough Trade, the UK label that had discovered the Smiths and the Strokes. Collective bands with ten-plus members became the newest Canadian export – Montreal's Arcade Fire and Vancouver's The New Pornographers representing the country's other two big cities.

The summer of 2003 saw the birth of 'Torontopia' – not really a movement, more a complicated, deeply ironic expression of civic pride – and a term that remains sadly divisive and misunderstood. Coinciding with the election of cultured, progressive mayor David Miller – mercifully replacing Mayor Mel – Torontopia roughly included all those aforementioned early-2000s institutions: Spacing, Trampoline Hall, Vaseline, the Hidden Cameras, Three Gut Records, and Wavelength.

Torontopia was coined, or at least semi-popularized, by Steve Kado, then of Hidden Cameras splinter group the Barcelona Pavilion, who brought a much-needed sense of confrontation to Toronto indie stages with dance-punk songs about architecture and housecleaning. To me, Torontopia was the once-sleepy, standoff-ish city coming to life and falling in love with itself: it was an ecstatic crowd sweatily dancing to Anagram or controller.controller or Kids on TV. Kado's co-op label Blocks Recording Club captured this musical era with the essential CD comp *Toronto Is Great!!!*

Torontopia was also Sunday soccer matches in Trinity Bellwoods, before the park became a mini-Coachella each weekend. It was running into a friend at the corner of Queen and Spadina and having them run into another friend, and another, watching a random agglomeration of strangers become new friends, before Facebook ruined everything. It was giant games of Tag played downtown, it was seven a.m. subway dance parties, it was artists building lofts in bus shelters in protest against runaway development. It was the multicultural crowd at a Femi Kuti show at Harbourfront – or a Movement party at the Rivoli. And it was Toronto coming alive, with strangers becoming friends on darkened street corners when the power died during the blackout that August. There's a reason Steve Kado still talks about 2003.

The floodgates had opened, and the stream of great music continued through the mid-2000s – witness records by the Constantines (their masterpiece *Shine a Light*), FemBots, Pony da Look, Great Lake Swimmers, Final Fantasy (a.k.a. Owen Pallett), Jon-Rae & the River, Holy Fuck, the Bicycles, Laura Barrett, Ohbijou – as well as Broken Social Scene's family of Arts & Crafts bands: Stars, Metric, Feist. The success of A&C and Paper Bag marked another sea change for Toronto music – we now had homegrown labels with an international reach, a trend that continued in the 2010s with Buzz Records, Hand Drawn Dracula, and OVO Sound. And starting in 2006, the Polaris Music Prize began to recognize innovative Canadian albums on the basis of artistic merit.

West Queen West pushed further west with the 2004 opening of the renovated Drake and Gladstone Hotels, and venues ventured further into Parkdale with Wrongbar and Stones Place. In 2005, the music scene became truly adventurous with the advent of Extermination Music Night, guerrilla indie shows held in abandoned buildings like the Don Valley Brickworks.

Toronto really began to discover itself in 2006, when the first Nuit Blanche began bringing the city to life after hours with an all-night contemporary art extravaganza. That same year, long-awaited new cultural facilities opened, like the Canadian Opera Company's Four Seasons Centre for the Arts, followed by the controversial ROM 'Crystal,' and Frank Gehry's beloved redesign of the AGO. But everyone I knew was more excited about Vaseline's Will Munro opening his own bar, the Beaver, on 'Queer West.'

The problem with Torontopia is that it was overwhelmingly downtown and white. We conveniently ignored the demographic realities of the city post-amalgamation. There was a huge class divide growing in Toronto, exacerbated by issues related to transit, housing, sprawl, and wealth concentration, resulting in racialized poverty in the suburban outskirts.

Mayor Miller, re-elected in 2006, was keenly aware of these issues, and aimed to address them by the TTC through 'Transit City,' an array of light rail lines that would have better connected the distant suburbs to downtown. But a neo-conservative wave was rising, starting with the election of PM Stephen Harper. Is it a coincidence that 2006 was the year Torontopia was declared dead?

Through the second half of the 2000s, the city got meaner and angrier. Perhaps in response to the group-hug collectivism of Broken Social Scene, but more likely an amplification of this anxious era, indie Toronto produced harder-edged bands like Fucked Up, Crystal Castles, and later METZ. The rapid growth of the city brought it to a boiling point of congestion.

Perpetually overlooked Dundas Street West, around the intersection of Ossington, became the new centre of cool. Sure, this was started in '03–'04 by hipster bars the Communist Daughter and Sweaty Betty's, but the 'hood was amplified by the '07 opening of the Dakota Tavern – marking the triumphant return of roots-rock – followed by the Garrison in 2009. Though it should be noted that global music venue Lula Lounge beat them all to it, back in 2005.

Toronto hip-hop, meanwhile, went global with Somali-born rapper K'Naan, whose song 'Waving Flag' became a World Cup anthem, and hyperlocal with More Or Les, who rapped about the city's finest brunch spots.

After seven great long years at Sneaky Dee's, the Garrison became the new home of Wavelength, right before we ended our weekly series in 2010. Our second decade saw us stretch out and try different things, including an artist incubator series, pop-up gallery shows, and bigger festivals on Toronto Island, such as the ALL CAPS! Island Festival and its successor, Camp Wavelength.

Two thousand ten was an annus horribilis for Toronto. The G20 Summit saw our downtown under siege by out-of-control police forces, and dozens of innocent people 'kettled' in the rain and jailed in inhumane facilities. Rob Ford got elected mayor by declaring war on downtown's supposed 'War on the Car,' exploiting suburban thirst for 'Subways, Subways, Subways!' Horrified progressives wondered how we'd get through the next four years. But no one could have predicted 2013's Crack-Mayor-Gate, or that *this* would be what got Toronto discovered by US talk shows.

But another civic icon emerged, who became our Anti-Ford figure. Aubrey Graham Drake, a bi-racial kid from Forest Hill and former *Degrassi* TV star, successfully made Toronto seem mysterious and cosmopolitan to the rest of the world. Drake's own OVO Sound label helped popularize the 'New Toronto Sound' of hazy, decadent R&B/hip-hop by the likes of Daniel Caesar, Majid Jordan, PARTYNEXTDOOR, and dvsn.

The early 2010s also saw a new golden era for DIY punk venues – though Soybomb had been throwing hardcore shows in the half-pipe in their Bathurst apartment since the early aughts, and artist collective space Double Double Land opened in '09, everything took off when the Garage opened – a venue run out of an actual car garage near Kensington Market. The Garage was affiliated with Buzz Records, who repped the millennial wave of Toronto noise-punk with the likes of Weaves, Dilly Dally, HSY, and Casper Skulls.

Artists like Weaves' Jasmyn Burke were part of a long-overdue movement toward more representation for BIPOC people in independent music, alongside Zaki Ibrahim, Yamantaka // Sonic Titan, Tanya Tagaq, Maylee Todd, Pantayo, and Hooded Fang. Since 2014, there's been more crossover between hip-hop, indie, and electronic musics, with artists like Harrison, Charlotte Day Wilson, SlowPitchSound, Just John, and Obuxum blurring the boundaries, as well as powerful women emcees rising up, like Haviah Mighty, Han Han, and LolaBunz.

Toronto music venues aren't extinct quite yet, but the affordability crisis of the late 2010s has endangered them, and the DIY spaces so prevalent less than a decade ago are now all but gone. New live clubs have opened in recent years in what was once the far west end, such as the Junction City Music Hall and the Baby G at Dundas and Brock. The east end has been more challenged for venues, with a monthly show series, Feast in the East – which includes dinner and art along with the bands – starting up specifically to fill this void, though it's often bouncing from space to space.

Feast in the East have also made efforts to present events 'beyond the core,' in locations such as Prairie Drive Park in Scarborough. Finding consistent performance spaces in Toronto's suburban neighbourhoods is more of a challenge, but there are signs of hope, whether it be library concerts on Albion Road in Rexdale, or Nuit Blanche creating an art zone around the Scarborough Civic Centre. As the city grows and downtown becomes more unaffordable, the future of Toronto's cultural vitality will depend on its inner suburbs attaining the kind of density that supports artistic amenities – such as live music venues. With artists' recording revenue decimated by digital streaming, the pressure is only increasing on live promoters to provide musicians with much-needed income.

The City can do much more to preserve music venues and back up its 'Music City' branding. It's made baby steps, including modernizing its noise bylaw and convening forums and studies to encourage music in alternative, DIY spaces, but more muscular measures are needed. Stronger heritage protections could have saved the Silver Dollar as a gritty, Dan Burke–booked indie rock'n'roll venue: current planning rules preserve its physical design and decor but don't require that it return to life as a live music venue. (Though it should be noted that heritage is in fact a provincial jurisdiction.)

More proactive zoning could designate a given street as a live music district – semi-industrial Geary Avenue being a commonly cited target site – which could potentially create a new Yorkville, if we dream big enough.

And more public assistance for local entrepreneurs and non-profits to own their own performance spaces would be the biggest investment in Toronto's musical future. It's the *ownership* of the Cameron House, the Horseshoe Tavern, the Rivoli, and the Rex by music-loving entrepreneurs that has allowed Queen West to survive the onslaught of three decades of gentrification.

As of this writing, the latest incarnation of the El Mocambo is still getting ready to open its doors.

BIBLIOGRAPHY

This book would not have been possible without the following secondary sources. Thanks to all that have come before and done their part to document Toronto's rich musical history.

BOOKS

Arthur, Eric. Toronto, *No Mean City*. University of Toronto Press, 2003 (third edition; originally published 1964).

Barclay, Michael, and Ian A.D. Jack, Jason Schneider. *Have Not Been the Same: The CanRock Renaissance 1985–1995*. ECW Press, 2011 (second edition; originally published 2001).

Barclay, Michael. *The Never-Ending Present: The Story of Gord Downie and the Tragically Hip*. ECW Press, 2018.

Benson, Denise. *Then and Now: Toronto Nightlife History*. Three O'Clock Press, 2015.

Berman, Stuart. *This Book Is Broken: A Broken Social Scene Story*. House of Anansi Press, 2009.

———. *Too Much Trouble: A Very Oral History of Danko Jones*. ECW Press, 2012.

Bidini, Dave. *On a Cold Road: Tales of Adventure in Canadian Rock*. McClelland & Stewart, 1998.

Bingham, Dave. *Noise From the North End: The Amazing Story of the Ugly Ducklings*. Friesen Press, 2015.

Bonnet, Frédéric, editor. *General Idea: A Retrospective (1969–1994)*. JRP | Ringier, 2011.

Campbell, Dr. Mark V., editor. *For The Record: An Idea of the North*. Northside Hip Hop Archive & Vivid Simulacra, 2019.

Crouse, Richard, and John Goddard. *Rock and Roll Toronto*. Doubleday Canada, 1997.

Cullen, Don. *The Bohemian Embassy: Memories and Poems*. Wolsak and Wynn Publishers Ltd., 2006.

Deppe, Gord. *SpoonFed: My Life With the Spoons*. Manor House Publishing Inc., 2014.

Edwardson, Ryan. *Canuck Rock: A History of Canadian Popular Music*. University of Toronto Press, 2009.

Einarson, John. *Four Strong Winds: Ian and Sylvia.* Emblem Editions, 2012.

Emerson, Derek, and Shawn Chirrey, Simon Harvey. *Tomorrow Is Too Late: Toronto Hardcore Punk in the 1980s.* UXB Press, 2018.

Fraser, Malcolm. *The Wooden Stars: Innocent Gears.* Invisible Publishing, 2013.

Helm, Levon, and Stephen Davis. *This Wheel's on Fire: Levon Helm and the Story of The Band.* Chicago Review Press, 2000.

Higgins, Dalton. *Hip Hop World: A Groundwork Guide.* House of Anansi Press, 2009.

Henderson, Stuart. *Making the Scene: Yorkville and Hip Toronto in the 1960s.* University of Toronto Press, 2011.

Hoskyns, Barney. *Across the Great Divide: The Band and America.* Hal Leonard, 2006.

Jennings, Nicholas. *Before the Gold Rush: Flashbacks to the Dawn of the Canadian Sound.* Viking Canada/Penguin Canada, 1997.

Jennings, Nicholas. *Lightfoot.* Penguin Canada, 2018.

Levine, Allan. *Toronto: Biography of a City.* Douglas & McIntyre, 2014.

Liss, Sarah. *Army of Lovers: A Community History of Will Munro.* Coach House Books, 2013.

Locke, Jesse. *Heavy Metalloid Music: The Story of Simply Saucer.* Mosaic Press, 2016.

Lorinc, John, and Jane Farrow, Stephanie Chambers, Tim McCaskill, editors. *Any Other Way: How Toronto Got Queer.* Coach House Books, 2017.

Marom, Malka. *Joni Mitchell: In Her Own Words.* ECW Press, 2014.

McDonough, Jimmy. *Shakey: Neil Young's Biography.* Anchor Books, 2003.

McPherson, David. *The Legendary Horseshoe Tavern: A Complete History.* Dundurn Press, 2017.

Melhuish, Martin. *Oh What a Feeling: A Vital History of Canadian Music.* Quarry Press, 1996.

Mersereau, Bob. *The History of Canadian Rock 'n' Roll.* Backbeat, 2015.

Miller, Mark. *Such Melodious Racket: The Lost History of Jazz in Canada, 1914–1949.* The Mercury Press, 1999.

Miller, Mark. *Jazz in Canada: Fourteen Lives.* Nightwood Editions, 1988.

Monk, Philip. *Is Toronto Burning? Three Years in the Making (and Unmaking) of the Toronto Art Scene.* Black Dog Publishing, 2016

Pevere, Geoff. *Gods of the Hammer: The Teenage Head Story.* Coach House Books, 2014.

Pope, Carole. *Anti Diva*. Vintage Canada, 2000.

———. *Contents Under Pressure: 30 Years of Rush at Home and Away*. ECW Press, 2004.

Popoff, Martin. *Rush: The Illustrated History*. Voyageur Press, 2013.

Pyle, Don. *Trouble in the Camera Club: A Photographic Narrative of Toronto's Punk History 1976-1980*. ECW Press, 2011.

Robertson, Robbie. *Testimony: A Memoir*. Vintage Canada, 2016.

Sewell, John. *How We Changed Toronto: The Inside Story of Twelve Creative, Tumultuous Years in Civic Life, 1969-1980*. Lorimer, 2015.

Silcott, Mireille. *Rave America: New School Dancescapes*. ECW Press, 1999.

Smash, Nick. *Alone and Gone: The Story of Toronto's Post Punk Underground*. Smashbook, 2015.

———. *What You Don't Want Is What You Get*. Smashbook, 2018.

Snow, Michael. *The Michael Snow Project: Music/Sound 1948–1993*. Art Gallery of Ontario/The Power Plant, 1994.

Staniforth, J.B. *The Deadly Snakes: Real Rock and Roll Tonight*. Invisible Publishing, 2012.

Sutherland, Sam. *Perfect Youth: The Birth of Canadian Punk*. ECW Press, 2012.

Von Essen, Derek, and Phil Saunders. *No Flash Please! (Underground Music in Toronto 1987–92)*. Anvil Press, 2016.

Walker, Klive. *Dubwise: Reasoning From the Reggae Underground*. Idiomatic, 2006.

Wallis, Ian. *The Hawk: The Story of Ronnie Hawkins & The Hawks*. Quarry Press, 1997.

Ward, Christopher. *Is This Live? Inside the Wild Early Years of MuchMusic: The Nation's Music Station*. Random House Canada, 2016.

Warner, Andrea. *Buffy Sainte-Marie: The Authorized Biography*. Greystone Books, 2018.

Worth, Liz. *Treat Me Like Dirt: An Oral History of Punk in Toronto and Beyond 1977-1981*. ECW Press, 2009.

Yaffe, David. *Reckless Daughter: A Portrait of Joni Mitchell*. Sarah Crichton Books, 2017.

Yorke, Ritchie. *Axes Chops & Hot Licks: Maple Music 1968-1975*. Rock 'n Roo, 2015 (originally published 1971).

Young, Neil. *Waging Heavy Peace: A Hippie Dream*. Plume, 2013.

BLOGS, PODCASTS, WEBSITES, ETC.

Alternative Toronto – alternativetoronto.ca
CanadianBands.com
The Canadian Encyclopedia – thecanadianencyclopedia.ca
Canadian Music Blog – musiccanada.wordpress.com
Canuckistan Music – canuckistanmusic.com
The Communic8r – thecommunic8r.com
Equalizing X-Distort – equalizingxdistort.blogspot.com
FlatPhil's Blog – flatphil.wordpress.com
The Flyer Vault – instagram.com/theflyervault
Historic Toronto – tayloronhistory.com
A Journal of Musical Things (by Alan Cross), ajournalofmusicalthings.com
Kreative Kontrol with Vish Khanna – vishkhanna.com/kreative-kontrol
LCBO Corporate Timeline – lcbo.com
MAR Productions – YouTube.com
The Museum of Canadian Music – citizenfreak.com
Musical Urbanism, by Leonard Nevarez – pages.vassar.edu/musicalurbanism
Nicholas Jennings – nicholasjennings.com
Northside Hip Hop Archives – nshharchive.ca
Russ & Gary's 'The Best Years in Music' – strathdee.wordpress.com
Some Old Pictures I Took, by Rick McGinnis – someoldpicturesitook.
  blogspot.com
The Spirit of Radio CFNY 102.1 FM Fan Site – spiritofradio.ca
Views Before the 6 – soundcloud.com/viewsbeforethe6
Voluntary in Nature – voluntaryinnature.blogspot.com
Weird Canada – weirdcanada.com

NEWSPAPERS/PUBLICATIONS

Eye Weekly (1991–2011): reporting by Jason Anderson, Denise Benson, Stuart
  Berman, Elizabeth Mendez Berry, Mary Dickie, J. Alexander Ferron,
  Kieran Grant, Erin Hawkins, Joanne Huffa, C. J. O'Connor, Bill Reynolds,
  and others.
Exclaim (1992–): reporting by Ron Anicich, Michael Barclay, Lori Beckstead,
  Denise Benson, Prasad Bidaye, Ian Blurton, Jen Campbell, Lorraine
  Carpenter, Sylvia Chow, Del Cowie, David Dacks, Craig Daniels, Ian

Danzig, Christian deBrujin, Andrew Duke, Ewan Exall, Neil Exall, Matt Galloway, Erin Hawkins, Scott Ingram, Daihbid James, James Keast, I. Khider, Phil Klygo, Matt McMillan, Glenn Milchem, Bruce Lam, Cindy McGuinn, Joshua Ostroff, Ryan B. Patrick, Kevin Press, Don Pyle, Thomas Quinlan, Dave Rave, Phil Saunders, Craig Thompson, Chris Twomey, Christopher Waters, Mike White, Chris Wodskou, others.

The Globe and Mail (1957–): reporting by Jack Batten, Marilyn Beker, Rebecca Caldwell, Simona Chiose, Guy Dixon, Robert Everett-Green, Katherine Gilday, Liam Lacey, Carl Wilson, Brad Wheeler, others.

Graffiti (1984–86): reporting by Mary Dickie, Howard Druckman, Morgan Gerard, Dan Hughes, Rick McGinnis, others.

Now Magazine (1981–): reporting by Susan G. Cole, Steven Davey, Matt Galloway, Michael Hollett, Kim Hughes, Christopher Jones, Daryl Jung, Ellie Kirzner, Alice Klein, Elliott Lefko, Helen Lee, Suzanne Little, Sarah Liss, James Marck, Peter Noble, Tim Perlich, Kevin Ritchie, Rick Robertson, Andrew Sun, Kwame Younge, others.

The Toronto Star (1957–): reporting by Dave Bidini, Margaret Daly, Peter Goddard, Paul Irish, Edward Keenan, Craig MacInnis, Betsy Powell, Jennie Punter, Ben Rayner, Eric Veillete, Murray Whyte, others.

FILMS/DOCUMENTARIES

Christopher's Movie Matinee. Dir. Mort Ransen, 1968. NFB.ca.
City Sonic (video series). Various directors, 2009. kensingtontv.com/citysonic
Crash 'n' Burn. Dir. Ross McLaren, 1977. YouTube.com.
The Evolution of Drum & Bass in Toronto. Dir. Chris McKee. 2016. YouTube.com.
Festival Express. Dirs. Bob Smeaton, Frank Cvitanovich, 2003. DVD.
I Got Mine: The Jackie Shane Story (audio). Dir. Elaine Banks, 2010. CBC.ca.
The Last Pogo Jumps Again. Dirs. Colin Brunton and Kire Paputts, 2013. Vimeo.com.
The Legend of 23 Hop. Dir. Colm Hogan, 2019. YouTube.com.
Make Some Noise. Dir. Andrew Munger, 1994. YouTube.com.
Remember Who's Emma. Dir. Lyndall Musselman, 2009. YouTube.com.
QSW: The Rebel Zone. Dir. Lorraine Segato, 2001. Supplied by the filmmaker.
Right, Right Time: The Summer Records Story (audio). Prod. Ian Cauthery, 2013. Soundcloud.com. (Originally produced for CBC Radio, *Inside the Music.*)

Rise Up: Canadian Pop Music in the 1980s. Dir. Gary McGroarty, 2009. DVD.

She Said Boom: The Story of Fifth Column. Dir. Kevin Hegge, 2012. Vimeo.com

Symptom Hall (audio). Dir. Jonathan Culp, 2016. Unpopulararts.com

This Beat Goes On: Canadian Pop Music in the 1970s. Dir. Gary McGroarty, 2009. DVD.

Toronto Jazz. Dir. Don Owen, 1963. NFB.ca.

Yonge Street: Toronto Rock & Roll Stories. Dir. Bruce McDonald, 2011. Vimeo.com. (Originally produced for Bravo! TV.)

You Left Me Blue: The Handsome Ned Story. Dir. Chris Terry & Ross Edmunds, 2017. YouTube.com.

ACADEMIC PAPERS, ARTICLES, ETC.

Bidini, Dave. 'An oral history of The Edge, Toronto's hippest club, from the people who lived and loved it.' *National Post*, 2013.

Boles, Benjamin. 'A brief history of Lee's Palace.' *BlogTO*, 2014. 'A brief history of no fun Toronto.' *BlogTO*, 2014. 'From Science Centre Parties to Rave Buses, Relive Toronto 90s History with This Flyer Collection.' *Noisey/Vice*, 2016. 'Remembering the Time 20,000 Ravers Went to City Hall to Protest Toronto's Rave Ban.' *Noisey/Vice*, 2017.

Bronson, AA. 'The Humiliation of the Bureaucrat: Artist-run Centres as Museums by Artists.' *Art Metropole*, 1983

Bradburn, Jamie. 'Ghost City: 925 Bloor Street West.' *The Grid*, 2013. 'Vintage Toronto Ads: The Electric Circus.' *Torontoist*, 2013.

Brown, Nicholas & Bruneau, Jaclyn. 'Are Artist Run Centres Still Relevant?' *Canadian Art*, 2015.

Caldwell, Rob. 'From Lions to Evidence: Bruce Cockburn, Leroy Sibbles and the Reggae Connection.' The Cockburn Project, 2016.

Callendar, Tyrone (producer). 'Let Your Backbone Slide at 30: Maestro Fresh Wes shares his oral history of Canada's most loved rap song.' CBC Radio, 2019.

Caradeuc, Anna. 'Synth Pioneer John Mills-Cockell Of Syrinx on the Rise and Impact of Electronic Music.' Uproxx.com, 2017.

Dacks, David. 'A brief history of reggae in Toronto.' BlogTO, 2014.

Duffy, Rob. 'Sites & Sounds.' *The Varsity*, 2009.

Elliott, Paul. 'The History Of Rush by Geddy Lee & Alex Lifeson: The Early Years.' Loudersound.com, 2016.

Green, Richard. 'RPM, 1964–2000: The Conscience of Canada's Music Industry.' Library and Archives Canada, 2015.

Jagger, Juliette. 'Historic Venue Spotlight: Le Coq d'Or.' *Noisey/Vice*, 2014.

McCuaig, Keith. 'Jamaican Canadian Music in Toronto in the 1970s and 1980s: A Preliminary History.' Ottawa: Carleton University (MA thesis), 2012.

Lee, David Neil. '"We Can Draw!": Toronto Improvisation, Abstract Expressionism, and the Artists' Jazz Band' in *Critical Studies in Improvisation*, Vol 11, No 1-2, 2016.

Leigh, Nathan. 'The Strange History of The Mynah Birds, the Lost R&B Supergroup ft. Rick James and Neil Young.' Afropunk.com, 2014.

Levi, Charles. 'Sex, Drugs, Rock & Roll, and the University College Lit: The University of Toronto Festivals, 1965-69.' Historicalstudiesineducation.ca, 2006.

Levy, Joseph. 'A Brief History of Rough Trade with Carole Pope and Kevan Staples.' Laventure.net, 2014.

Lifeson, Alex. 'The Ghosted Victory Burlesque Theatre.' *West End Phoenix*, 2018.

Locke, Jesse. 'The Astral Excursions of John Mills-Cockell.' Musicworks, 2017.

Munroe, Jim. 'Ask Us About Anarchist-Retail Opportunities! A short history of Who's Emma, a Toronto punk collective. Punk Planet, 1997.

O'Connor, Alan. Who's Emma and the Limits of Cultural Studies.' *Cultural Studies* 13(4), 1999.

Peters, Vicky. 'Old But Not the Least Bit Tired.' *Torontoist*, 2008.

Plummer, Kevin. 'Historicist: The Hawk's Nest in Toronto.' *Torontoist*, 2011. 'Historicist: Elvis in Toronto, 1957.' *Torontoist*, 2013. 'Historicist: Sounds of Home I & II.' *Torontoist*, 2013.

Rayner, Gordon.' Mnemonica: Artist's Statement.' Catalogue, Robert McLaughlin Gallery, 1979.

Rancic, Michael. 'A Nation of Tinkerers: How a Canadian University Shaped Electronic Music in North America.' *Noisey/Vice*, 2016.

Schabas, Jake. 'Throwback Thursday: Yorkville and the death of Toronto's first scene.' *Spacing*, 2009.

Scott, Andrew. 'The El Mocambo Tavern and the Toronto music scene: A historical exegesis.' Soundscapes.info, 2003.

Shedden, Jim. DIY *Toronto ca. 1975–1989*. Jim Shedden Editions, 2017.

Strachan, Jeremy James. 'Music, Communications, Place: Udo Kasemets and Experimentalism in 1960s Toronto.' Toronto: Faculty of Music, University of Toronto (PhD thesis), 2015.

Storring, Nick. Liner notes, Syrinx: *Tumblers From the Vault*. RVNG Intl., 2016.

Sylvester, Erin. 'Yorkville's Riverboat Coffee House, Which Helped Launch Gordon Lightfoot, Neil Young, and Joni Mitchell.' *Torontoist*, 2016.

Ugwu, Reggie. 'Jackie Shane, a Transgender Soul Pioneer, Re-emerges After Four Decades.' *The New York Times*, 2017.

IMAGE CREDITS

p. 9, Courtesy of Simon White; p. 11, Courtesy of Jonny Dovercourt; p. 18, Courtesy of Tommy Wilson; p. 19, Courtesy of Numero Group; p. 24, Courtesy of Buffy Sainte-Marie; p. 28, York University Libraries, Clara Thomas Archives & Special Collections, Toronto Telegram fonds, ASC27707; p. 36, Courtesy of the Mullings Family and Light in the Attic Records; p. 37, Courtesy of the Mullings Family and Light in the Attic Records; p. 41, Courtesy of Massey Hall; p. 45, Courtesy of John Mills-Cockell; p. 48, Courtesy of John Mills-Cockell; p. 52, Courtesy of Richard Flohil; p. 58, Courtesy of Paul Till, rockandroll-portfolio.com; p. 64, Courtesy of Vilam Hrubovcak; p. 67, Courtesy of Light in the Attic Records; p. 73, Courtesy of Don Pyle; p. 74, Courtesy of Peter MacCallum; p. 76, Courtesy of Don Pyle; p. 77, Courtesy of Don Pyle; p. 79, Courtesy of Don Pyle; p. 83, Courtesy of Peter Noble; p. 86, Courtesy of Deborah Palloway; p. 87, Courtesy of Deborah Palloway; p. 88, Courtesy of Martha and the Muffins; p. 91, Courtesy of Karl Jirgens; p. 96, Courtesy of Paul Till, rockandrollportfolio.com; p. 99, Courtesy of Nick Smash; p. 101, Courtesy of Allison Wardman; p. 104, Courtesy of Gord Deppe; p. 106, Courtesy of Isobel Harry; p. 110, Courtesy of Nick Smash; p. 112, Courtesy of Simon White; p. 119, Courtesy of Leroy Sibbles; p. 122, Courtesy of Luis Marmelo; p. 124, Courtesy of Jena von Brucker; p. 134, Courtesy of Trevor Hughes; p. 136, Courtesy of Simon White; p. 139, Courtesy of Mark Mowatt; p. 142, Courtesy of Heather Cameron; p. 144, Courtesy of Dave Bidini and Darrin Cappe; p. 147, Courtesy of Cathy Bidini; p. 153. Courtesy of Derek von Essen; p. 155, Courtesy of Paul Till, rockandrollportfolio.com; p. 157, Courtesy of Derek von Essen; p. 158, Courtesy of Rick McGinnis; p. 165, Courtesy of Nick Smash; p. 169, Courtesy of Rob Ben; p. 173, Courtesy of Rob Ben; p. 178, Courtesy of Andrew McAllister; p. 181, Courtesy of Rick McGinnis; p. 182, Courtesy of Rob Ben; p. 186, Courtesy of Derek von Essen; p. 189, Courtesy of Kevin Lynn; p. 192, Courtesy of Ladan Behbin; p. 197, Courtesy of Jonny Dovercourt; p. 200, Courtesy of Rob Ben; p. 207, Courtesy of Andrew McAllister; p. 209, Courtesy of Jonny Dovercourt; p. 210, Courtesy of Michelle Breslin; p. 212, Courtesy of Phil Klygo; p. 216, Courtesy of Brendan Donaghey; p. 219, Courtesy of Brendan Donaghey; p. 222, Courtesy of Sheinina Raj; p. 230, Courtesy of Sean Dignan; p. 233, Courtesy of alexd, TRIBE MAGAZINE; p. 234, Courtesy of Constellation Records; p. 239, Courtesy of Constellation Records; p. 245, Courtesy of Mondo Lulu; p. 248, Courtesy of Public Transit Recordings; p. 257, Courtesy of Lisa Kannakko; p. 260, Courtesy of Michelle Breslin; p. 264, Courtesy of Dawn Wilkinson; p. 266, Courtesy of Dawn Wilkinson; p. 269, Courtesy of Natalie Galaska; p. 272, Courtesy of Jonny Dovercourt; p. 277, Courtesy of Jonny Dovercourt; p. 280, Courtesy of Mike Olsen; p. 285, Courtesy of Michelle Breslin; p. 288, Courtesy of Amit Dahan; p. 293, Courtesy of Stephen Chung; p. 294, Courtesy of Amit Dahan; p. 297, Courtesy of Jeffrey Remedios.

ACKNOWLEDGEMENTS

To my parents, Michael Bunce and Barbara Jenkins, who decided to call Toronto home. Thank you for everything – and for playing the Beatles non-stop.

To my sister, Sue Bunce, who first turned me on to 'good music' via CFNY in the eighties, and who shares my love of cities – and our strange, humble hometown.

To my 'brother from another mother' Dave Rodgers, who started me on this crazy journey when he suggested we start a band back in Grade 9. And to our Scarberian fellow travellers Andrew McAllister and Paul Boddum, who also couldn't get off the ride.

To everyone I've ever played in a band with – thank you for being brave enough to get up on stage and see what happens. I'm grateful that some of you are still among my best friends.

To the whole extended Wavelength family – thank you for believing in the cause of local music and for all the hours you've devoted to making Toronto a better place for music lovers. There are far too many of you to thank, but I want to give extra special shoutouts to Aaron Dawson for stepping up when I was head down in my manuscript, and to Adam Bradley for our many conversations that initially inspired this book.

To my first work family, at *Eye Weekly* in the late nineties and early 2000s – especially everyone in the editorial and design departments. Thanks for opening my eyes to a wider world of culture and for teaching me the value of humour, research, and copy editing.

To the Coach House Books team – in particular Alana Wilcox for her belief in this project and her endless patience; to editors John Lorinc, Peter Norman, and Carl Wilson for fleshing out the vision, and to Dave Gee, Crystal Sikma, Nick Hilton, James Lindsay, Yasmin Emery, Tali Voron, and Rick/Simon for pulling it all together.

To the writers who inspired me when I started this project and kept fuelling the beast as it grew – and especially those who generously shared your wisdom and experiences along the way: Michael Barclay, Denise Benson, Stuart Berman, Dave Bidini, Shawn Chirrey, Del Cowie, Nicholas Jennings, Sarah Liss, Don Pyle, Nick Smash, Sam Sutherland, Liz Worth. (Extra massive shoutout to those who offered fact-checking and proofreading assistance!)

The people who connected me with others and helped spin the web: Eric Alper, Caroline Azar, Benjamin Boles, Kevan Byrne, Richard Flohil, Grasshopper, Brandon Hocura, Keram Malicki-Sanchez, Yvonne Matsell, Glenn Milchem, John Mills-Cockell, Nicholas Murray, Andrew J. Paterson, Justin Peroff, Lorraine Segato, Rich Taylor, Gary Topp.

To all those who shared their life stories, dug deep, and entrusted me with the formative tales of their youth. Thank you for opening up – and for helping solve some decades-long mysteries. Apologies to anyone that I have forgotten, or didn't have the space to mention or say more about. Deciding who and what to include was the most heartbreaking part of this process.

To all the photographers who so generously shared their work – I'm so grateful you were enthusiastic to help me tell the rich visual side of this story.

To the zine-makers who lent or donated their teenage treasures, in particular Pam Hong, Dave 'Rave' MacIntosh, and Jim Shedden.

To the Toronto Public Library for your access to knowledge and your fantastic online system. Thanks also to Ian Danzig for letting me spend hours digging through the *Exclaim!* archives – and for being there to document the indie nineties. To Mary Dickie, for letting me peruse the stacks of old music mags. And to *Now Magazine*, for making your back issues available online.

To all the show promoters and venue owners – thank you for creating a place for live music in this city. It would be a much duller place without you. And to all the flyer designers, record pressers, tape dupers, bloggers, bartenders, and poster gluers – for bringing the scene to life.

To the friends who opened up their homes and gave me beautiful spaces to write: Tyler Belluz in the City of Guelph, Glen Newbury and Elana White on Toronto Island, Chloe Town on Crozier Lake. And all my friends who offered me healthy distractions and went on nature hikes.

Finally and most importantly, to Kimberley Brown, for your boundless love, support, and patience.

ABOUT THE AUTHOR

Jonny Dovercourt is a writer, musician, and concert presenter based in Toronto. He is a co-founder and the Artistic Director of the Wavelength Music Series, and has also worked for the Images Festival and the Music Gallery. His writing has appeared in *Exclaim!*, *Eye Weekly*, *Huffington Post*, *Musicworks*, *Now*, and *Spacing*. He has performed with numerous indie bands, including Republic of Safety, Secret Agent, Several Futures, and A Tuesday Weld.

Typeset in Laurentian and Slate.

Printed at the Coach House on bpNichol Lane in Toronto, Ontario, on Zephyr
Antique Laid paper, which was manufactured, acid-free, in Saint-Jérôme, Quebec,
from second-growth forests. This book was printed with vegetable-based ink on a
1973 Heidelberg KORD offset litho press. Its pages were folded on a Baumfolder,
gathered by hand, bound on a Sulby Auto-Minabinda and trimmed on a Polar single-
knife cutter.

Edited by Alana Wilcox and Peter Norman
Designed by Crystal Sikma
Cover design by David Gee
Author photo by Kate Mulvale

Coach House Books
80 bpNichol Lane
Toronto ON M5S 3J4
Canada

416 979 2217
800 367 6360

mail@chbooks.com
www.chbooks.com